To Dunstan

Lots of love on your 8th birthday.

Mum

x x x
x x

The Illustrated
Children's Bible

The Illustrated
Children's Bible

Retold by
Geoffrey Marshall-Taylor

Illustrated by
Andrew Aloof
Jon Davis
Dick Eastland
Colin Shearing
Barrie Thorpe

OCTOPUS

Foreword

by David Konstant, R.C. Bishop in Central London

There is a stage in a young child's life when the only word he seems to know is 'why?'. It can be a little irritating at times, but it reminds us how important it is to be curious. We only discover truth when we start asking questions. People like Aristotle, Marco Polo, Leonardo da Vinci, Amundsen and Einstein are remembered because they discovered some right answers. The world would be different without them. It is good to be curious.

Most of us are curious about ourselves and where we have come from. It is fascinating to see how far back we can trace our family history. When we get all the way back, to the very beginning of time, what then? How did it all begin? How will it all end? Why am I here? Have people always been the same? Is there a God? Where is God? What is God like? Are there rules for living properly? Is there life after death? Why is there evil in the world? Why doesn't good overcome evil? . . .

About 4000 years ago there was a Middle Eastern people who were curious about their origins. They asked the same sort of questions that we ask. They believed that God was telling them about himself and was showing them how to find the right answers. Very slowly, over many hundreds of years, they wrote down the story of their dealings with God. The Bible brings together some of these writings.

Jews and Christians believe that the Bible contains an account of God's message to mankind. It is written in many different styles by hundreds of different people. In the Bible there are prayers, hymns, letters, bits of history, legend, parable, prophecy, gospel and so on. In some way God speaks through all of them. That is why we still read the Bible. We are curious to know our origins.

I warmly recommend this Children's Bible. It is clearly presented, well put together and effectively illustrated. The first requirement of any version of the scriptures is that it should render the meaning of the original text faithfully. A second, equally important, requirement is that it should readily be comprehensible to its readers. It is clear that in producing this text great care has been taken to ensure that these two requirements are met. Children are introduced to the main themes of the Bible in such a way as to encourage them to read further. It is good to be able to welcome this instructive, helpful and readable bible for children.

David Konstant

Foreword

by the Archbishop of York, Dr Stuart Blanch

I am glad to have had an opportunity of seeing
sections of this book before publication and I warmly
commend it for use by children, parents and teachers
— and indeed by any who find the traditional format
of the Bible difficult to cope with. This is not a
complete Bible, nor is it a word-by-word translation,
but a series of extracts presented in a vivid and
readable way. The illustrations are, as far as I am able
to judge, true to the history and customs of the day.

The Bible remains the Word of God for the present
generation as it was for every previous generation —
and it is important that it should be available to the
people of the next generation as well in a form which
will enable them not only to understand it but to
enjoy it. This book, I believe, admirably fulfils the
purpose which the author and the publishers have in
mind.

Stuart Ebor:

Preface

The Bible is an important book — Christians would say that it is the most important book a person can ever read. They think this because it is about God, and also because it is about the sense of direction and fulfilment that God can give to people's lives. But the Bible can be a daunting book to approach. After all, the Bible is made up of 66 different books, written a long time ago by many authors who lived in the area of the world we now call the Middle East. These 66 books were not arranged in chronological order and sometimes the meaning of their words is not clear to readers in the 20th century. I have written this book to help young people to understand the Bible. It is not the whole Bible. I have acted partly as a storyteller and partly as a guide. After placing the stories in a sequence, on occasions I added to them other related writings, such as poems, proverbs or letters. Sometimes I have explained events or concepts which might otherwise be unclear. For those who want to read further in a complete Bible, the relevant references are printed under each title.

I have read many of the stories in this Children's Bible in schools and churches. The most rigorous test, however, was to read them to my own children, Andrew, Stephen, Paul and Anna. I'm grateful to them and to others who have told me honestly what they thought. My hope is that the imperfections of my writing will not prevent anyone from grasping one of the great central themes of the Bible: that to discover Jesus Christ is to discover God and to discover God is to discover ourselves.

Christians believe that God can speak through the Bible today as He spoke to many of the people in the stories. They don't mean that they hear an actual voice, but that, as they think about the words of the Bible, they find that they are learning about God, about their fellow human beings and about themselves. This is one of the ways God speaks. The Bible can guide us, encourage us, inspire us and challenge us — if we will let it.

Geoffrey Marshall-Taylor

Contents

Old Testament

The Creation	10	Saul's Jealousy	82
The Garden of Eden	12	David and Jonathan	84
Cain and Abel	14	The Hunt for David	86
Noah's Boat	15	The Death of Saul	87
The Great Flood	16	David and Mephibosheth	88
God's Promise to Abraham	18	David and Bathsheba	89
Abraham and Isaac	20	David and Nathan	90
Isaac and Rebecca	22	David and Absalom	91
Isaac's Two Sons	24	Absalom's Rebellion	92
Jacob's Dream	26	Solomon is King	94
Jacob and Esau are Reunited	28	The Wisdom of Solomon	96
Joseph and his Brothers	30	Solomon's Temple	98
Joseph is Sold	32	The Queen of Sheba Visits Solomon	100
Joseph and his Dreams	34	The Kingdom is Divided	102
Joseph Meets his Brothers Again	36	God Provides for Elijah	103
Moses Grows Up	38	Elijah Challenges Baal	104
The Burning Bush	40	The Drought Ends	106
Moses Returns	41	Elisha is Chosen	107
The Disasters in Egypt	42	Naboth's Vineyard	108
The Passover	43	The Chariot of Fire	110
The Israelites Cross the Red Sea	44	Elisha and the Shunamite Boy	112
God Cares for His People in the Desert	46	The General's Leprosy	114
The Ten Commandments	48	Jehu and Queen Jezebel	116
The Tabernacle	50	Amos, the Farmer	118
The Spies and the Fruit	52	Jonah and the Great Fish	120
The People Reach Canaan	54	Isaiah	122
The Capture of Jericho	56	King Hezekiah and the Assyrians	124
Achan and the City of Ai	58	Josiah's Discovery	126
Deborah and Barak	60	Jeremiah	128
Gideon Becomes a Leader	62	The Destruction of Jerusalem	130
Gideon and the Midianites	64	Daniel and the King's Dreams	132
Samson and the Lion	66	The Fiery Furnace	134
Samson and Delilah	68	The Writing on the Wall	136
Ruth	70	Daniel in the Lion Pit	138
Eli and Samuel	72	Rebuilding the Temple in Jerusalem	140
The Death of Eli	74	Nehemiah Rebuilds the City Walls	142
The Return of the Ark	75	Esther, the Young Queen	144
Saul is Anointed King	76	The Maccabees	146
Samuel Meets David	78	The Promise of the Messiah	148
David and Goliath	80		

New Testament

God's Message to Mary 150
The Birth of John the Baptist 152
Jesus is Born 154
Jesus is Taken to the Temple 156
King Herod and the Wise Travellers 158
John Baptizes Jesus 160
John the Baptist Dies 162
The Temptation in the Desert 164
Jesus and the Fishermen 166
The Wedding in Cana 168
The Teaching of Jesus 170
The Lord's Prayer 172
The Centurion's Servant 174
A Paralysed Man is Healed 175
The Storm on the Lake 176
Jairus' Daughter 178
Matthew's Call 180
The Sower 181
Jesus Tells More Stories 182
Feeding the Five Thousand 184
The Good Samaritan 186
The Woman at the Well 188
The Lost Sheep 190
The Lost Coin 191
The Lost Son 192
The Vineyard Workers 193
Jesus Heals a Blind Man 194
Who Was Jesus? 196
The Vision on the Mountain 198
Jesus and the Children 200
Jesus and Nicodemus 202
Zacchaeus Comes to Jesus 203
Jesus and Lazarus 204
Jesus Rides into Jerusalem 206
Jesus in the Temple 208
A Gift for Jesus 210
Jesus Washes the Disciples' Feet 211
The Last Supper 212
The Garden of Gethsemane 214
The Arrest 215

The Trial of Jesus 216
Jesus Meets Pontius Pilate 218
The Soldiers Mock Jesus 220
Jesus Carries his Cross 221
The Crucifixion 222
The Empty Tomb 224
Jesus and Thomas 226
Jesus at the Lakeside 228
The Ascension 230
The Gift of the Holy Spirit 232
Peter Preaches 233
A Lame Man is Healed 234
Peter and John Face the Council 235
Peter's Vision 236
Peter in Prison 238
Philip and the Ethiopian 239
Stephen 240
Paul at Damascus 242
Paul at Philippi 244
Paul's Shipwreck 246
Paul and Onesimus 248
Paul the Letter Writer 250
More Christian Letters 251
Everything is New! 251

The Story Behind the Bible 252
Life in Bible Times 253

The Creation of the World

Genesis 1 & 2

In the beginning, everything was darkness, nothing but empty darkness. Then over the deep darkness God's power began to move. Day by day, stage by stage, God created the world.

On the first day of God's creation He brought light into the darkness. As light began to shine throughout the universe, He was pleased with it. He then divided time into day and night: during the daytime the light shone brightly; during the night-time the light dimmed and gave way again to darkness.

On the second day God made the sky and filled it with clouds. At that stage all that could be seen beneath the sky was a world of water.

God intended there to be dry land in His world, so on the third day He caused the land, which He called 'earth', to appear. The land now divided up the waters into many large areas which God called 'seas'. As the land dried out, it became possible for plants to grow on the earth. Each plant produced its own seeds, so that it could spread quickly to other places.

During the fourth day God made great lights to shine from the skies: the moon, the stars and the sun. The moon and stars gave some brightness to the world at night, while the most dazzling of them all, the sun, lit up everything by day.

God looked at the universe He had created so far and He was delighted with every stage of His work. It was far from finished because He wanted the waters and the skies to be alive with the movement of creatures. So, on the fifth day He made some, such as the fish, to live in the waters and He made others,

such as the insects and birds, to live in the skies. He formed them in such a way that in days to come they would increase in number and exist throughout the world.

Now that creatures were flying and swimming in every part of the world, God decided to create some to live on the earth itself. 'The earth must produce animals of many kinds,' He thought. 'They should be different sizes, from very small to very large; some will become tamed, but most of them will roam wild.' This happened on the sixth day.

God enjoyed seeing the animals developing. He was pleased, because everything was now ready for Him to create the most important being of all. 'I will now make mankind,' God said on the same day. 'In many ways mankind will be like me and will become the masters of every other living creature: they will control the birds of the skies, the fish of the seas, and the animals of the earth.' God then gave His blessing to mankind. 'Increase in number,' He went on. 'Populate and rule the earth, for you are the masters of all living things. I have provided all kinds of grain and fruit for your food; the animals will eat the grasses and plants which I have provided for them.'

This was the last stage of God's creation. It was now complete and He was pleased with what He had done. On the seventh day God rested. From then on, the seventh day was always special to Him. It was to become special for mankind too; a day when everyone would be able to rest from work, and praise the One who had made the world.

The Garden of Eden

Genesis 2 & 3

When God first made man, He provided a delightful garden, called Eden, in which he could live. It was thick with beautiful trees which bore delicious fruit. Right in the heart of the garden stood two trees which were more important than any others: the Tree of Life and the Tree of Knowledge. Anyone who ate the fruit of the first tree would enjoy everlasting life, and anyone who ate the fruit of the second tree would understand the difference between goodness and wrong and would start to do wrong rather than right.

God asked the man, whose name was Adam, to take care of the garden and to tend the plants that grew in it, but He also gave him a warning. 'You may eat the fruit of any tree except one. You must not touch the Tree of Knowledge. If you do, you will die.'

Later God showed Adam all the plants and creatures He had made and He asked him to give each one a name. He then realized that although the garden was full of life, Adam had no companion to share it all. God made him fall into a deep sleep, during which he took a rib from his side. From this rib He made a woman. Adam was overjoyed when he saw her and he gave her the name 'Eve'.

Adam and Eve enjoyed living in the garden. They never thought or did anything wrong. Then, for the first time, wrongdoing crept into God's world.

The most cunning creature God had made was the snake. One day it spoke to Eve when she was on her own. 'Has God warned you not to eat any of the fruit in the garden?'

'We can eat whatever we like, except from the Tree of Knowledge,' she told him. 'If we taste its fruit we will die.'

'Don't believe it,' the snake replied. 'You won't die. God only said that, because if you eat that fruit, you will be like Him and know everything there is to know.'

Eve thought about this and walked up to the attractive tree. The fruit looked delicious and she began to imagine what it might be like to know what was bad and what was good. Then she made up her mind to try the fruit. With a quick movement she picked some and ate it at once. Then she took some to Adam and he also ate it.

From that moment things began to spoil their lives.

Until then, for example, they had not worn any clothes; but now they felt ashamed and embarrassed to be naked, so they found some fig leaves and sewed them together to cover their bodies. That evening they realized that God was in the garden and they tried to hide from Him among the trees. 'Where are you, Adam?' God called out.

'I hid from you, because I was naked,' Adam answered.

'How did you know that? Have you eaten the fruit I warned you about?' God asked.

'The woman gave some to me and I ate it,' Adam explained.

'Why did you do it?' God asked Eve.

'It was the snake's fault. He tricked me into it.'

As each tried to pass on the blame, it was clear that the happiness of the garden had been spoiled by their wrongdoing. God decided to punish them and the

snake. 'You will have to crawl in the dust for ever,' He told the snake. 'Man will always be your enemy.' Then He turned to Eve. 'I will make child-bearing painful for you and from now on man will be your master.' Lastly He spoke to Adam. 'Because of this, the ground will become hard to cultivate. Weeds and thorns will become entangled with the plants and you will have to work hard all your life in order to grow enough to eat. In the end you will die and your body will return to the earth from which it came.'

God then drove Adam and Eve from the garden. They were no longer able to eat the fruit of the Tree of Life so they would not be able to live for ever. So Adam gave up his chance to live in close friendship with God, but God never gave up showing His love to people, and He hoped that they would want to serve Him in return.

13

Cain and Abel

Genesis 4

Adam and Eve were very pleased when their first son was born. They were so thankful to God that they called him Cain, which means 'Given by God'. They had many more children after him.

When Cain grew up, he became a farmer and worked hard growing crops. He had a brother named Abel, who was a shepherd. One day they both decided that they ought to give something to God to show that they were grateful for His help. Each built a fire and placed on it the gift he was offering to God.

First, Cain brought some corn and burnt it, but God was not pleased because he knew that Cain was filled with wrong thoughts. Then Abel offered one of his few lambs to God gladly, who was pleased.

As soon as Cain realized that God did not like his offering, he became furious with jealousy. God saw this and spoke to him. 'Cain,' he warned, 'get rid of those evil thoughts. If you don't, there will be trouble.'

Cain refused to listen and his hatred for Abel grew so strong that one day, as they walked together, he attacked him and killed him. Cain thought that no one would know about it, but God knew and challenged him. 'Cain, tell me where Abel is?'

'How do I know?' he snapped. 'Am I supposed to look after my brother?'

'The blood of Abel cries out to me,' God replied, 'so you must be punished. Your crops will never grow again. You will have nowhere to settle and work: for the rest of your life you will be a wanderer.'

Cain left Adam and Eve and soon afterwards another son was born to them. They called him Seth, which means 'Chosen by God', because they believed that God had given him to take the place of Abel.

14

Noah's Boat

Genesis 6

The sons and daughters of Adam and Eve had many children themselves, and the population of the Earth increased. God was sad because people took no notice of Him and lived to please themselves. He felt sorry that He had made the human race and so He decided to change the world. 'I will remove them all from the surface of the earth,' He thought.

Only one family pleased God by the way they lived, and as a result He planned to spare them. This was the family of a man called Noah. One day God told Noah about His plan for him. 'I want you, Noah, to build a huge boat with three decks. Choose the best wood and make it 133 metres long, 22 metres wide and 13 metres high. This will be your home for

many months, so build it well.'

God went on to explain why Noah had to do this. 'I am going to send a great flood which will destroy all living creatures on the earth. You and your family will not be harmed if you all go into the boat when the flood waters begin to rise. You will be safe there. Your three sons, Shem, Ham and Japheth may take their wives and children too. It is important that you take a male and female of every kind of creature you can find, so that when the flood is over they may survive and breed. Make sure that you load the boat with enough food for them and your relatives. Don't be afraid, Noah. Trust me and I will keep you safe.'

Noah did as God asked, although his friends and neighbours probably laughed at him and his enormous boat. After several months' hard work it was ready, and God told Noah to move into his new floating home. A week after all the people and creatures had gone inside, heavy rain began to fall.

15

The Great Flood

Genesis 6–9

The heavy rain poured down continuously for forty days. Rivers and streams burst their banks and water started to cover the land. As the level rose, Noah's boat began to float. The flood destroyed buildings and trees; then it lapped even the tops of hills and mountains. Eventually there was nothing but water in every direction as far as the eye could see. Every creature died except those in Noah's boat, which was drifting safely on the surface of the water.

When at last the rain stopped, the water level remained the same for about four months. Then it slowly began to go down. Five months later the boat ran aground on a mountain called Ararat, which was still hidden beneath the waves. There were no side windows in the boat, so Noah and his family could not see what was happening. They knew that the boat had come to rest somewhere, but they didn't see

the peaks emerging from the flood or the mud-covered land drying in the wind.

To find out what was happening, Noah opened a small window in the roof and released a raven through it. This was to see if it could find any trees to perch on. The bird flew off, but did not return. Next he sent out a dove, which came back on the same day, but showing no sign that it had found anywhere to shelter or anything to eat. A week later, he let the dove go again. This time it arrived back as before, but in its beak was a fresh olive leaf, which meant that it had found some trees and bushes above the water. Noah waited a further week before letting the dove free again. It did not return, so he was sure that it had found food and that now the other animals would survive, if he released them.

His sons helped him to unbolt the huge door in the

side of the boat. They pushed it open and, when their eyes had grown used to the strong sunlight, they saw that the surface of the earth was almost completely dry.

Noah and his family led all the creatures out of the boat. They kept the domestic animals, but set the others free. Everyone was so pleased to be on land again that they decided to give thanks to God for keeping them alive. First they built an altar out of a raised platform of stones and lit a fire on it. As a gift for God, they killed an animal and a bird and placed them on the flames.

As the smoke of their sacrifice rose into the sky, God was pleased with them. 'I will never again destroy mankind,' He promised, 'even if people's lives become full of wrong once more. As long as the earth exists, life will go on year after year. There will always be winter and summer, cold and heat, night and day. Sowing and harvesting will never stop. Look, I will put a rainbow in the sky, as a sign of my promise to the world. Whenever you see it, it will remind you of what I have said.'

As they stood around the altar, a brilliant rainbow appeared and spanned the sky. Feeling sure that God's strength was with them, they collected their belongings and their animals and made their way down the mountain to build new homes for themselves and for those who would live after them.

From that time the population of the earth began to increase again. Noah had so many descendants that they had to live in many different places and they began to speak in many different languages. It was not long before they had to form themselves into separate groups and nations.

17

God's Promise to Abraham

Genesis 11 & 12

Between the two great rivers, the Tigris and the Euphrates, was a country called Sumeria, which became famous for its magnificent cities, where the people lived surrounded by comfort and riches.

A man called Terah once decided to leave the splendid city of Ur to try to reach the distant land of Canaan. He took with him his son Abram, his young grandson, Lot, and Abram's wife, Sarai. Terah never reached Canaan, because they stopped at a town called Haran.

After a while Abram became certain that God wanted him to leave Haran to make the long journey to Canaan alone. 'If you do this,' God seemed to be saying, 'I will bless you. You will have many descendants and they will become a great nation.' It was a

hard decision for Abram to leave his father and his new home at Haran, but he made up his mind to trust God and to go wherever He led him.

Abram and Sarai set off with their nephew, Lot. Abram was quite rich, so he took his wealth with him and a great many servants. After months of hard desert travel, they at last reached the land of Canaan. While they were there, God spoke to them at a place named Shechem. 'This', he said, 'is the land which I will give to you and to your children.' As a thanksgiving, Abram offered God a sacrifice.

For a while they moved on from place to place in Canaan, but they could not find anywhere to settle. The problem was that it was a very hot summer. Water and food were hard to find. Naturally the

Canaanites who lived there didn't want to share the little which they had with strangers like Abram, Sarai and Lot. Abram knew that his family, his servants and his animals would die without food and water, so he decided to leave Canaan for a while and travel further south to Egypt where there was no shortage.

They lived in Egypt for several years. At first they got on well with the king of Egypt, but later he turned against them and made them leave his country. So, Abram set off again with his family and servants. They made their way back to Canaan again.

When they returned, Abram and Lot decided to live in different places, so that they would each have enough land for their flocks and herds. Abram stayed in Canaan. One night, when he was lying awake, God spoke to him again.

'Don't be afraid of the future,' He said. 'I will guard you from danger and will reward you richly for trusting me.'

But Abram was sad, when he heard this.

'What is the use of making me rich,' he answered. 'Sarai and I are old and we have no children, so when I die, I will have no one to carry on my work and inherit my money.'

'Don't worry, Abram,' God said. 'Look out at the night sky. You see the stars. Try to count them.'

'I can't, Lord, there are too many.'

'You're right,' said God, 'and I promise you, Abram, that you will have as many descendants as there are stars in the sky. Remember how I brought you safely from Ur to Canaan. I will not let you down. I will give you a son and the whole of this land will belong to your descendants. They will be my people and I will be their God. My promise is for ever.'

Abram was pleased when he heard God's words and he decided to trust what He said. To prove that he believed it, God asked Abram to change his name to Abraham, which means 'Father of nations'. Sarai was to be called Sarah, to show that she would be the 'Mother of the nations'.

Abraham and Isaac

Genesis 18, 21 & 22

God wanted Abram and Sarah to be certain about his promise, so he sent some messengers to speak to them. It was midday and Abraham was sitting in the shade of his tent doorway, trying to keep cool, away from the burning heat of the sun. It was so hot that he had dozed off for a while. Suddenly he woke up and realized that three strangers were standing a few metres away near a tree. He blinked and then stood up and went towards them.

It was the custom to offer travellers food and drink, so Abraham invited them to rest with him. 'Sirs', he said to the men, 'you must stay a while. I am your humble servant. Rest in the shade of this tree. I will wash the dust off your feet and bring you something to eat.'

'Thank you,' they answered and sat down.

Abraham quickly went into his tent. 'Hurry, Sarah,' he told his wife. 'Find the sack of best flour and bake some bread. We have visitors.' Then he ordered a servant to kill a calf for the meal. When everything was ready, Abraham served the food himself. After they had eaten, the men surprised Abraham by talking to him about Sarah. 'In nine months' time,' one of them said, 'your wife will have a son.'

Sarah overheard them say this and she laughed out loud. 'How can I possibly have a baby? It just doesn't happen to women as old as I am.'

The men then got up and rode off into the desert.

But God kept His word and soon she was amazed to discover that she was going to have a baby. She was very excited at the news.

When at last the baby was born, Abraham and Sarah were happy because it was a son, as God had promised, and they called him Isaac. He was very precious to them because he was the only baby Sarah ever had and because he was born when they were so old.

Abraham trusted God throughout his life and God was certain that Abraham would never let Him down yet He decided to put him to the test. When Isaac was older, He asked Abraham to do the most difficult thing he had ever done.

'Abraham, I know that you love your son Isaac very much because he is your only son. Well, I want you to do this for me. Take him to Mount Moriah and offer him there as a sacrifice to me.'

Abraham must have been very sad. There was nothing more terrible to him than the thought of killing Isaac. Although he was unhappy, he still trusted God and believed that he should do what God asked. So, he got up at sunrise the next day to cut the wood for the sacrifice. He loaded it on the back of a donkey and set off for Mount Moriah with Isaac and two servants. The journey took three days and when they were approaching the place, Abraham told the servants to wait with the donkey. They both walked on a little further, out of sight of the servants. Isaac carried the firewood and his father took the knives and the fire. As they walked up the hillside, Isaac grew puzzled.

'Father,' he said to Abraham, 'we've brought everything we need for the sacrifice except the lamb we have to kill. Where is it?'

'Don't worry,' his father replied, 'God will give us one.'

They walked on and found a suitable spot for the

sacrifice. Abraham collected some large stones and piled them up to make an altar. He then put the firewood on top. Then to Isaac's horror, his father tied his arms and legs and put him on the wood. Abraham reached for his knife and was just about to kill Isaac when God spoke clearly to him. 'Abraham, you must not harm him. I now know that you put me first in your life. You trust me so much that you would have killed your own son for me. Look behind you.'

Abraham turned and there, in a thorn bush, was a ram. It was caught by its horns and could not escape.

Abraham knew that God meant him to kill the ram instead of Isaac, so he cut Isaac's ropes and lifted him off the wood. Abraham then took the ram and killed it as a sacrifice to God. God was so pleased with Abraham that He again promised that he would be the father of a great nation. 'You will have as many descendants,' declared God, 'as the stars in the sky and I will bless them in the future. I promise this because today you have trusted and obeyed Me.'

After this, Abraham and Isaac went down the hillside to rejoin the servants and then they returned home.

Isaac and Rebecca

Genesis 24

After many years Isaac's mother, Sarah, died. Abraham, who was very old, often thought about God's promise that he would be the father of many descendants. Before this could happen, Isaac would have to marry. Abraham was determined that before he died, he would find a wife for his son, who by now was a grown man.

So one day, he called his oldest and most trusted servant to him. 'I want you to go on a journey,' Abraham told him. 'Travel north to the place where I was born and visit all my relatives. Find a wife for Isaac from among them and then bring her back here.'

'But, sir, it's a great distance away,' the servant protested, 'and you haven't been there for years. Even if I find a suitable girl, she probably won't come with me.'

'Trust the Lord God,' Abraham replied. 'I'm sure He will make everything possible.'

The man set off, taking with him ten fully laden camels to show how wealthy and important Abraham was.

After a very long journey, he saw in the distance the city of Haran, where many of Abraham's relatives lived. It was late afternoon when he stopped at a well just outside the city to water the camels. While he was there, several women came to draw water and he wondered whether one of them might be the right person to marry Isaac. As they approached, he asked God for help. 'I will ask them for a drink,' he thought. 'If anyone offers to water my camels, that will be a sign that she is Isaac's future wife.'

He had hardly finished praying when a very beautiful girl called Rebecca walked up carrying a water pot on her shoulder. She went down the steps to the water and filled the pot. As she was coming back up, Abraham's servant called out to her.

'I'm very thirsty,' he said. 'Would you please give me a drink?'

'Here you are,' she replied. 'Have some of this water.' She tipped her pot so that he could drink. Then she said to him, 'I'll give your camels some water too.'

He thanked her as she filled a nearby water trough for the animals, making several trips to and from the well. The servant watched her, excited that God had led him so quickly to Isaac's wife. To her surprise, when she had finished what she was doing, he went up to her and gave her a gold ring and two gold bracelets. 'Tell me,' he asked, 'who is your father?'

'He is a man called Bethuel,' she replied. 'His father is called Nahor.'

The servant was astonished, because Nahor was

none other than his master Abraham's brother. Full of thanks to God, he returned to Rebecca's house to meet her family. He told them how God had blessed Abraham and made him a rich man. He then described his search for a wife for Isaac. When Rebecca's family heard about this and about the way he had met her, Bethuel knew what to do.

'I don't have to decide,' he said. 'God has made all this happen. If Rebecca agrees, she may return with you and become Isaac's wife.'

Rebecca said that she would go, so the next morning, after loading some camels with supplies for the journey and gifts for Abraham, she and the servant set off on the long journey back to Canaan. When at last they reached the place where Abraham lived, Isaac and Rebecca were married. Abraham was pleased that God would be able to bless his family in the future through the children of Isaac and Rebecca.

Not long after the marriage had taken place, Abraham died.

Isaac's Two Sons

Genesis 25–27

After some time Isaac and Rebecca became the parents of twin sons. They called the one who was born first Esau. From the time of his birth he had a mass of auburn hair all over his body. His brother was given the name Jacob. In those days, if there were more than two children in a family, when their father died, the eldest son became the head of the family and was given his father's money and possessions. Esau was a few minutes older than Jacob, so he would become the head of the family after Isaac's death. As the two boys grew up, this made Jacob very jealous. One day, he decided to try to change things. Esau had been out hunting and returned home hungry and exhausted. As he came in, he smelt the supper which Jacob had been cooking. 'Jacob,' he said, 'I've never felt so hungry. Please give me some of your stew.'

Jacob realized that his brother was desperate for something to eat, so he saw this as his chance.

'Of course, Esau,' he replied. 'You can have some, but I want something in return.'

'What? Tell me. I'll give you anything.' Esau blurted out.

'When our father dies, I want to be the leader of the family. I want to be in charge of his possessions.'

'All right!' said Esau. 'I agree.'

'You must promise to give up your place to me,' Jacob said.

'Yes. I've already said I will,' Esau shouted. Jacob sighed with delight and gave his brother some of the stew. So Esau gave up everything that could have been his in return for a bowl of stew.

Years later Isaac, who was by now old and blind, felt sure that he would soon die. He still wanted Esau to be the leader of the family, so he sent for him. 'Esau,' he said, 'you know how I like the food you prepare. I want you to hunt a deer for me. Make me a meal with it and then I will give you my special blessing before I die.'

Unknown to them both, Rebecca had overheard them. She became very angry, because Jacob was her favourite son and she wanted Isaac to bless him instead. She worked out a plan to trick Isaac into doing what she wished. Isaac could tell which son was which by touching their arms: Esau's arms were covered with thick hair, but Jacob had smooth skin.

Jacob killed two goats and tied their skins around his arms. He then put on Esau's clothes and, pretending to be his brother, he went to his father carrying a dish of goats' meat and some bread. Isaac was puzzled at first. 'You're back quickly, Esau.'

'God helped me find an animal almost at once,' Jacob replied. 'Have some meat, Father, and then give me your blessing.'

'Is that really Esau?' Isaac asked suspiciously. 'Come here, let me touch your arms.' Jacob went nearer. 'You sound like Jacob, but your arms feel like Esau's. Are you really Esau?'

'Of course I am,' Jacob lied.

Then Isaac kissed him and gave him his blessing. 'May God give you good fortune, my son,' he said. 'May you be powerful and prosperous all your days. I give you all that is mine.' Jacob was very pleased and left his father just before his brother returned. As soon as Isaac talked to Esau, they realized that Jacob had tricked them both, but they could do nothing about it as Isaac's promise to Jacob could not be broken. Esau hated Jacob and made up his mind to kill him. Rebecca learned of this and told Jacob to leave home, so he left. It was the last time he saw his parents because they died soon afterwards.

Jacob's Dream

Genesis 28 & 29

Jacob travelled alone through the desert. He thought about the way he had tricked Esau and wondered if God would ever forgive him. The nights were warm, so he would sleep in the open and not bother with a tent. One night, as he was sleeping with his head on a stone, he had a dream. He pictured a great stairway reaching from the ground up into heaven. Then he saw angels walking up and down it. It seemed as if God Himself was near him speaking to him.

'I am the God of Abraham and Isaac. I will give this land to you and your children. You will have as many descendants as there are specks of dust on the earth. Never forget that I am with you. I will protect you and bring you back to this land in safety.'

Suddenly Jacob woke up, amazed at his dream. 'To think that God is here and I did not realize it,' he cried. Jacob was filled with wonder that God should speak to him after all that he had done. He knew then that God would forgive him. As dawn broke, he took the stone which he had used as a pillow and fixed it upright in the ground. He poured olive oil over it to show that the stone was to be a reminder for ever of what had happened to him there. Jacob made a solemn promise to God.

'If you will protect and guide me,' he said, 'I will serve you all my life. This stone will become a place where you will be worshipped.'

Jacob continued on his journey and eventually came to a well not far from Haran. Some shepherds were watering their flocks and told him that his cousin Rachel was on her way to that very place with his uncle Laban's sheep. When she arrived, his eyes filled with tears and he kissed her. 'I'm a relative of your father Laban,' he said excitedly. 'My mother is his sister Rebecca.'

Rachel was so pleased to meet him that she ran home to tell Laban the news. He came out to meet Jacob and welcomed him with a kiss. Without hesitation he invited Jacob to stay with them as long as he liked.

Jacob worked for Laban while he was at Haran. He would not take any money from his uncle for what he did, so, after he had been there about a month, Laban talked to him about it. 'I insist on paying you something, Jacob,' he said. 'Tell me what can I give you in return for all the work you've done?'

'During my stay here,' he replied, 'I have begun to love Rachel very much. What I would like more than anything is to marry her. If you wish I will work another seven years for you, if you will give her to me.'

It was the custom then that girls could not marry until their older sisters were married. Laban was sure that Rachel's elder sister, Leah, would be married by the time the seven years had come to an end, so he gladly agreed and promised that Jacob could marry Rachel.

Towards the end of the seven years Laban was becoming worried because had not found a husband for his elder daughter, Leah. On the day of the marriage Laban tricked Jacob. During weddings the women and girls all wore thick veils which hid their

faces and the bridegroom was not allowed to see his bride's face until after the ceremony. What Laban did was to bring Leah, not Rachel, as the bride.

Jacob was so angry when he found out, that Laban let him marry Rachel as well for in those days it was not unusual to have two wives. But in return he made Jacob work with him for another seven years.

Jacob and Esau are Reunited

Genesis 31–33

Jacob became rich working for Laban and he had eleven sons from his marriages with Leah and Rachel. Not long after the youngest, Joseph, had been born, Jacob felt that he would like to return to Canaan where he had been brought up. He wanted to go partly because Laban was no longer as friendly towards him as he had been, and because Laban's sons had become jealous of his wealth. One day, when Laban was in the fields shearing the sheep, Jacob, without telling his father-in-law, took Rachel, Leah and their children, together with all that he owned, and set out for Canaan in the south. As soon as Laban heard that he had gone, he chased after Jacob. When at last the two men met, they spoke harshly to one another, but there was no fighting between them. Laban decided to let them carry on towards Canaan and, before he left, they promised never to do any harm to the other.

As Jacob and his family neared Canaan, he sent a message to his brother Esau, whom he had tricked so many years before. He wanted Esau to forgive him and be his friend again. Then he learned that Esau was setting out to meet him with a great number of men and he became frightened. He prayed to God for protection, and then he sent 530 animals to Esau as a gift.

During that night, Jacob was out walking alone when he suddenly met a man who started to fight and wrestle with him. They fought throughout the night and as they tussled, Jacob felt sure that there was something strange about this person. He seemed different from an ordinary man. Just before

dawn the man hit Jacob on the hip and threw it out of joint. Although weakened by the pain, Jacob still struggled until his opponent gave up. Before the man went away, he turned to Jacob and said, 'Your name should no longer be called Jacob, but Israel, which means the "One who struggles with God". Your life has been a struggle against other people and against God, but now your struggle is at an end.' He blessed Jacob and then left. When he was alone again, Jacob knew that God had been with him. As he limped back to join his children, he felt sure that all would be well when he met Esau.

Soon Jacob saw several hundred people approaching in the distance making clouds of dust as they

rode. He knew it must be Esau and his men. He walked on his own towards them and bowed deeply seven times as they drew nearer. To his surprise and delight, Esau dismounted and ran to meet him. They hugged one another and tears flowed down their faces. Jacob knew that his brother now forgave him for the wrong he had done many years before. He then brought Rachel, Leah and his children to meet Esau, and after they had talked together for many hours, they parted again to live happily in different parts of Canaan.

God helped Jacob and his family to do well in their new home and they became prosperous and powerful. Jacob had not forgotten God's words to him

when he had dreamed about the stairway: 'I will give this land to you and to your children.' God had kept His promise, so Jacob went back to the place where it had happened and, filled with thankfulness, he worshipped God there. He called the place Bethel, which means 'the House of God'.

Soon after leaving Bethel, another son, called Benjamin, was born to Rachel. During the birth she became very sick and she died a few hours after seeing her new baby. Jacob buried Rachel at the place which we now call Bethlehem. He brought up his twelve sons by himself and as they grew older, they began to work for him, tending the crops and the animals.

Joseph and his Brothers

Genesis 37

As his twelve sons grew older, Jacob came to love one of them more than the others. This was Joseph, who was then about seventeen. His father made no secret that he was his favourite son and to show this, one day he gave Joseph a special gift. It was a new, full-length robe. It was special because the sleeves were long and wide. Parents usually gave a long-sleeved robe to the child they wanted to become the head of the family. Except for Benjamin, who was still very young, all the brothers hated Joseph for this. He had already annoyed them by telling Jacob the things they said and did when their father was not there. They hated Joseph so much that they would never speak to him in a kindly way.

One day, while they were all working in the fields together, Joseph told his brothers about something which had happened the night before.

'Hey, listen!' he said, 'last night I had a peculiar dream.'

'What dream?' one of them asked.

'Well, it was like this,' he explained. 'It was harvest time and we were all in the fields tying up wheat sheaves. Suddenly the sheaf I was holding stood up straight, all by itself. Then the sheaves you were holding moved towards mine and made a circle around it. Then an amazing thing happened—all your sheaves bowed down to my sheaf.'

Joseph's brothers were furious when they heard what he said. 'I suppose you think it'll come true, do you?' they scoffed. 'You'll become a king and we'll be your slaves. Is that it?'

Joseph said nothing, but his brothers disliked him all the more. Later on he had yet another dream and again made the mistake of telling them. In it he saw the sun, the moon and eleven stars all bowing down to him. Again his brothers were enraged as he described it. Even Jacob was angry when he heard about it. 'Don't be so conceited, Joseph,' his father shouted. 'Do you imagine that the rest of your family would bow down to you?' Although Jacob sent Joseph to get on with his work, the dreams stayed in the young man's mind and he wondered whether they might ever come true.

A few weeks later Joseph's older brothers were all away from home, looking after their father's flock of sheep. Joseph and Benjamin had stayed at home. Jacob wanted to know how they were managing, so he decided to send Joseph to find out. 'Go and make sure they're safe,' he told him, 'and see if the sheep are being well looked after.'

Joseph left straight away. When his brothers saw him in the distance, they knew that this was the chance they had been waiting for. They would get even with him and their father would know nothing about it. 'Here comes Joseph, the dream boy,' one of them called out.

'If we killed him out here in the desert, no one would know,' suggested another. 'How about all those dry wells in the area. All we do is throw him down one and leave him for dead. When we go back home, we'll tell Father that a wild animal killed him. That'll be the end of his dreams.'

'No,' shouted Reuben, the eldest, 'we can't kill him. He is our own brother. I say we should throw him into a dry well, but we mustn't harm him.' Reuben's words persuaded the others, but they didn't realize what he was planning. He thought he would be able to come back later and help Joseph to climb out of the pit. Then they had to stop talking as Joseph approached.

Joseph is Sold

Genesis 37

When Joseph walked up to his brothers, they all stood around him and tore his long-sleeved robe off his back. Then they dragged him to a dried-up well and pushed him down into it. The sides were steep so he could not escape. Reuben made an excuse and left them, intending to return later to rescue him. Ignoring Joseph's shouts, the rest of the brothers sat down to have a meal. As they were eating, they saw a

camel train passing by, laden with spices on its way to Egypt. Judah, another of the brothers who thought it was wrong to kill Joseph, had an idea.

'Listen,' he said, 'why not sell him to those travellers? That way we'll get our revenge without killing him.' The idea pleased the others, so they shouted over to the camel riders and asked some of them to stop. They had no difficulty selling Joseph for twenty silver pieces. When they had made the deal, they pulled their brother out of the well, tied his arms and lifted him on to a camel. The travellers then continued on their way to Egypt where they planned to sell Joseph as a slave.

Later that day, when the place was deserted, Reuben returned only to find that the well was empty. Joseph had gone. He was very sad and went at once to find out from the others what had happened. He heard their story and was heartbroken. Then they all had to return home to face Jacob, so they decided that before they arrived, they would dip Joseph's robe in goat's blood. When they met their father, they handed it to him. 'We found this,' they said. 'Is it Joseph's?'

Jacob sobbed when he saw it. 'Of course it's Joseph's,' he cried. 'Some wild animal's killed him and torn him to pieces. My son, Joseph, my son.' He never forgot Joseph, the son he loved so much and his heart was always sad when he thought of him.

It must have seemed to them all that Joseph's dreams had come to nothing; but while all this was happening, Joseph was alive in Egypt. He had been sold as a slave to a man called Potiphar, who was the captain of the king's guard.

Joseph worked hard for Potiphar, who was so pleased with him that he made him the chief servant and allowed him to take charge of his household. At first Potiphar's wife liked Joseph, but then she turned against him and, in order to get him into trouble, she made up a story that he had attacked her. Joseph was arrested and put into prison for something he had not done.

Even in prison Joseph showed that he had many skills and, after a while, the jailer asked him to take charge of the other prisoners.

Joseph and his Dreams

Genesis 40 & 41

While he was in prison, Joseph was in charge of two men who had once been the king's special servants—the chief baker and the wine steward. One night they each had a dream which made them very unhappy when they woke up. Joseph believed that God could tell him the meaning of the dreams, so he asked them to tell him what had happened in them.

The wine steward remembered his very clearly. 'I saw a grapevine with three branches,' he said. 'The leaves grew and were quickly followed by the flowers and the grapes themselves. I seemed to be holding the king's cup, so I put it under the grapes, squeezed their juice into it, and handed it to the king.'

Joseph saw at once what it meant. 'The three branches mean three days,' he declared. 'In three days' time, you will once again serve the king's wine in the palace. In return for telling you what the dream means, I only ask you tell the king about me.'

Then the baker told what he had dreamt. 'I saw three bread-baskets, one on top of another, balanced

on my head. The top one was full of cakes which were being pecked by birds. What can it mean?'

'I think I know,' replied Joseph. 'The three baskets mean three days. In three days' time, the king will have you killed and the birds will come to peck at your body.'

On hearing Joseph's words, the wine steward cheered up, but the baker was even more miserable. Three days went by and everything happened exactly as Joseph had forecast.

Unhappily for Joseph the wine steward forgot about him for over two years. Then one day the king himself had two dreams. In the first he saw seven fat cows grazing on the banks of the River Nile. Suddenly seven very thin cows came along and ate the seven fat ones. In the second dream the king pictured a corn stalk which sprouted seven ripe ears of corn, full of splendid grain. Then seven more ears grew bearing hardly any grain at all. As the poor corn appeared, the good corn seemed to vanish.

The king was puzzled and anxious when he woke up, so he sent for the wisest men in the land, but no one could understand the dreams. Just then the wine steward remembered Joseph. At once the king sent for Joseph and told him his own dreams.

God showed Joseph at once what they meant. 'Sir,' he said to the king, 'God is warning you about the future. The dreams mean that for seven years Egypt will prosper; there will be good harvests and you will become rich. However, after the seven excellent years there will be seven terrible harvests and the people will become poor and hungry.'

'But if this is true, what can be done?' asked the king.

'There is one way to stop Egypt from starving. Choose someone with great wisdom to take charge of the country. Give him the power in the first seven years to order food to be stored and guarded, so that there is plenty for the seven bad years.'

When he heard his words, the king realized that Joseph had the wisdom to do such a job, so there and then he made him the governor of all Egypt.

Joseph, who was thirty years old, did his work well. Egypt saved plenty of grain to last during the seven years of bad harvest which came. Because other countries had not saved any corn, people flocked to Egypt to buy corn from Joseph.

Joseph Meets his Brothers Again

Genesis 42–50

The famine was very bad in the land of Canaan where Joseph's family still lived. Jacob, his father, heard about the corn in Egypt and sent ten of Joseph's brothers on the long journey south to buy some. Jacob kept his youngest son, Benjamin, at home.

When at last they arrived in Egypt, they had to buy the corn from Joseph, because he was in charge of selling it. When they went into the room where Joseph was sitting, none of the brothers recognized him, because he was wearing fine Egyptian clothes.

Joseph knew who they were as soon as he saw them and, as they bowed down in front of him, he remembered the dreams about the corn and the stars. After all the years that had gone by, the dreams had come true. He pretended that he did not know them and spoke roughly to them. 'You haven't come to buy corn. You are spies and enemies of Egypt.'

'No, sir,' they answered nervously. 'We swear before you: we have come to buy corn.'

'Then why are there ten of you?' Joseph asked.

'We're all brothers, sir,' they replied. 'There are twelve in all, but one died and the youngest son is at home with our father.'

'I don't believe you,' Joseph retorted. 'I intend to test your story. Guards, arrest that one.' He pointed to Simeon. 'He will stay in my prison while the rest of you return to Canaan to fetch your youngest brother. If you return, I will know you have spoken the truth. I will allow you to take some corn back with you.'

Nine of the brothers then paid for their corn and sadly started out on their journey. When they reached home, they told Jacob what had happened. He was broken-hearted to hear about Simeon. As they were discussing what to do, they opened their corn sacks. To their surprise and horror, in the top of each sack was a bag of money, the money they had paid Joseph for the corn.

For some months Jacob refused to let them go back with Benjamin, but then they used up all the corn and so they realized that they had to return to Egypt with him. When they arrived, Joseph invited them to his own house for a meal. They still did not realize that he was their brother. Joseph began to weep with happiness when he saw Benjamin, so he had to leave the room until he could control his tears.

After eating, Joseph ordered that his brothers should be given more corn to take back with them. As they prepared to leave, he could not bear to be parted from Benjamin. He thought up an idea to keep him in Egypt. Unknown to his brothers, he hid a silver cup in Benjamin's sack. They had hardly begun their journey, when Joseph sent a messenger after them to accuse them of stealing the cup. 'No, sir,' they protested, 'if any one of us has done this, he deserves to die.'

'Open your sacks,' ordered the messenger. 'If I find the cup, the person who has taken it must return with me to be my slave.'

When Benjamin's sack was opened, there on top of the corn was the missing cup. The brothers were all horrified and went back to face Joseph again. Joseph insisted that they must all return to Canaan except Benjamin, who was to stay in Egypt. 'But, sir,' pleaded Judah, 'if we do that our father Jacob will die of sorrow. Take me as your slave instead.'

Joseph, too, loved his father with all his heart. After Judah had spoken, he ordered the Egyptians to leave him alone with his brothers. He couldn't hold back the tears any longer. To his brothers' amazement he began to cry. The sound of his sobs filled the house. At last he managed to look up. 'I am Joseph your brother,' he said. 'No, don't be afraid. God has planned all along that I should save you from hunger and suffering.' He threw his arms around each of his brothers in turn and wept for joy.

Joseph gave them clothing, money and carts loaded with corn. He asked them to return home quickly to tell Jacob that he was still alive and to ask him to return with them to Egypt. They did this without delay, and as soon as Jacob heard about Joseph, he set off with his sons to meet him again.

Joseph heard that they were on the way and rode out in his chariot to welcome his father. When they met, they threw their arms round each other and cried with happiness. 'My son,' said Jacob to Joseph, 'now I don't mind if I die soon, because I have seen you alive after so many years.'

Joseph invited his father and brothers, together with their wives and children, to live in Egypt, where they would be sure of having plenty of food. They agreed to do this and made that country their home. Jacob died soon afterwards, but Joseph and his brothers stayed in Egypt for the rest of their lives.

Moses Grows Up

Exodus 1 & 2

Jacob's sons had many descendants and after hundreds of years there were thousands of them living in Egypt. Jacob had once been given a special name by God: He called him 'Israel'. This was how his descendants in Egypt came to be known as the 'Children of Israel' or the 'Israelites'. The king of Egypt became afraid because there were so many of them. He thought that they might want to rule the land themselves, so he took away their jobs, their money and their houses and made them all slaves. The Egyptians forced the Israelites to work very hard, building and farming. Although many of them died through the cruelty of their masters, the king was still worried because their numbers were still increasing.

For a period he ordered all Israelite boys to be killed as soon as they had been born. Sadness filled the

people as their babies were taken from them. One of the mothers tried to stop this happening. She hid her baby boy for three months and no one knew that she had him. When he was too big to stay unnoticed in the house, she decided to abandon him, in the hope that some Egyptian might find him and look after him. First, she made a watertight basket out of reeds and pitch. Then, one night, she put the baby in it, placed a lid on top and carried it down to the banks of the River Nile. She chose a spot near the royal palace where Egyptians used to go to bathe. The water near the bank was full of tall plants, so she left the basket floating among them with the baby asleep inside. Her daughter Miriam stayed nearby to see what would happen.

Sure enough, in the morning, the king's daughter left the palace with her servants and began to bathe in the river. She was puzzled to hear the sound of a baby crying, so she went to see where it was coming from. She was surprised to find a small floating basket amongst the bullrushes. She could hardly believe her eyes when she lifted the lid and saw a

small baby crying with all its might. Although the princess knew that it was an Israelite baby, she wanted to look after it. Miriam watched all this and thought that the princess seemed kind, so she came forward and spoke to her. 'Excuse me, your highness, but if you want to keep the baby, I know someone who would look after it for you. Shall I fetch her?'

'Yes, please,' replied the king's daughter. 'Go at once.'

Miriam ran home and asked her own mother to go to talk to the princess. Her mother was overjoyed to hear what had happened and went as quickly as possible to the palace. The princess, not knowing that this was the baby's own mother, asked her to take care of him for a while. 'I will pay you to look after him,' she said. 'Then when he is older, he will come to live with me as my own son.'

Miriam's mother did as the princess asked and was thrilled to have her own son in her arms again. 'You were taken out of the water,' she said looking at him, 'so I shall call you Moses, which means the "one who was taken out".'

Later Moses went to live in the palace with the princess. Although he was brought up as an Egyptian nobleman, he never forgot that his parents were Israelites. One day when he was older, he saw an Egyptian cruelly murder one of the Israelite slaves. Moses was so angry at this that he hit the Egyptian and killed him. Someone must have seen Moses attack the man, because eventually the king heard about it. The king tried to have him arrested and put to death, but before he could do anything, Moses escaped to a safe place in the desert called Midian.

The Burning Bush

Exodus 3

Moses was once resting at a well in the desert when a large flock of sheep and goats came to drink there, led by seven young women. He found out that they were all the daughters of a farmer called Jethro. Some other shepherds tried to stop them getting near the water, but Moses stood up for the girls and made sure that their animals had enough to drink. When Jethro heard of this, he invited Moses to work for him and then gave him his daughter Zipporah for his wife.

Moses became a shepherd for Jethro and often led the flock through the quiet hilly areas of the desert. One day, after he had taken the animals up a mountain called Sinai, he noticed something very strange. He saw a bush on fire. He had often seen dry bushes burning in the desert, but this one was different. Although it was on fire, it wasn't being burnt up.

He went nearer to look at it and, as he did so, it seemed as if a voice was calling to him from the centre of the flames. 'Moses! Moses!' it called.

'Yes, I am Moses,' he replied. He felt sure it was God speaking to him.

'Moses,' God said. 'This is a holy place. Take off your sandals. I am the God of Abraham, Isaac and Jacob. My people are being treated cruelly in Egypt. I want you to go to the king of Egypt and ask him to let my people leave that land. You will be their leader.'

Moses was frightened when he heard this. Although there was now a new king there, he felt sure that he could never be a leader and speak at the palace or in large meetings. But God promised to be with him. 'I will help you to lead my people out of Egypt and I will give them a new land which will be rich and fertile. In all that you do, Moses, I will give you my power.'

Moses was still nervous at the thought of leading the People of Israel, but he decided to trust God and, after saying goodbye to Jethro, he took Zipporah and his children to Egypt.

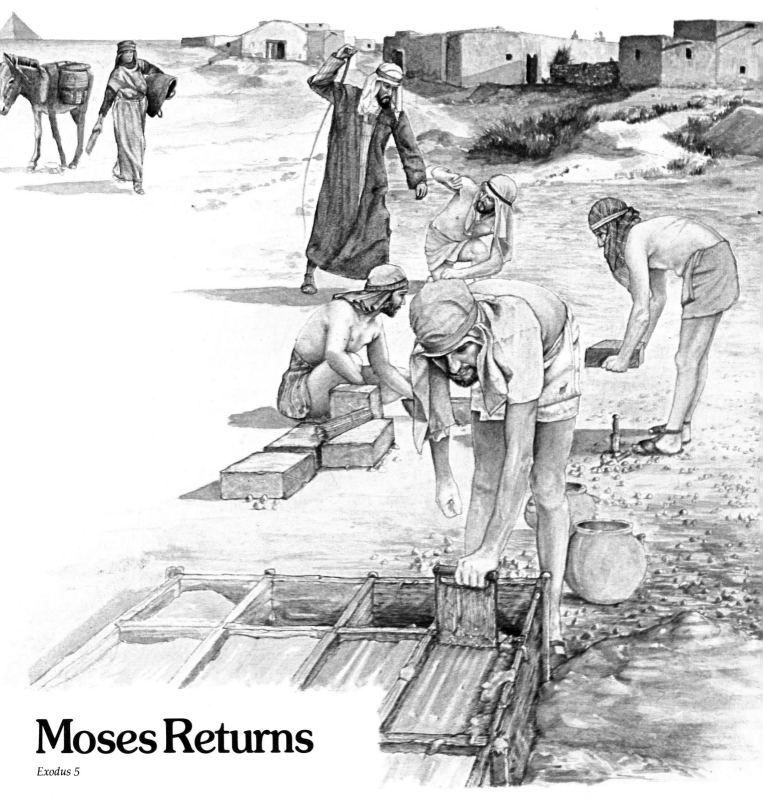

Moses Returns

Exodus 5

Moses had a brother called Aaron who still lived in Egypt. Aaron was a very good speaker, so, when Moses reached Egypt, he went everywhere with him, advising him and talking for him. Both men went to the palace and met the king. They asked him to let the Israelites leave the country, but the king refused. Instead, he worked the slaves harder than ever, until they begged Moses to leave them alone.

But Moses knew that what he was doing was right. God wanted His people to leave Egypt. 'Tell the people this,' God said to him, 'I am the Lord your God. I will set you free from your slavery. You will be my people and I will be your God. I will give you a new land to live in, the land of Canaan.'

'But, Lord,' said Moses, 'who am I to do this? The king won't take any notice of me.'

'He will,' God assured him. 'Even though the king may refuse to listen at first, I will show him that you speak for me. He will learn the hard way.'

So Moses and Aaron went again to see the king, but he was hard-hearted and ignored what they said. God then tried another way to make the king agree to let the Israelites go. He struck Egypt with the first of several disasters. God turned all the river and canal water into blood for seven days, but the king was not impressed and still refused to free the people.

The Disasters in Egypt

Exodus 7–10

God wanted Moses to give a warning to the king of Egypt, so once more he and Aaron went to the palace. 'My lord the king,' he said, 'unless you set my people free, God will bring trouble to your land by sending millions of frogs to infest it.' Again the king took no notice, so Aaron held out his stick and at once millions of frogs left the ponds and rivers and went everywhere.

The king quickly sent for Moses and Aaron and he seemed to have changed his mind. 'If your God will remove these revolting frogs, I will set your people free.' Moses believed him and asked God to take away the animals. The frogs began to return to the water, but as soon as the king realized that they were no longer a nuisance, he changed his mind.

God sent one disaster after another. When each one struck, the king agreed to let the people go, but then, after it was over, he broke his word. The hordes of frogs were followed by swarms of gnats and flies; then a disease killed large numbers of animals belonging to the Egyptians and painful boils appeared on people's bodies; after a terrible hail-storm had ruined crops and plants, millions of locusts ate what was left, so that there was hardly a green leaf to be seen in the whole of Egypt. Even when God completely covered the sky with black clouds for three days, still the king behaved in the same way.

He was so stubborn that God decided to send one more disaster, far worse than all the others, to make him give in. 'At midnight,' Moses told him, 'the Lord my God will kill the eldest son of every family in Egypt. It will not matter how old they are, nor who their parents happen to be. Among them, your majesty's own son will die.'

The Passover

Exodus 12

God was ready to carry out His threat, but He did not want any harm to come to the Israelites. God told Moses how their first-born sons could be saved: each Israelite family had to do something very special as a sign that they were willing to trust him. 'Each house-hold,' Moses explained, 'must kill a lamb or a goat and pour some of its blood into a bowl. Then pick a sprig from a hyssop plant, dip it in the blood and daub it around the doorposts of your houses. When God's power sweeps through Egypt tonight, everyone in the houses marked with blood will be safe: no one in those families will die. You must all be ready to travel quickly, because at any moment God will lead us out of this land. Each year in the future we will remember the way God saved our sons and helped us to escape from Egypt: we will hold a festival which we will call the Passover, because the Lord God "passed over" our homes and no harm came to us.'

As soon as Moses' instructions reached them, the thousands of Israelite families quickly carried them out.

At midnight God's power moved through the land, bringing death to the eldest son of every Egyptian family, but the Israelites were kept safe. The night sky rang with the wailing of the sorrowful Egyptians. The king's own son died and the sound of weeping echoed through the royal palace. The king realized that he had to let the Israelites leave before something even worse happened, so he sent an urgent message to Moses. 'Go at once. Leave Egypt for ever. Serve your God in another land.'

Moses passed the news quickly to all the Israelite families, who left their homes in order to escape while the Egyptians were still stunned with grief. When they had assembled together, Moses and Aaron led them towards the east in search of a new land where they would be free.

The Israelites Cross the Red Sea

Exodus 14 & 15

So Moses led the Israelites out of Egypt across the desert towards the Red Sea. There were thousands of them, all carrying their belongings and driving their animals. God guided them as they travelled and at last they reached the shore of the Red Sea where they camped for a while. They knew that they would have to cross the water, because that was where they hoped to find the new land they wanted to live in.

While they were camped there, the king of Egypt was changing his mind. He was now raging with fury that the Israelites had escaped and he wanted

revenge for the death of all the Egyptian sons. He quickly alerted his army, and ordered them to go with him to force the people to return.

As soon as the Israelites saw the dust clouds coming towards them, they knew it must be the Egyptians. They were afraid of what might happen.

'Have you brought us all this way to die in the desert?' they complained to Moses. 'We asked you not to interfere with us in Egypt. We'd rather be Egyptian slaves again than be killed here.'

'There's no need to be afraid,' Moses reassured

them. 'God will protect you. He will fight for you.'

Moses then pointed his stick at the waters of the Red Sea. As he did so, the waves divided and rolled back in front of him, leaving a pathway across to the opposite bank. As the sea bed dried in the warm wind, Moses was able to lead the people along the pathway to the other side of the Red Sea.

They all hurried across, knowing that the Egyptians were not far behind. When the Israelites reached the other side, they looked back to see the army trying to follow them through the Red Sea. The chariots were heavy and soon the wheels sank and stuck in the sea bed. The soldiers and charioteers struggled to push them out, but the water started to return and the waves swept over the Egyptians. Their chariots, men and horses were all drowned.

The people knew that God had been with them, because they had seen His power save them from death at the hands of their Egyptian masters. They were ready to trust Him and their leader Moses to guide and protect them in the future.

'I will sing to the Lord, because He has won a
  glorious victory.
He has hurled horses and soldiers into the waves.
The Lord is my strength; I will sing about the way
  He has saved me.
He is my God and I will praise Him;
He is the God of my fathers, and I will proclaim His
  greatness.
There is no other god like you, O Lord.
You will reign, the King for ever and ever.'

God Cares for His People in the Desert

Exodus 17; Numbers 20

Once the Israelites had reached safety on the other side of the Red Sea, they set out, led by Moses and Aaron, in search of somewhere to live. They wanted to reach the land of Canaan, but that meant travelling for a long time across a huge desert area where food and water would be hard to find. They had all seen how God had helped them by saving them from the Egyptians, so they were sure that He would help them as they made their way through the desert. Twice each day God provided food for them all, so that no one would go hungry. Each morning when the people woke up, they found the desert sand carpeted with a dew. As the sun rose and the dew disappeared, the sand was covered with a thin, white powder. This was a special food called 'manna', which tasted something like honey biscuits. Then each evening God sent flocks of small birds called quails, which the people caught and killed. God's daily supply of manna and quails meant that no one went without food.

After travelling for several weeks, many of the people became tired of eating the same thing day after day. To make matters worse, they reached a rocky area and ran out of water, so a group of them went to see Moses and Aaron. 'Do you want us to die in this desert?' they asked. 'We'd rather have stayed where we were, in Egypt. There we had corn, figs, grapes—food of all sorts. Now there's no water to drink either.'

Moses and Aaron went to a quiet part of the camp and asked God to show them what to do. When God had spoken to them, they went back and called all the

Israelites to meet at once near an outcrop of rock. God wanted the people to see His power, so He told Moses to stand at the rock-face and speak to it. Water would then pour out of it.

In front of the thousands of Israelites Moses stood near the rock, but instead of speaking to it, he hit it with his stick. At once a torrent of water gushed out. The people were amazed and forgot their grumbles as they drank from the cooling stream.

God was not pleased with Moses, because he had hit the rock, and some people would now think it was Moses, not God, who had given them the water. So God told Moses and Aaron that, as they had done this, they would die before the people reached the land of Canaan.

The Israelites travelled on across the desert. At a place named Rephidim they were attacked by some people called Amalekites. Moses decided that they had to defend themselves, so he asked a brave man named Joshua to choose a band of men to fight the Amalekites.

The next day Joshua led his soldiers to meet the enemy. Moses wanted to see what would happen, so he took two men, Aaron and Hur, with him and climbed a hill overlooking the place where the battle was going on. As he watched, he lifted up his arms and prayed that God would help Joshua and his men to win. While he did this, the Israelites managed to drive the Amalekites back.

The battle went on for a long time. Although Moses still prayed, his arms became more and more tired and he had to lower them. As soon as they dropped to his sides, the Amalekites started winning. When he made a great effort and lifted his arms again, the Israelites began to win once more.

In the afternoon, when he was exhausted, he sat on a large stone, still praying to God. After some time Aaron and Hur held his arms up until, at sunset, Joshua defeated the enemy completely.

The Israelites then thanked God for the way He had answered Moses' prayers and protected them from the Amalekites.

The Ten Commandments

Exodus 20 & 32

Three months after the Israelites had escaped from Egypt, they reached a rocky area called Mount Sinai. While they camped there, Moses climbed the mountain alone to be by himself and to pray to God. As he was praying, God spoke to him and made a promise. 'If you and the people will trust me and do as I say, in return I will make you my special people for ever.'

Moses went back and reported this to his leaders, who were very pleased and made up their minds to serve and obey the Lord God, as He had asked.

Three days later Mount Sinai was covered by thick clouds; lightning flashed around the peaks, and thunder boomed through the valleys. A loud trumpet blast seemed to come from the skies. Everyone knew that God wanted to say something very important to them all, but they were afraid to go nearer than the foot of the mountain, so Moses climbed up alone to talk again to God.

The words God spoke to Moses became very important to the Israelites: they were the rules and laws by which He wanted them to live. Of all the instructions He gave them, the Ten Commandments were the most important:

1 You must not worship any other gods but Me.

2 You must not make for yourselves images of anything in heaven or on the earth, because I alone am the Lord your God.

3 You must not use my name wrongly.

4 You must keep the seventh day of each week for resting and worshipping. Finish all your work in the other six days.

5 Always respect your parents.

6 Never murder anyone.

7 Husbands must be faithful to their wives; wives must be faithful to their husbands.

8 Never steal anything.

9 Never invent lies or untrue stories about people.

10 Never long for other people's property.

God carved these rules on two pieces of stone, which He gave to Moses, together with other laws.

Moses was gone for several days, and the people feared that he would never return. They decided to make a statue to worship, and Aaron was foolish enough to agree. They melted down gold jewellery to make a statue of a golden bull.

When Moses came down the mountain, carrying the stone slabs on which the Ten Commandments were engraved, he saw what was happening and was furious. The people were breaking some of the very laws which he held in his hands.

In his rage he hurled down the slabs, smashing them on the rocks below. He stormed into the camp and ordered the golden bull to be melted. He went up the mountain again to ask God to forgive them. God said that although He would have to punish them, He would forgive them, because they were His people, and He loved them. He promised to guide them as they travelled on through the desert and He gave Moses two more stone slabs, on which He again wrote the Ten Commandments. The Israelites kept these and guarded them very carefully, because they were a reminder of God's laws and their own promise to obey Him.

The Tabernacle

Exodus 35–40

While the Israelites were travelling through the desert, they were never in any one place long enough to build a Temple in which they could worship God. They decided that they would make a special tent which could be dismantled easily and carried with them and they called it the Tabernacle.

Moses asked all the people to make gifts to him of precious metals, fine materials and the best wood. These would then be used to make not only the new Tabernacle, but also all the items which were needed for the ceremonies.

Wherever the Israelites stopped, they erected the large tent and made a courtyard around it with some portable screens. They then pitched their own family tents in groups, according to the tribes they belonged to, around the outer screens. Having the Tabernacle in the middle of the camp was a reminder that God was always at the centre of their lives.

If an Israelite wanted to attend a ceremony at the Tabernacle, he first walked through the entrance in the screens. The entrance curtain was two metres high and made of fine linen woven with blue, purple and red wool. The rectangular courtyard was quite large, measuring 44 metres by 22 metres.

Walking forward he would come to the great Altar of Sacrifice which had been made of wood overlaid with metal. It was square with horn-shaped pieces rising from each corner. Sacrifices were burned and offered by the priests on the grid on top of the altar.

Between this altar and the tent itself was a large bronze basin made from mirrors given by the Israelite women. Here the priests had to wash before being dressed in special robes to perform the ceremonies. Beyond the basin was the magnificent Tabernacle.

It was made of a rectangular frame of gold-covered wood which stood four metres high, over the top of which they laid a covering of fine linen woven like the entrance in blue, purple and red, and then three layers of animal skins. The outer cover was made of the finest leather. It took up an area which measured over 13 metres long by about 4 metres wide. Only the priests were allowed to go through the doorway, which was a huge curtain of linen woven as before. Inside, the tent was divided into two rooms. In the first, called the Holy Place, the priests kept three pieces of furniture: a golden seven-branched candlestick, the Altar of Incense and the Table of Showbread, on which twelve loaves were placed as a reminder of all that God provided for His people.

Once a year, one person, the High Priest, was allowed to enter the second room which was called the Most Holy Place. There he made a special offering to God and asked Him to forgive the wrongs of the people. It was here that they kept a piece of furniture which was most precious to them all. The Ark of the Covenant, as it was called, was a golden chest in which were kept the stone slabs on which God gave Moses the Ten Commandments. On the lid of the Ark were two winged figures of hammered gold. The Ark was precious to the Israelites because it was always a reminder that God was with them and they believed that they would all prosper as long as it stayed with them. When they had to move on and the Tabernacle was dismantled, the Ark was covered by a cloth, so that no one could see it, and it was carried along by men with shoulder poles.

Wherever the Israelites went, the tent went with them and for 300 years it was the place where they all worshipped God.

The Spies and the Fruit

Numbers 13

It was a hard life for the people of Israel, to keep travelling month after month through the desert. They longed to stop and settle down in a place where they could grow their crops and build proper houses. They became curious about Canaan, the land which God had promised to give them. So Moses chose twelve men to go ahead as spies to explore the area. Before they left, he called them together and gave them their instructions.

'I want you to come back and tell us what sort of place Canaan is. For instance, how many people live there already? Are they well armed? Do they live in tents, villages, or walled cities? Is the soil suitable for farming? And, as it will soon be the grape harvest, bring us some of the fruit that grows there, so that we can see how good it is.'

The spies were away for forty days. They brought back pomegranates, figs and branches of grapes. The grapes they had brought were so huge that two men had to fasten each branch onto a pole and carry it between them.

Although the fruit was better than they had hoped

for, ten of the spies brought back gloomy reports about the people of Canaan. They said that everyone there was so strong and the cities so well defended that Moses could not possibly lead the Israelites into that land.

Two of the spies, however, Caleb and Joshua, said something very different. 'We must go,' they urged Moses. 'If the Lord God is with us, He will give us the land. He will protect us. You must not be afraid.'

But the people didn't believe Caleb and Joshua, and as a result God became angry with them. He told them that they would have to spend many more years travelling in the desert and that, apart from Caleb and Joshua, no one over twenty years old would live to see their new country.

So, on they travelled. The Israelites frequently grumbled against God and many wished they had never left Egypt. God became so annoyed at this that He sent hundreds of poisonous snakes among their tents, in order to bring them to their senses. When people began to die from the snake bites, everyone cried out to God for forgiveness. Moses also prayed to God, begging Him to spare them.

God heard them all and told Moses how the people would be saved. He must make a snake of bronze and fix it to a tall pole, which then had to be put up in the middle of the camp. Everyone who looked at the bronze snake would live. Moses did as God instructed. Dying people were carried from their tents to look at the snake and as they looked, so they began to recover. Once again the Israelites began to put their trust in God.

The People Reach Canaan

Joshua 2 & 3

The years went by and very few were left alive who could remember life in Egypt. They had travelled in a huge circle around the desert and now were approaching Canaan again. For years Moses had led the Israelites towards this new land which God had promised to them, but he never set foot in it. He merely glimpsed it from a distant hilltop and died before he reached it.

Joshua, one of the two spies who earlier had trusted God, took over from Moses as leader of the People of Israel. He decided that after they had crossed the River Jordan and were actually in Canaan, they would all head for the city of Jericho. Before giving the order to set out, Joshua sent two of his own spies to Jericho to see how well it was guarded.

When the men reached the city, a woman called Rahab sheltered them for the night. She had a house built into the city wall. Somehow the king of Jericho heard that they were there, so he sent soldiers to arrest them. They searched, but didn't find anyone, because Rahab had hidden them under the flax which she kept on the flat roof of her house.

In return for her kindness the spies promised Rahab that she would not be harmed when the Israelite army attacked Jericho. 'What you must do,' they told her, 'is to tie this red cord to your window. When our army sees it, they will not harm anyone in the house.'

The men returned and reported that they were sure that God would help the army to capture Jericho. When he heard the news, Joshua ordered all the people to get ready to travel at once. There was great excitement, because everyone knew that after forty years of desert life, they would be entering the promised land of Canaan.

Canaan was on the other side of the River Jordan. The Israelites had to cross it, so after they had all assembled on the east bank, the priests, who were carrying the Ark of the Covenant, stepped into the water first. The river flow became less and less, until it trickled and then stopped. This meant that the priests were able to cross over to the west bank, followed by the army and the rest of the people.

At last they had set foot in the land of Canaan. They knew that God had kept His word and they were so sure of His protection that they marched on hopefully towards the city of Jericho.

The Capture of Jericho

Joshua 6

When the Israelite army reached the hilltop city of Jericho, they found the gates firmly closed and barred against them. As Joshua looked up at the well-guarded walls, God spoke to him and told him what to do.

'Don't be afraid,' He said. 'Jericho will be yours. You have to march with the army around the city once a day for six days. Seven priests holding trumpets and carrying the Ark will walk in front of the soldiers to remind everyone that the God of Moses is with you. On the seventh day you will march seven times around the walls, with the priests blowing the trumpets. After that, sound one long trumpet blast. As soon as the soldiers hear it, they must all shout as loudly as they can. When this happens, the walls of Jericho will crumble and you will be able to capture it easily.'

Joshua told the priests and soldiers what to do. 'I want seven priests with trumpets to go with an armed guard ahead of the Ark. All other priests and soldiers will then march behind the Ark as it is carried around the city.' The procession lined up and then, on Joshua's orders, it began to move slowly forward. The priests blew the trumpets as loudly as possible, but no-one else was allowed to make a sound. The Ark was paraded once around Jericho and then, at night, it was brought back to the Israelites' camp.

The next day Joshua and his army got up early and everyone did exactly the same thing: they spent the whole day walking slowly around the foot of the hill. The people in the city must have been puzzled and nervous at such strange happenings, because Joshua gave the same orders for six days.

On the seventh day, as God had told him, Joshua

changed the instructions slightly. This time the procession had to walk faster and go around the hill seven times. On the first six circuits, they were to stay completely silent, without even blowing the trumpets. On the seventh circuit, as soon as the trumpets had sounded, every soldier and priest was to shout at the top of his voice. Before they did, Joshua spoke to the army. 'You can be sure,' he shouted, 'that the Lord God has won this battle for us. You must destroy everyone in the city, except for Rahab and anyone else in her house. If you find any silver, gold, bronze or iron, you may not keep it for yourselves. Now, get ready and blow the trumpets!'

The trumpets rang out around the city walls and the whole army sent up a great shout. Immediately the walls cracked open and crashed down. The army marched quickly up the hill and, clambering through the dust and rubble, entered the city. They captured it without any difficulty and, after making sure that Rahab and her family were safe, they set light to broken buildings and burnt them to the ground.

Rahab and her family were led through the smoke-filled streets out of the city, and taken to the safety of the Israelite camp.

The People of Israel were even more certain now that God was with Joshua and with them. The news of their victory spread rapidly throughout Canaan and everyone began to fear these new invaders.

Achan and the City of Ai

Joshua 7 & 8

Joshua's army went on from Jericho to capture another city called Ai. They were amazed and disheartened when the citizens of Ai drove off their attack. Because they felt that God had let them down, Joshua prayed, asking God for His help.

When God spoke to Joshua, He told him why the army had lost the battle at Ai. It was because someone had done wrong by disobeying Joshua's order and stealing some valuable articles from the ruins of Jericho. God said that He could not bless and protect the Israelites with a thief in the army.

Joshua at once began to hunt for the man. The culprit was found to be a soldier called Achan. When Joshua questioned him, he admitted everything. 'It is true, sir,' he said. 'I have done wrong. I stole an expensive cloak, some silver and a gold bar. If you search my tent, you'll find it all buried there.'

Some men went and found the items as Achan had described and brought them to Joshua. He had to punish Achan, so he ordered him to be killed and all his property destroyed.

Joshua could now think about Ai again and he managed to capture it by a trick. The night before he

planned to attack, half the Israelite army hid within striking distance of the city. The next morning Joshua took the other half up to the walls and then pretended to run away. At this the soldiers of Ai streamed out of the gates to chase them. When the city had no one to defend it, the other half of Joshua's men captured it and set it alight. They then followed the army of Ai and, after catching up with them, helped Joshua's section to defeat them in battle.

The people of Israel carried on fighting their way throughout the land of Canaan. Wherever they went, they had success until eventually they owned the whole area. Joshua divided it between all the people who were at last able to settle and begin a new peaceful life for themselves.

Some years later, when Joshua was sure that he would soon die, he called all the people together and spoke to them for the last time. He reminded them how God had led and protected them from the days of Abraham until that moment. He then went on to encourage them for the future. 'Honour the Lord,' he called out. 'Serve Him faithfully. Do not worship other gods. I want you to know this: as for myself and my family, we will serve the Lord!'

The people promised the same thing themselves. 'We will also serve the Lord,' they said. 'He is our God. We will obey His commands.'

It pleased Joshua to hear the people speak like this and he longed for them to keep their word. Soon after this great meeting Joshua died.

Deborah and Barak

Judges 4 & 5

For a while after Joshua's death the people of Israel kept their promise and served God faithfully. After some years they began to worship other gods and statues. Because of this they lost battles and then cried to the Lord God for help. This happened time after time. On each occasion, when they asked for God's forgiveness, He gave it to them, and on each occasion someone was found to lead them back to God and back to the success they had once enjoyed.

These leaders, who had to keep rescuing the people from disaster, were called 'judges'. One of them was a very clever woman called Deborah. Israelites would go to her when they had serious problems and she would give them her advice. Sometimes she would tell them what God wanted them to do.

An enemy king called Jabin kept attacking the Israelites until they were very afraid and asked God to help them. Deborah believed that God wanted them to defend themselves, so she asked a man named Barak to visit her. 'Barak,' she said when he came, 'I want you to pick 10,000 men to form an army. You must then attack Sisera, who is the leader of Jabin's soldiers. Even though he has a great many chariots, you will win.'

'I'll fight if you promise to come with me,' he replied. So Deborah agreed and the day of the battle finally arrived.

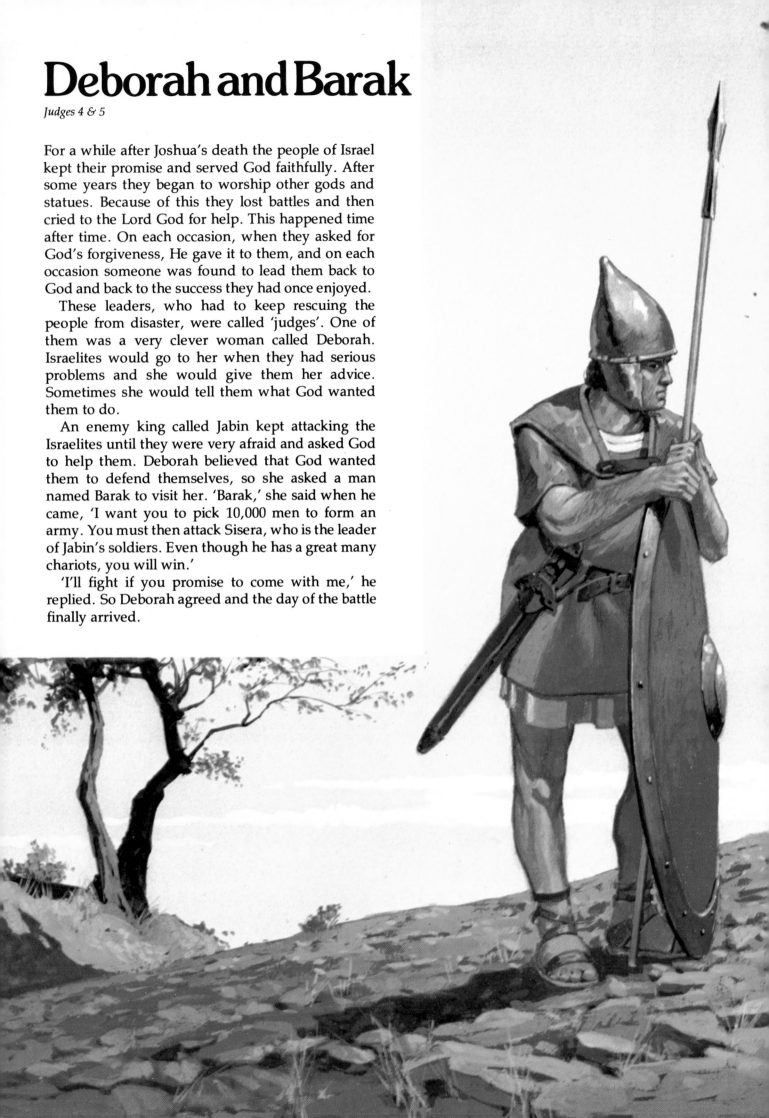

'Go,' she told him. 'The Lord is with you!'

The two armies fought fiercely until Barak won a complete victory. Most of Jabin's army was destroyed, but Sisera, the commander, managed to escape. He ran and ran until, exhausted, he reached the tent of a woman he knew called Jael. She took him into the tent and drew a curtain across to hide him. 'Please,' he gasped. 'I'm so thirsty. Give me a drink of water.'

She gave him some milk and then he asked her to keep watch outside the tent while he rested. He was fast asleep within moments. What he did not realize was that Jael was not on his side. When she was sure that he was sound asleep, she crept up to him with a hammer and a tent-peg. She then killed him by driving the peg right through his head.

It was not long before Barak and his men passed by, hunting for Sisera, so Jael showed him what she had done. Deborah and Barak were so pleased with the victory that they sang a song of rejoicing:

'Praised be our Lord God!
Hear this, kings! Listen, rulers!
The words I sing and the music I play
Are in honour of the Lord God of Israel!
O Lord, may all your enemies be destroyed;
But let those who serve you shine
Like the light of the rising sun!'

Gideon Becomes a Leader

Judges 6

There was peace for about forty years after the defeat of Sisera and Jabin, but then the Israelites came under attack from people called the Midianites. In their raids they used to destroy crops and take any animals they could find. The Israelites felt helpless and soon ran out of food.

One night a young man named Gideon was threshing some wheat. So as not to be seen by the Midianites, he was doing it in a wine press which was out of sight of the surrounding countryside. He was in the middle of his work when he suddenly noticed someone standing near him. At first he was afraid, but then he realized that it was a messenger from God. 'Gideon,' the messenger said, 'God is with you, and because you are strong He commands you to save Israel from the Midianites.'

'But how can I?' protested Gideon. 'I'm a nobody!'

'God will be with you,' the Lord's messenger replied. 'You will destroy the Midianites.'

'All right,' said Gideon. 'If the Lord God wants me to lead His people, give me a sign. Prove it to me, but first let me bring you some food.'

'Very well,' answered the messenger. 'I'll wait here until you come back.'

Gideon went home and prepared a meal. He cooked some goat's meat, baked some bread and boiled up some soup. He then returned to the wine press and offered it all to the messenger, who asked him to do something very strange. 'I want you to place the bread and meat here, on this rock,' he said. 'Then pour the soup over it.'

Gideon did as he was told. To his amazement the man touched it with a stick and at once fire burst from the rock and burned up the food. This was the sign he had asked for, so now he knew that God would be with him, helping him to lead the Israelites to victory against their enemies.

Gideon was unhappy because his own family and most of their neighbours did not worship the Lord God. One night he took ten servants and smashed the statues of the other gods which his father had made. In the morning, when people woke up and saw what he had done, most of them were very angry. But to Gideon's relief his father stood up for him and said that he had done the right thing.

Gideon's courage grew, as over 30,000 men joined him to fight the Midianites. He still wanted to be absolutely certain that he was doing the right thing, so he asked God for another sign. 'Tonight I am going to put a woollen fleece outside on the ground. In the morning I will look at it, and if the ground is dry, but the fleece wet with dew, then I will know that you are with me.'

The next day the wool was just as Gideon had asked, but even so he asked God for another sign. This time he wanted the fleece to be dry and the ground wet. Again God did as he asked. Gideon no longer had any doubts at all, so he began to prepare his soldiers to meet the Midianites.

Gideon and the Midianites

Judges 7

Gideon was preparing to fight the Midianites when God told him that he had too many soldiers. 'If you have too many,' God said, 'they will all think that they've won the battle without my help.'

Gideon then gave his men the chance to leave the army if they were afraid. Of the men 22,000 gladly went home, but still God said that there were too many, so He asked Gideon to watch them when they next went to drink from the nearby stream. He could only keep the ones who lay on the bank and drank like dogs straight from the water. When they came to do it, Gideon was dismayed to find there were only 300 who drank in this way. But God was not dismayed. 'You will win against the Midianites with only those 300 soldiers,' He promised.

Although he trusted God, Gideon was naturally worried that night at the thought of attacking with such a small army, so he decided on a dangerous

plan. He would secretly visit the enemy camp to find out as much as he could.

He woke his servant Purah and the two of them moved stealthily down the valley towards the Midianites. They were staggered to see the size of the enemy forces: their camels, tents and supplies seemed to cover the entire ground. Just then, they heard two guards talking together, so Gideon and Purah crawled as close as they could to hear what they were saying without being discovered. 'I had a strange dream last night,' said one of the Midianites. 'A barley loaf came hurtling down the hillside, rolled right into the camp here, collided with a tent and flattened it. What do you make of that?'

There was fear in his companion's voice when he answered. 'It must mean Gideon and the Israelite army. They're going to come down the hillside and destroy us all.'

Hearing this made Gideon confident again that God would help him to defeat the Midianites, so he went quickly back to his own camp and began to wake the 300 soldiers. 'Come on! Get up! We're going to attack now, tonight. The Lord will give us the victory!'

Next he made them form into three sections, each with 100 men. Every soldier was given a trumpet, and a jar with a flaming torch inside. 'This is the plan,' Gideon told them. 'We will surround the enemy tents. My group will try to reach the edge of the camp unseen. As soon as we get there, I will give a signal for you all, so listen and watch carefully. I want no fighting. When we're ready, my men will blow their trumpets and shout, "For God and for Gideon". The moment you hear that, I want the rest of you to do the same and to break the jars you're holding.'

Concealed by the shadows of the valley, Gideon and his 300 Israelites made their way down to the Midianite camp and positioned themselves right around it. Then, at Gideon's signal, the silence of the night was shattered by the blasts of 300 trumpets, the shouts of 300 men and the smashing of 300 jars. The sleeping enemy woke suddenly, as the din echoed around the hillsides, sounding more like the noise of thousands. The Midianites saw the flames of the torches making a ring of fire around their camp and they panicked, certain that they had been surrounded by a vast army. In the half light of the camp, they began to kill one another and then fled screaming into the darkness of the desert. Gideon's men followed them that night and for several days until they had been completely defeated. Afterwards Gideon gave thanks to God for giving him the victory over the Midianites and for making the land of Canaan a place of peace.

Samson and the Lion

Judges 14–16

As time went by, many different armies tried to invade Canaan to capture it from the Israelites. One of these was the army of the Philistines, who were always trying to force their way inland from their settlements on the sea coast. For a while they captured and ruled large areas of Israelite territory. A very strong Israelite boy called Samson grew up in this part of the land and when he was old enough to marry, he decided that he wanted one of the Philistine girls to be his wife. His parents were not pleased, but Samson went ahead.

On the way to the wedding he passed the body of a lion which he had killed in a vineyard some days before. When he went to look at it, he found a swarm of bees around it and inside the body some honey which they had made. He scooped out a handful and ate it going along. At last he reached the girl's home and the seven-day wedding feast began. Most of the people there were Philistines and many of the young men were upset that an Israelite was marrying a Philistine girl. This annoyed Samson, so he challenged them to answer a riddle. 'Listen,' he called out, 'I will give each of you some linen and a set of new clothes if you can tell what this means before the wedding is over. Here's a riddle: From the hungry came food; from the strong came sweetness. Now

answer that for me. What does it mean?'

The Philistine men went silent, and even three days later none of them knew the answer. They became embarrassed and angry that an Israelite had caught them out, so they persuaded Samson's new wife to find out what it meant.

She did this for them and on the last day of the feast, they gave Samson the answer. 'You found honey in a hungry lion; that's how sweetness came from the strong.'

Samson was so furious at their trick that he gave his wife to another man. He then had to give the young men their linen and clothes, so he killed thirty Philistines from another city and took what they had been wearing.

The Philistines came to hate Samson and he took every chance to fight them. One day he trapped 300 foxes and tied them together in pairs. He fastened burning torches to their tails and drove them into the Philistine's cornfields and burnt all the crops.

Samson was then hunted by his enemies, who wanted to kill him. He was forced to hide in the hills, but some Israelites betrayed him and he was captured. He was so strong that he broke the ropes which they had put around his arms. As he made his escape, he killed a great many Philistines using a donkey's jaw-bone as a weapon.

Once, Samson went at night to Gaza, the most important Philistine city, hoping that he would not be recognized. But he was, so the Philistines shut the city gate, and planned to capture him the next morning. Samson managed to outwit them by deciding to leave at midnight. When he found the gate barred, he pulled the whole thing out of the ground and made off safely into the countryside with the pieces of the wooden gate on his shoulders.

Samson and Delilah

Judges 16

Later Samson met a girl called Delilah and loved her so much that he would do anything for her. The Philistine leaders discovered that he was visiting her, so they offered her a great deal of money if she would tell them how Samson could be made weak, so that they could capture him easily.

She agreed to find out and, on Samson's next visit, she asked him gently, 'What makes you so strong, Samson? Tell me what would someone have to do to make you their prisoner?'

'They'd have to bind me with seven new bowstrings,' he replied. She then got seven bowstrings and tied Samson up when he was asleep. As soon as all was ready she signalled to the waiting Philistines, who rushed into the room. Samson woke up, but the bowstrings snapped like a burnt thread, so they were not able to seize him.

Twice more Delilah tried to find out the secret of his strength: she bound him with brand new ropes and then wove his plaited hair on to a loom, but on each occasion Samson tricked her and so managed to stay free. He loved her so much that, even though she kept betraying him, he kept coming back to her.

The fourth time she asked him for his secret, he told her what it was. 'From my boyhood I have promised to serve God and as a sign of this I have never cut my hair. If anyone were to cut it, I would feel I had broken my promise. God would no longer give me His strength and I would become weak.'

Delilah informed some of the Philistines, who came at once and waited outside until Samson had fallen asleep. Then one of them crept in and cut off his seven locks of hair as he lay sleeping in Delilah's arms. She began to shout loudly at him, 'Samson! The Philistines are here! Samson!'

He woke up immediately, but was too weak to hold off the men who attacked him. At last their hated enemy was in their hands. They shackled him with strong, bronze chains and then cruelly attacked his eyes until he was blind. He was taken to the city of Gaza where they made him work grinding corn in the prison. As the months passed, his hair slowly grew again and his strength began to return.

The Philistines were so delighted to have captured him that they held a great feast to celebrate. Thousands of people came and, while they were singing and dancing, the leaders had Samson dragged from prison so that they could laugh at him.

Samson asked the boy who was guiding him to let him lean against the huge pillars which held up the roof. As soon as he felt the pillars, he prayed to God for his old strength again and then heaved with all his colossal power against the great stones. They gave way and the roof crashed down with a thunderous roar crushing the Philistines and Samson to death beneath the rubble.

Ruth

The Book of Ruth

All this fighting made life very hard for the Israelites but having these problems also made families very close in their love and loyalty for one another.

Once, during a terrible famine, a man from Bethlehem called Elimelech decided to travel to the country of Moab to find food. With him went his wife, Naomi, and their two sons, Mahlon and Chilion. They lived there for many years and their sons married Moabite girls called Orphah and Ruth. All went well until first Elimelech and then his two sons died.

Naomi, who was old by now, made up her mind to return to Bethlehem where some of her relatives still lived. Although it meant leaving their home country, Ruth and Orphah set off with her. They had not travelled very far when Naomi stopped and tried to persuade them to return to Moab. Orphah really wanted to do this, so she sadly said goodbye to Naomi and went back. Ruth was determined to stay with Naomi. 'I want to be with you wherever you go,' she said. 'Your people will be my people. Your God will be my God.'

Naomi agreed, and they travelled on to Bethlehem. When they arrived, everyone was excited to see Naomi again after so many years. They both needed some grain for food, so, as it was harvest time, Ruth went to see if she could find some. She came to a field where barley was being cut, and followed behind the reapers to pick up anything they dropped. She did not realize that the field belonged to a man called Boaz, or that he was a relative of

Naomi's husband Elimelech.

Later that day Boaz himself came up, saw Ruth and asked his workers who she was. As soon as they had told him, he spoke to her in a kindly way. 'I know how much you have given up to stay with Naomi,' he said. 'May God bless and repay you well for all your love.'

After they had talked, Boaz told his workers to drop some barley deliberately so that Ruth would have plenty to take away. He also offered her food and drink. In the evening, when Ruth told Naomi how Boaz had looked after her during the day, this gave Naomi an idea. At that time, if a woman's husband died, usually the close relatives of the dead man would look after her. As Boaz was a close relative of Elimelech, Naomi told Ruth to visit him that very night to ask him to care for her.

Boaz had finished his meal and fallen asleep outside where he had been sorting the grain from the straw. He was lying on a mound of barley when Ruth found him. She said nothing, but lay down at his feet. In the middle of the night he woke and was startled to see someone there. 'Who is it? What do you want?' he said, not recognizing her.

'I'm Ruth,' she answered. 'Naomi's daughter-in-law. Sir, you are my nearest relative, so I've come to ask if you will care for me by making me your wife.'

Boaz was pleased that she had come. 'May God bless you,' he said. 'In the morning I will try to do as you have asked.'

The next day Boaz made all the necessary arrangements and soon he and Ruth were married. Later they had a son, who brought them and Naomi a great deal of joy. So although Ruth had given up everything to be with Naomi, God blessed her and gave her a new life of happiness with Boaz.

Eli and Samuel

I Samuel 1–3

For many years the Israelites worshipped God at a place called Shiloh. A priest named Eli looked after the Tabernacle there and arranged all the ceremonies.

One day he saw a woman come in who was in tears. She prayed silently, and Eli saw that she was very upset. 'Don't be anxious,' he said quietly, 'I hope that the God of Israel will give you what you want.' She was encouraged by his words.

The woman, whose name was Hannah, was crying because she wanted to have a son. Soon, to her joy, she found that she was going to have a baby. When it was born, she called the boy Samuel. She was very grateful to God, so she decided that when he was a little older she would take him to Shiloh and leave him to serve God there with Eli.

The old priest was pleased to have the young boy to help him, since his own sons, Hophni and Phinehas, set a bad example by cheating and bullying the Israelites who went there to worship God. Each year Hannah used to visit Samuel.

As Samuel grew older, he pleased God and the people who came to the Tabernacle by the way he behaved. It was the opposite with Eli's sons, and, because of the wrong things they did, God told Eli

that unhappiness awaited him. 'The time will come,' He said, 'when the rest of your family will die before they are old. You are to blame, since you have let Hophni and Phinehas spoil my Tabernacle.'

One night Samuel was asleep in the Tabernacle when, just before dawn, God called to him, 'Samuel! Samuel!' The boy thought it was Eli, so he ran and woke him up. The old man looked puzzled. 'You called me, sir,' Samuel explained, 'so I came at once.'

'I didn't say anything,' he replied. 'You must have been dreaming. Go straight to bed.'

Samuel did as he was told, but then God spoke to him again. Once more he went to Eli and once more Eli sent him back. When he had returned to his room, he heard someone calling a third time. He made straight for Eli's room and was insistent. 'You did call me. I heard it clearly.'

Eli suddenly realized who it was. 'No, I'm not the one calling you, Samuel. It is God. I want you to go back to your room yet again and when you hear his voice, say, "Speak, Lord, your servant is listening".'

He did just as Eli suggested and when God called him for the fourth time, he answered straightaway. 'Speak, Lord, I am listening.' God's message was that He would have to punish Eli and his family for the wrongs they had done.

The next morning Samuel told this to Eli, who said, 'He is the Lord. He will do what is right.'

During the years to come God spoke more and more to Samuel so that, as he became older, all the Israelites began to see that he was going to be God's special messenger, a prophet of the Lord.

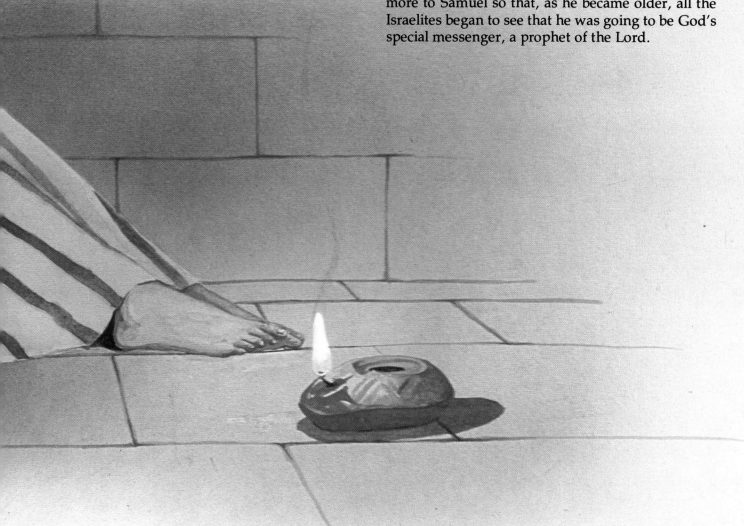

The Death of Eli

I Samuel 4

The Philistines kept up their efforts to capture the land of Canaan, so the Israelites formed an army again and met them in a fierce battle. The Philistines won, killing about 4,000 soldiers in the fighting.

This dismayed the Israelite leaders who decided that the only thing they could do was to bring the Ark of the Covenant from the Tabernacle at Shiloh. This was the special box in which they kept the Ten Commandments which God had given to Moses. They believed that if they did this, God would be close to them when they fought the enemy again.

The Israelite army was full of hope when they next marched to meet the Philistines. Even though they carried the Ark into the middle of the battle, they were heavily defeated and thousands of Israelites were killed. Eli's two sons, Hophni and Phinehas, were among the dead. What happened to the Ark was even worse. The Philistines managed to capture it and took it back with them to their camp.

This was a disaster for the Israelites, because the Ark reminded them of God's goodness and they believed that without it God would not help them.

After the battle a messenger ran to Shiloh where Eli was waiting for news. The old man was so eager to hear what had happened that he was sitting on a seat by the roadside. When the messenger spotted him, he rushed up and told him everything. The shock was too great for Eli, who fainted and fell backwards off the seat. He was so heavy that the fall broke his neck and killed him. As God had told Samuel many years before, Eli and his family ended their lives in unhappiness.

The Return of the Ark

I Samuel 6

The Philistines realized that things were starting to go wrong for them because they had captured the Ark of the Covenant. They had put it in their temple at Ashdod near the statue of their god Dagon, and twice they discovered the statue knocked over. The second time its head and arms came off.

Later a terrible disease began to infect the people who lived in and around Ashdod. They knew these things had happened because of the Ark, so they tried to send it to another city. Everywhere it went the same disease broke out, so in desperation the Philistines decided to send it back to the Israelites.

They harnessed two cows to a new cart and placed the Ark on it. In a box next to it they put a gift of gold. Then the cows pulled the cart towards an Israelite town called Beth Shemesh, without anyone leading or guiding them. The Philistine leaders followed it at a safe distance to make sure it arrived.

Most of the people of Beth Shemesh were harvesting in the fields when someone spotted the cart coming towards them with the golden Ark shining in the sunlight. They were delighted and stopped work to celebrate. When they had lifted the Ark carefully on to the ground, there and then they made a sacrifice to show that they were thankful.

Although most of the Israelites were pleased to have the Ark back again and to know that the Lord God was with them, some were not interested because they had begun to worship other gods. Samuel, who was by now respected as the leader of the people, gave orders that all these statues of other gods should be destroyed.

Saul is Anointed King

I Samuel 10

When Samuel was old, the people had to decide who should follow him as leader. Samuel's two sons were dishonest and unpopular, so someone else was needed. The Israelites soon began to insist on having a king to rule over them for the first time in their history. Although Samuel was against the idea, it became his task to find the right person to lead the people in this way.

The first king of Israel was a tall young man named Saul, and it all came about because of a few stray donkeys! Saul's father, Kish, had lost the animals and he sent his son with a servant to look for them.

They travelled for days, but could not find them anywhere. They had run out of food and were on the point of giving up, when Saul's servant remembered that the prophet Samuel was living in the next town. They decided to go to see him, hoping that he would tell them where the donkeys had gone.

Meanwhile God had told Samuel that someone would be coming to see him and that he would be the new king. So when Saul arrived, the prophet surprised him by inviting him to a meal. 'Come and eat with me today,' said Samuel, 'and tomorrow I will answer your questions. And, by the way, forget about the donkeys—they've already been found! I am more interested in you, as are all the people of Israel.'

Saul did not understand his words and was even more puzzled when Samuel woke him at dawn the next day and told him to start on his way home. Saul and his servant got ready and then Samuel walked with them along the road. They stopped just outside the town where no one would see them. Samuel asked the servant to leave him alone with Saul.

'Saul,' he said when they were by themselves, 'God has told me to anoint you as ruler of all Israel. You are to govern and defend our people.' With that he took out a small jar which he had been carrying and poured the oil from it onto Saul's head. This was a sign that Saul was to be king.

Samuel saw that Saul could not believe what was happening to him, so he told him that on his way home he would meet two men who would talk about the lost donkeys and that later on he would meet three people who would offer him some bread.

Saul and his servant then took their leave of Samuel and went home. As they travelled, they met people who did just as the prophet had described. This made Saul certain that God wanted him to be king, but he told no one about it.

Samuel next had to show all the people of Israel that Saul was the right person to rule over them. He called the Israelites to a special meeting. They all wanted to see their first king and they came in their thousands. Every person belonged to one of the twelve tribes of Israel, so Samuel began by picking out one of the small tribes. 'Your new king,' he called

out, 'belongs to the tribe of Benjamin.' From this tribe he then pointed to the family of Matri, the one to which Saul belonged. 'Your new king is a member of this family.'

When this family walked forward, Saul was not there. He was afraid of what was going to happen, so he had hidden near the food store. Samuel waited until they had fetched him and then, in front of all the people, he asked Saul to come out. He was head and shoulders taller than most people and he looked an impressive young man as he stood beside Samuel. 'This is the man whom God has chosen!' Samuel declared. A great shout went up from everyone. 'Long live the king!'

Samuel Meets David

I Samuel 16; Psalm 23

Saul's reign began well. For several years he served God faithfully and won many victories against the Philistines. But after a while things started to go wrong and he began to disobey God.

Because God was not pleased with the way Saul was disobeying Him, He asked Samuel to find the person who would eventually become the new king after Saul's death. God sent Samuel to the small town of Bethlehem to look for the son of a farmer called Jesse, who was the grandson of Ruth and Boaz.

Samuel was afraid in case Saul found out, but God said that all would be well if the prophet carried out his wishes. When Samuel reached Bethlehem, he announced that he was going to hold a sacrifice and that he wanted Jesse and his family to be there.

Jesse soon came, together with seven of his sons. As Samuel looked at the young men, he was sure that none of them was the future king. The prophet could not understand it and asked Jesse if he had any more sons. 'Well, yes,' he replied. 'There's David, the youngest. He's out in the fields. We left him to look after the sheep.'

'I'd like you to fetch him,' Samuel said. 'We won't start the sacrifice until he comes.'

They had to wait a while until at last David arrived. Samuel was in no doubt when he saw this lively, auburn-haired boy, that he was to be the future ruler of Israel.

Then in front of Jesse and the rest of his family he anointed David with oil as a sign that one day he would be king. From then on God strengthened David and blessed everything he did.

It was not long before David met King Saul. Their meeting came about because David played the harp very well.

Saul had so many problems and worries that he found it hard to rest and sleep. One thing that seemed to calm him was the sound of a harp. He heard about David's musical talents and invited him to come to court to play for him. Saul liked him immediately and asked him to stay. Among the songs he played were many that he had written himself. He would have had plenty of time to think of words and tunes as he sat alone on the hillsides looking after the sheep. His most famous song tells how God cares for people with as much love as a shepherd cares for his sheep.

'The Lord is my shepherd: He gives me everything I need.
He makes me rest in grassy meadows and takes me to pools of clear water; He strengthens me again.
He is true to His word and leads me along the right paths.
Even though suffering surrounds me like a shadow-filled valley, yet you stay near me.
Your stick and staff keep me safe.
Upon my head You pour your healing oil.
You provide food for me, while my enemies surround me, and You fill my cup until it overflows.
I am sure that goodness and mercy will be with me every day of my life and I will be your companion for ever.'

One day, while David was with Saul, news came that the Philistines were preparing to attack the Israelites, so Saul decided to lead his army to face them.

David and Goliath

I Samuel 17

Saul found the Philistines camped on a hill-top and ordered the Israelite soldiers to pitch their tents on the opposite hill-top, with a valley between them. Neither army wanted to make the first move, but then one of the Philistines came forward to challenge his enemies. Goliath, as he was called, was a huge soldier nearly three metres tall. Heavy bronze armour covered this enormous man who shouted scornfully across the valley to the Israelites. 'Choose one of your men to fight with me. If he kills me, our whole army will be your slaves; if I win, you will be our slaves!'

His words terrified the Israelites. They had to accept the challenge, but did not know whom to send. Each day Goliath repeated the challenge.

One day David's father asked him to take some food to his brothers who were in Saul's army. When he got there, Goliath was shouting his daily challenge. The Israelite soldiers told David all about it and explained that king Saul was offering a reward to anyone who would fight him; he would give him money and his own daughter as a wife.

David startled everybody by boldly going straight to Saul and offering to challenge Goliath himself. 'What could you do?' snapped Saul. 'You're no more than a boy; he's a trained soldier!'

'Sir,' answered David, 'I have been a shepherd for many years. When lions and bears have attacked my

sheep, I have chased and killed them. God has protected me in the past; He will protect me now.'

'Very well,' Saul agreed. 'Go and fight him. I pray that God will be with you.'

David tried on Saul's own armour, but it was too heavy for him, so he made his way down the valley armed only with a stick and a shepherd's sling. As he crossed the brook at the bottom, he picked up five smooth stones for the sling and set off up the other side of the valley. Goliath saw him coming and started down to meet him. He roared with laughter when he saw David. 'Come on, boy, and I'll throw your dead body to the animals and birds.'

David did not flinch. 'You may be well armed, but I come in the name of the Lord God of Israel. Today you and the Philistine army will be destroyed.

Everyone will know that the God of Israel is powerful in battle.' He ran nimbly uphill towards Goliath and, when he got within range, he put a stone in the sling, whirled it round and shot it at great speed at the huge man. It hurled straight to his uncovered forehead and Goliath dropped to the ground. A single stone from David's sling had killed him. When he reached the body, David drew the Philistine's heavy sword and cut off his head.

As soon as the rest of the Philistine army saw that their champion had been killed, they deserted their camp and fled into the desert.

All Israel congratulated David and thanked God for the victory He had given them. From then David lived all the time in Saul's household and became as close as a brother to Jonathan, Saul's son.

Saul's Jealousy

I Samuel 18

As Saul and David returned from defeating Goliath, people in every town cheered as they went by. They danced and made up songs to celebrate the victory. One of the songs made Saul angry because it said that Saul had killed thousands of the enemy, while David had killed tens of thousands. From that moment Saul began to be jealous of David and at times his envy flared into terrible hatred.

The day after hearing the song, David was playing his harp to make Saul calm. A sudden rage gripped the king, who twice hurled a spear at him. He missed from close range and so became convinced that God was protecting David.

As a reward for killing Goliath, Saul had promised David that he could marry one of his two daughters.

Michal, the younger of them, loved the young man very much, but before Saul would let them marry, he demanded a high price from him. He had first to kill one hundred Philistines. The king hoped that in doing this, David would be killed. To Saul's surprise he killed two hundred men, and so earned the right to marry Michal.

Jonathan found out that his father still wanted to kill David, so he persuaded his friend to hide for a short time until Saul's temper had died down. While he was away, Jonathan pleaded with his father to stop this hatred and he made him promise never to harm David in the future.

David returned to the palace, but soon Saul's jealousy increased and he broke his word by hurling

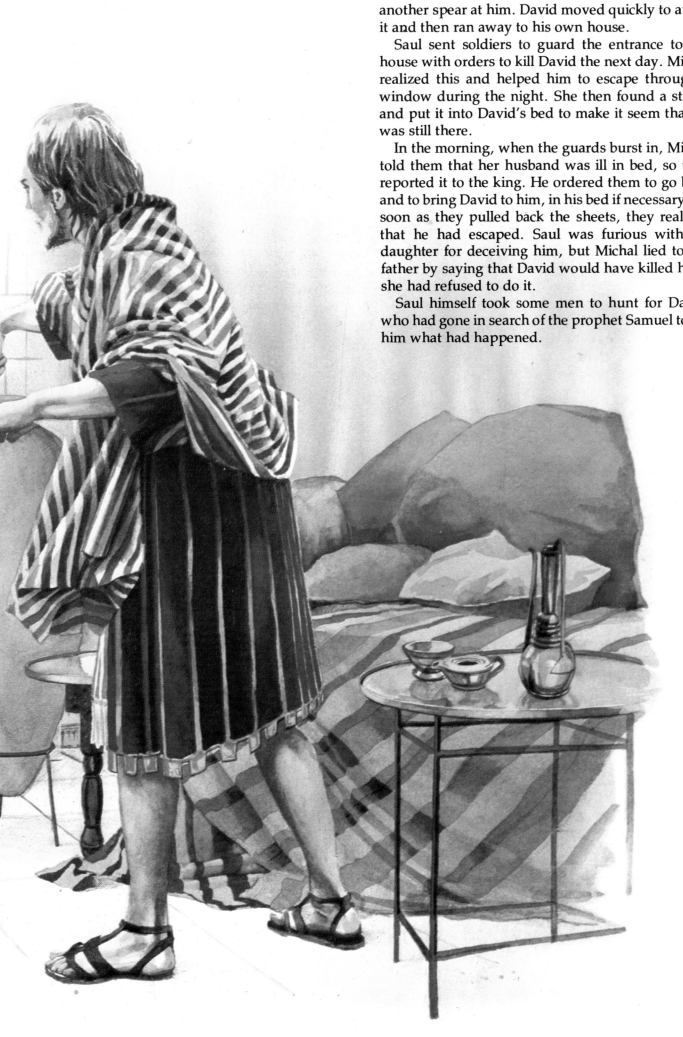

another spear at him. David moved quickly to avoid it and then ran away to his own house.

Saul sent soldiers to guard the entrance to the house with orders to kill David the next day. Michal realized this and helped him to escape through a window during the night. She then found a statue and put it into David's bed to make it seem that he was still there.

In the morning, when the guards burst in, Michal told them that her husband was ill in bed, so they reported it to the king. He ordered them to go back and to bring David to him, in his bed if necessary. As soon as they pulled back the sheets, they realized that he had escaped. Saul was furious with his daughter for deceiving him, but Michal lied to her father by saying that David would have killed her if she had refused to do it.

Saul himself took some men to hunt for David, who had gone in search of the prophet Samuel to tell him what had happened.

David and Jonathan

I Samuel 19, 20; Psalm 7

After a while Saul gave up the search and David managed to return secretly to talk to Jonathan. 'What have I done?' asked David. 'Your father does nothing but try to kill me.'

'I don't believe it!' his friend protested. 'My father promised not to harm you.'

'He has kept it from you, Jonathan. Believe me, I have been close to death for some time.'

'All right, but what can I do to help?'

'Every month I'm supposed to be at the palace to eat with your father,' David explained. 'Will you ask him if I can miss tomorrow's banquet? Tell him that you said I needn't go this month in order to be with my family at Bethlehem? I won't go, of course. I'll be here all the time. If he doesn't mind and agrees, I

shall know that he won't harm me; if the mention of me makes him angry, I shall be sure that I'm still in danger.'

They arranged for Jonathan to let David know the king's feelings by a special signal. David was to hide in a particular field behind a pile of stones. Jonathan would go to the place with a servant and shoot three arrows into the air. Then Jonathan would send the servant to look for them. If he shouted, 'Look, they're this side of you,' then it would be safe for David to return to the palace; if he shouted, 'They're on the other side of you,' then his life was in danger and he would have to escape.

With this plan agreed, the two young men made a solemn promise that they would always love one

another whatever happened. Then they said good-bye and Jonathan returned to the palace.

That evening Jonathan sat opposite King Saul at the meal table. One place was empty: it was the place reserved for David, but Saul did not mention him at all. The next evening David's place was empty again. While they were eating, Jonathan explained that he had given David permission to be away from the palace in order to visit his family.

Jonathan carried out the plan, but Saul burst into a rage when he heard David's name and turned on Jonathan for taking his friend's side. The king was so out of his mind with fury that he seized a spear and hurled it at his own son.

Jonathan was in no doubt that Saul would have no mercy for David, so the next morning he went with his servant to the prearranged place and gave David the arrow signal to escape without delay. He then sent the servant back to the town, and with sad hearts the two young friends parted company.

Saul became determined to hunt for David, so he sent soldiers to search for him and kill him. David had to lead the life of a criminal, moving on from place to place without proper food or shelter.

David cried out to God for His help and one day he put his feelings into the words of a song:

'O Lord my God, I take refuge in You.
Save me from those who pursue me,
Or they will tear me apart like a lion
And no one will rescue me.
O Lord my God, if I have done wrong,
If I have ever treated a friend with harshness,
Then let my enemies destroy me
And let them trample me into the dust.
O Lord, let wickedness come to an end;
Protect those who do what is right.
God is my shield; He is a fair judge.
I will give thanks to the Lord for He is good;
I will praise His name, the mighty God.'

The Hunt for David

I Samuel 21–30

Saul himself joined the search for David and he put to death anyone who sheltered him or gave him food. David and the men who were with him managed to avoid the king by staying in the hilly areas where it was hard to track anyone down. On one occasion only a valley separated the two groups and Saul would probably have caught up with David had not a messenger arrived to say that Saul's soldiers were needed elsewhere to fight off some attacking Philistines.

When Saul was able to start the hunt again, he used 3,000 men to comb the area where David had been last seen. One day by chance the king went into the very cave where David and his soldiers happened to be hiding. Saul did not notice them because the cave was very deep and they had moved well out of sight when he went in.

David's soldiers saw that he would be able to kill Saul and they tried to make him do it. He crept forward with a knife in his hand, but he refused to harm his enemy. Instead he managed to lift the corner of Saul's cloak and cut a piece from it. David went back to his men and told them not to harm Saul because he was God's chosen king.

As Saul left the cave, David called after him and showed him the piece of material he had cut off. 'My lord, I could have killed you, but I spared your life. Surely you can now see that I mean you no harm?'

Saul was sad when he heard David, because he knew that he was wrong to hunt him. 'May the Lord bless you for your kindness today,' he said. Saul then returned to his camp, but soon his old jealousy crept back and he started to hunt David again. Later on David had yet another chance to kill him, but he still would not do anything to hurt the king.

The Death of Saul

I Samuel 31; II Samuel 1

It was not long before the Philistines again made war against the Israelites, who lost a fierce battle at Mount Gilboa. After Saul and Jonathan had seen hundreds of soldiers killed around them, they made up their minds to try to escape with some of their men. They slipped away from the battlefield, but the Philistines caught up with them and killed Jonathan. Saul himself was badly wounded and shouted desperately to his armour-bearer, 'Don't let the enemy capture me and put me to death; draw your sword and kill me with it.' The young man could not bring himself to do it, so Saul fell on his own sword and died. All Saul's soldiers were killed in the fighting.

The Israelites were saddened at the news and David, when he heard it, tore his coat in sorrow. He took his harp and composed a song to show how he and everyone felt.

'All your greatness, Israel, has been cut down on
    the mountains!
The bravest of our men has fallen.
Let there be no more rain or dew on Mount Gilboa,
For there the shields of the great were spoiled,
And the shield of Saul has become dull.
We think of Saul and Jonathan, the ones we loved;
In life and in death they stayed together;
They were swifter than eagles and stronger than
    lions.
I grieve for you, my brother Jonathan,
For your love meant more to me than the love of
    any woman.'

David and Mephibosheth

II Samuel 4 & 9

After Saul's death David hoped to become the ruler of the Israelites, but not all the people wanted him as their king. Eventually they all agreed, and David, at the age of thirty, became king of Israel and lived in the palace in Jerusalem. He decided that the Ark of the Covenant, the special box containing the Ten Commandments, should be brought to the city as a reminder that God was with His people. It was carried and then placed in a newly made Tabernacle.

David's reign began well with many victories against the enemies of the Israelites. He often thought of the past and one day he wondered whether there were any relatives of Saul still alive. To his delight they found one of Jonathan's sons, a young man called Mephibosheth, who could not walk properly because of a fall he had had when he was five years old. Since that time everyone had forgotten about him.

David sent for him at once, but Mephibosheth did not want to go because he was afraid of meeting him. When he reached the palace, he nervously went in and was taken to the king.

'Don't be afraid,' David told him. 'I want to look after you, because of my love for your father, Jonathan.'

'But, sir,' he protested, 'I am useless. Why should you be kind to me?'

David cared for him, giving him some of Saul's former lands, and he asked him to eat at the king's table, as if he were his own son.

David and Bathsheba

II Samuel 11

One spring afternoon David was walking by himself on the roof of his Jerusalem palace, when suddenly he noticed a beautiful woman washing in a nearby courtyard. He found out that her name was Bathsheba, and invited her to the palace to see him. When they met, he fell in love with her and wanted to marry her, but he discovered that she was married already.

Although he knew that it was wrong, King David decided to arrange for Uriah, her husband, to be killed, so that she could become his wife. He sent a message to Joab, the commander of the Israelite army, telling him to put Uriah in the front line when they next had to fight.

It was not long before Joab and the army had to besiege a city, so he ordered Uriah to attack it at the place where the enemy was strongest. A number of Israelites were killed, and among them was Uriah.

Joab sent a messenger at once to the king to tell him what had happened. David would normally have been angry to learn that many of his men had died, but this time he was pleased because Uriah had lost his life. 'Go back to Joab,' he told the messenger, 'and tell him not to be worried at the number of our men who have been killed. I'm sure that if he attacks the city again, he will capture it.'

Soon afterwards David married Bathsheba. God was angry at the way David had arranged for Uriah to be killed, but at first the king did not seem to realize how wrong he had been. Because of this, God sent a messenger, the prophet Nathan, to talk to him.

89

David and Nathan

II Samuel 12; Psalm 51

Nathan dared not accuse the king of murder, so he found a different way to make him see the wickedness of what he had done. When he visited David, he told him a story. 'My lord,' he said, 'I'd like to hear your opinion about two men who both lived in the same town. One was rich and the other was poor.

The rich man owned a great many sheep and cattle, but the poor man had only one lamb. One day the rich man was entertaining guests and, rather than use one of his own animals for a meal, he took the poor man's lamb and killed it instead.'

David was furious when he heard about it. 'The man deserves nothing less than death!' he thundered. 'He ought to repay the poor man four times over.'

'Sir, forgive me,' Nathan interrupted, 'but you are the man in my story. The Lord God has given you everything: success, riches, the kingdom of Israel itself. Yet you saw the wife of an ordinary man, Uriah, and you wanted her for yourself, so you killed him in order to marry her. Be sure of this, God will bring trouble on your family in the future and all Israel will know why.'

David realized the terrible wrong he had done and he begged God for forgiveness. Although Nathan assured him that God would forgive him, David still felt ashamed and showed it in another of his songs:

'Lord God, have mercy on me and show me Your great love;
Wash away my wrongdoing and cleanse me from my sin.
I know I have done wrong; I never forget how I have failed.
I deserve to be judged: You are right to condemn me.
You expect me to be honest and truthful: help me to be full of your wisdom.
Forgive my wickedness and then I will be clean:
Wash me and then I will be whiter than the snow.
Put a new heart in me, O God; make me trustworthy once again.
Give me the joy of Your forgiveness and help me to obey you.
All I can offer you, O God, is a broken spirit; You will not despise a broken heart.
Save me, O Lord, and I will praise Your name.'

It was not long before Nathan's words to David came true and David's life became full of sadness.

David and Absalom

II Samuel 13 & 14

Among King David's many children there was one son who was well known throughout Israel because of his handsome appearance. This was Absalom, a strong young man with thick black hair, who had a sister, Tamar, who was also very attractive. One day their half-brother Amnon attacked and insulted Tamar. Absalom was furious and hated Amnon so much that he made up his mind to kill him.

His chance came two years later when Amnon came to a banquet at his house. Towards the end of the meal Absalom's servants carried out his orders and murdered their guest.

Although King David had been angry at Amnon's attack on Tamar, he was also enraged by Absalom's revenge. For his own safety Absalom left the country to escape from his father.

After about three years David's commander, Joab, realized that the king missed Absalom very much, so he persuaded him that it was not right to keep a son he loved in exile. David agreed to let him come back to Jerusalem, but he refused to allow him into the palace. For two whole years Absalom lived in the same city as his father, but without seeing him. This made him bitter, because when he had lived there before, he mixed fully in the life of the royal court.

Absalom thought that Joab could arrange for him to see David, but Joab would not come to his house to discuss it. This annoyed Absalom so much that he set fire to one of Joab's barley fields.

When his father realized how Absalom felt, he changed his mind and called him to the palace. David was pleased to see his son and welcomed him with a kiss. He then allowed Absalom to live in the style of a royal prince with chariots, horses and about fifty guards, but he still would not let him make his home in the palace itself.

Absalom's Rebellion

II Samuel 15–18

Absalom always wanted to be important and powerful in the kingdom. He often used to wait with his men at the main gateway of Jerusalem to talk to anyone who came to seek advice from King David. He told them that his father was not interested in them, so many people talked to Absalom instead. This made him more and more popular. It was all part of Absalom's scheme to win followers, so that he could lead a rebellion against his father.

About four years after he had been reunited with Absalom, David allowed him to leave Jerusalem to live in Hebron. No sooner had he arrived there than he made himself king and attracted a large number of followers who wanted to support him against David. When news of these events reached David it gave him the impression that all Israel was on Absalom's side. He imagined that his life was in danger, so without delay he left Jerusalem and hid in the desert with his family and a loyal escort of soldiers.

David remembered Nathan's words to him many years earlier. They seemed to be coming true, because he had never before had such trouble with his family or in the kingdom. He was heartbroken

that his own son had turned against him.

Absalom might have defeated David's soldiers if he had attacked them while they were disheartened, but he decided to wait until more men had joined his army. While he delayed, David became more determined and his army grew in size.

David sent two spies, Jonathan and Ahimaaz, to hide in the outskirts of Jerusalem to pick up any news they could about Absalom's plans. A servant girl used to give them information which they then took to him. One day they heard that Absalom was about to launch his major attack, but before they could tell David, they were spotted and they had to lie low.

A friend hid them down a well, sprinkling the cover with grain to camouflage it. When Absalom's men came to search for them, they found nothing and went away. The two spies then went quickly to warn David, who moved away to avoid the attack.

When David heard that Absalom and his army were in the same area looking for him, he divided his soldiers into three groups of about 1,000 in each, one of them under the command of Joab, and he sent them out to find his enemies, with strict orders not to harm Absalom himself.

The two armies met in the forest of Ephraim, and after a fierce battle David's men won and chased their enemies through the forest. Absalom was trying to escape on a mule when he met a few of David's men. He turned and galloped away, but as he rode under an oak tree he caught his head in the branches and his long hair became entangled. The mule sped on, leaving him hanging by the hair above the ground.

David's men did not know what to do, so they reported to Joab, who came at once and in spite of the king's orders he hurled three spears at Absalom and helped by some young soldiers he killed him. Joab then blew a trumpet as a sign that the battle was over.

David heard the news of the victory first, but his joy turned to sorrow when he was told about his son. 'O my son! Absalom, my son!' he cried. 'If only I could have died instead of you.'

Solomon is King

I Kings 3

When David was very old, one of his sons who was called Adonijah proclaimed himself king of Israel. David was angry at this because he wanted Solomon, another son, to succeed him. He ordered the prophet Nathan to anoint Solomon with oil at once as the sign that he was the new king.

Nathan did this in public, and after the trumpets had been sounded a shout went up, 'Long live Solomon the king!' When Adonijah's followers heard what had happened, they refused to support him any longer and they decided to follow Solomon.

As David was dying, he sent for Solomon and gave him some last advice. 'Obey the Lord your God and follow the law of Moses. In that way you will rule well in Israel.'

When Solomon began his reign, he realized that it would be a hard task for such a young man, so he prayed to God and asked Him for the gift of wisdom in all the decisions he would have to make. 'O Lord God,' he said, 'I am very young and have to rule a nation made up of thousands of people. Give me the wisdom to govern fairly and help me to know the right path from the wrong.'

God was pleased at his request and made a special promise to Solomon. 'Because you have asked not for yourself but for my people, I will give you more wisdom than anyone has ever had. In addition, you will have wealth, respect and a long life.'

Solomon became confident when he heard God's words and it was not long before he was able to prove his wisdom to the Israelites. Because he was the king, people came to him for a decision about their disagreements.

One day two women came with a small baby. 'Your majesty,' explained the first, 'we share the same house and not long ago I became the mother of a baby boy. Two days later this woman here also gave birth to a boy. One night her son suffocated and died, so she crept to my bedside and changed my baby for hers. When I woke up in the morning, I found a dead baby lying by me, but I knew it wasn't mine!'

'It's not true!' screamed the other woman. 'The baby that's alive is mine and no one else's!'

They both raised their voices in anger in front of the king and everyone wondered how he could possibly decide which of the women was telling the truth.

'Bring me a sword!' he called out to one of his servants. The women looked on, puzzled, as a sword was carried in and presented to the king. 'Now,' he commanded, 'cut the living baby in two. Give each woman half.'

There was a stunned silence, as the servant held the boy with one hand and raised the sword with the other. He was just about to bring it down on the child when one of the women rushed forward in tears.

'Your majesty I beg you, spare the child. I'd rather she had him than see him killed.'

The other woman showed no feelings. 'Don't give him to either of us,' she exclaimed. 'I don't care what you do.'

'Stop!' Solomon ordered the servant. 'Give the baby to the one who is sobbing. She must be the real mother, her love for the boy is so great.'

The way in which the king made up his mind impressed everyone who was there and soon news of his wisdom and fairness spread throughout Israel.

95

The Wisdom of Solomon

Ecclesiastes 3; Proverbs

Some books in the Bible contain wise sayings and stories from many different countries which have been written down in the hope that in the future people would read them and learn from them. Some of these may have been collected by King Solomon.

'Remember my words,' wrote a wise man, 'and keep my advice like precious treasure. Never let go of my teachings and engrave them in your mind. Wisdom and insight should stay close to you, just like a brother and sister who are never parted.

'There is a right time for everything under the sun: a time to be born and a time to die; a time to plant things and a time to pull them up; a time to demolish and a time to build; a time to laugh and a time to cry; a time to dance with joy and a time to be still with sorrow; a time for finding and a time for losing; a time for keeping and a time for letting go; a time for tearing and a time for mending; a time for silence and a time for speaking; a time for loving and a time for hating; a time for fighting and a time for making peace. There is a time for everything.

'Once a great king attacked a little city in which were only a few people. One of them was a poor man who had much wisdom. The great king hurled all the strength of his army against them, but he was outwitted by the wisdom of the poor man. Let me tell you this, wisdom is better than weapons of war.

'The tongue of someone who does right is as valuable as silver; the words of someone who does wrong are worth nothing.

'A person who listens to advice is travelling on the right path; a person who ignores advice will lose his way.

'God is against those who cheat, who weigh things dishonestly; he is pleased with those who are fair, whose scales are accurate.

'A good man looks after his animals; a wicked man is cruel to his.

'Someone who does right is like a lamp that is shining brightly; someone who does wrong is like a lamp that is going out.

'A wise child makes his father pleased; only a fool despises his mother.

'Wise people want to learn more; foolish people are satisfied with being ignorant.

'It is better to eat a simple meal among loving people, than to have a grand meal among hateful people.

'Once I went by a vineyard owned by a lazy person. I noticed that it was all overgrown with thorns; the ground was a mass of nettles; the wall around it was broken down. As I looked, I thought about it and it taught me a lesson: it's possible to forget work and to sleep for a while, but then, without realizing it, you will lose your money; poverty will creep up on you like a robber.

'A fire will go out without a supply of wood; arguing will stop if you cease idle chatter.

'Trust in the Lord with all your heart; do not depend on your own wisdom. Consider Him in everything you do and He will guide you along the right path.'

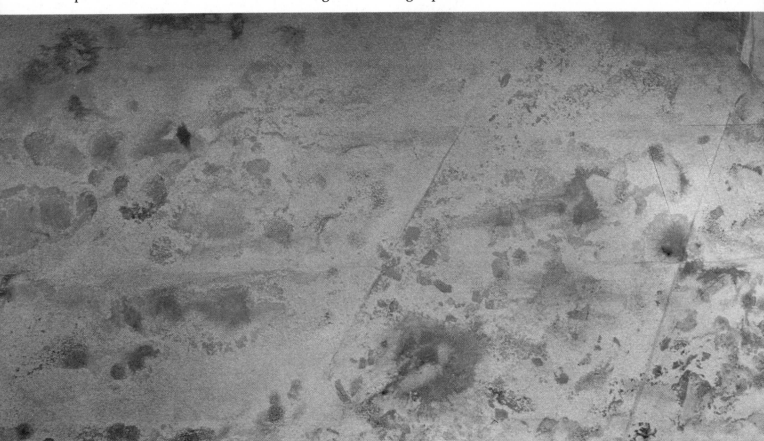

Solomon's Temple

I Kings 5–9

It was nearly 500 years since the people of Israel had escaped from slavery in Egypt, and during that time they had had no permanent place where they could make their sacrifices to God. Now that Jerusalem had become their chief city, King Solomon decided that he would build a magnificent Temple there. It would become the centre for the Israelites' worship and in it all their sacrifices would be carried out. The priests who performed the ceremonies would always live in the city to carry out their duties.

Solomon wanted the new Temple to be a splendid building, fitting for the worship of the Lord God. No expense would be spared, and people in their thousands would devote themselves to making it.

The main material used was stone, which was cut and transported by a work-force of about 150,000 men. Each of the huge stones was shaped at the quarry so that there would be much less noise in Jerusalem when it was being assembled.

The shape was similar to the Israelites' portable Tabernacle. The main area inside was 27 metres long, 9 metres wide and 13 metres high. At the rear they built a special room which they called the Most Holy Place, in which the Ark of the Covenant would eventually be kept.

The inner walls of the Temple were completely lined with cedar wood, while the floors were made of pine. Solomon obtained the splendid wood from Lebanon, a country in the north. Although Solomon used about 30,000 Israelites to supply and fit the wood, the king of Lebanon provided many of his own men to fell and shape the trees. In order to transport the trees easily, they lashed them together into rafts and floated them on the sea down the coast from Lebanon. They then carried them overland to the city of Jerusalem.

A person approaching the great steps into the Temple would first pass a bronze altar where sacrifices could be made, and then a huge bronze dish, four and a half metres across, which was held up by sixteen bronze oxen. He would next walk up some steps and pass through an entrance porch, on each side of which were two huge, decorated bronze pillars. He was now in a room called the Holy Place, where many ordinary ceremonies would take place, and, as he looked around, he would see a small altar for burning incense, ten lampstands, a table for the bread which would be offered to God and various implements for use in sacrifices. All these were made of gold, which would have glinted as the sunlight streamed in through windows near the roof.

At the back of the Holy Place were the great carved double doors which led into the Most Holy Place. Only one person was allowed into this room, the High Priest, and he entered it only once a year on the Day of Atonement. When he went inside, he would have seen two gold covered, winged creatures which stood about four and a half metres high. Their inner wings made a great arch underneath which was kept the Ark of the Covenant, containing the Ten Commandments of the Lord.

Seven years after the building work began King Solomon stood up at the altar of burnt offering in front of all the assembled people. He prayed that God would bless the new temple and the Israelites as they worshipped there. As his words rang around the courtyard, they also echoed in the hearts of those who heard him.

'May God be with us, as He was with our ancestors; may He never leave us; may He help us to love Him and obey the laws which He gave to our ancestors. May the Lord God hear my prayer and may He have mercy on the people of Israel, so that all the nations of the earth may know that the Lord is God; there is no other.'

The Queen of Sheba Visits Solomon

I Kings 10

Next to the Temple Solomon also built a new palace, which was made of the same magnificent materials. The nation of Israel prospered during his reign and the news of this wise king and his great new buildings spread from country to country.

One person who heard about Solomon was the queen of Sheba. She was eager to meet him and made the long journey to Jerusalem with a great many servants. Her camels were laden with gold, jewels and spices which were gifts for the king. As well as being gifts, all these riches showed to Solomon how rich and powerful she was.

When the queen was shown into the palace, she was amazed to discover how splendid and beautiful it was. She met King Solomon in the great Hall of the Forest of Lebanon, where the sunlight blazed through three rows of windows and shone on to the rows of cedar wood pillars. Solomon was pleased with the queen's gifts; he had never seen so many spices before.

During her stay the queen of Sheba was impressed by everything she saw: the food was exquisite; the music was played on the finest harps and lyres; the servants were smartly dressed and well cared for.

When she was left alone with Solomon, the queen tested his wisdom by asking him many questions, but he answered all of them easily. 'When I heard about you,' she told him, 'I could not believe it. I had to come to see you and your city for myself. I now know that you are even wiser and richer than people say.'

When the time came for the queen to leave Jerusalem, Solomon was very generous to her and he gave her many more gifts than a special visitor usually received.

King Solomon pleased God by the way he ruled Israel until, when he was an old man, he began to turn away from the Lord God to worship the gods of other nations. He even built a temple for Chemosh, one of the gods of the people of Moab. Because of this the Lord God of Israel became angry and told Solomon that when he died most of the kingdom would be ruled not by his own son, Rehoboam, as he expected, but by someone who was now one of his court officials.

Towards the end of his life several people turned against Solomon, one of whom was a young man named Jeroboam. One day Jeroboam was travelling from Jerusalem when he met a prophet called Ahijah on a lonely stretch of road. Ahijah took off his robe, tore it into twelve pieces, and, to Jeroboam's surprise, he handed him ten of them. 'This is a sign from God,' Ahijah said. 'After Solomon dies, you will rule over ten of the twelve tribes of Israel. This is because Solomon has done wrong and has disobeyed the Lord's commandments. If you will obey His laws and trust Him, then He will always be with you. You and your descendants will be kings in Israel.'

Solomon heard what Ahijah had done and said. He was so angry that he tried to kill Jeroboam, who was forced to leave the country to shelter in Egypt until after the king had died.

The Kingdom is Divided

I Kings 12

During the last years of Solomon's reign the people who lived in the northern part of the kingdom became tired of working hard for him, so when they heard that he had died, they were very relieved. After Rehoboam, Solomon's son, had been proclaimed as the new king in Jerusalem, he travelled to meet the northern tribes so that they could promise to obey him.

When the people learnt that he was coming, they decided to ask him how he would treat them in the future, because they did not want to serve a hard-hearted king. They realized that they had no leader who was brave enough to tell Rehoboam what they thought, so they sent a message to Egypt, where Jeroboam was in exile, asking him to return to help them.

Jeroboam came and went to meet King Rehoboam with the chief members of the northern tribes. 'If you will make life easier for us,' they told the king, 'we will serve you.'

Rehoboam was taken by surprise by what they said, so he spent three days listening to his advisers before giving his answer.

First he spoke with the elders, who advised him to treat the people fairly, but he ignored them and asked his friends, who urged him to be hard on them, so he replied, 'Listen, my little finger is thicker than my father's waist. I will make life harder, not easier for you. My father lashed you with whips; I will use horsewhips!'

When the northern people heard this, they were very angry and refused to serve Rehoboam. Most of the people of Israel rebelled and formed a new kingdom ruled by Jeroboam, leaving Rehoboam with only a small area in the south, called Judah. For many years to come there were two kingdoms each with its own king; the kingdom of Israel in the north and the kingdom of Judah in the south.

God Provides for Elijah

I Kings 17

About sixty years after the kingdom was split up, King Ahab was ruling in Israel. He displeased God because he did so much that was wrong. Things went from bad to worse when he married Jezebel, the daughter of the King of Sidon. Instead of serving the Lord God of Israel, she worshipped the god Baal and persuaded Ahab to build a temple in honour of him.

A man named Elijah had served God so faithfully that he became his special prophet, or messenger, in the land of Israel. He decided to risk his life by telling Ahab that he must stop doing wrong and offending the Lord God. He gave the king this message from God. 'Because of your actions, there will be no rain until I, the Lord, allow it. Your kingdom will suffer a terrible drought.'

The warning made no impression on Ahab and Jezebel, but, after being so outspoken, Elijah thought it best to hide for a while. God guided him to an isolated valley with a brook flowing through it. Even though the rest of the country was short of water, Elijah's brook did not dry up for several months. He never went short of food, because every morning and evening God sent ravens to him with bread and meat in their beaks.

When eventually his water supply ended, Elijah had to find somewhere else to hide. God led him to the town of Zarephath and told him that a widow would care for him there. Although she was very poor and had only a handful of flour and a drop of olive oil left in the house, she and her son shared it with Elijah, thinking it would be the last meal they could afford. God saw her kindness and made certain that while Elijah stayed there she did not go short of food. Each day she emptied her flour bowl and drained the oil jar, but the next day when she woke up she found to her surprise that there was enough in them both for that day's baking. God provided for them until the great drought ended.

Elijah Challenges Baal

I Kings 18

The water shortage had been going on for over two years when God told Elijah to visit King Ahab. When Ahab heard that the prophet was on his way, he went to meet him. 'At last I'm face to face with you,' the king said when he saw Elijah. 'You have brought nothing but trouble to Israel.'

'No, your majesty,' Elijah answered. 'You have caused the trouble by ignoring the laws of the Lord our God and by following the false god Baal. I intend to show you that there is only one God and you should worship only Him.'

'How will you do that?' asked Ahab.

'I will show you, if you will ask all the people to meet me at Mount Carmel. Above all make sure that the priests of Baal go too.'

Ahab said that he would do as Elijah asked, and not long afterwards thousands of people went to the mountain to see what would happen. Elijah was not afraid, although in that great crowd he was the only one who had remained faithful to the Lord God. He shouted out his challenge to them all. 'If the Lord is God, follow Him; if Baal, then follow him.' They were all silent, so he carried on. 'Let us see whether Baal has any power. I want two bulls to be brought here and killed. Then let the priests of Baal build an

altar, put wood on it and place one of the animals on top. Don't set light to it. I will do the same. Then your priests of Baal can call on your god to send down fire to burn your sacrifice. Afterwards I will call my God to send fire for mine. Whichever answers, then that one is the true God.'

All the people shouted out in agreement, so the priests of Baal prepared their sacrifice. From morning to midday they danced around their altar and cried out to Baal to send fire, but nothing happened. Elijah laughed at them. 'Shout louder,' he jeered. 'Perhaps Baal is asleep or maybe he's gone away for a while!' The priests carried on dancing and yelling until the middle of the afternoon, when they gave up.

Elijah gathered all the people around his altar, which had been damaged by the priests of Baal. He then rebuilt it and dug a trench around it. After he had put the wood and the bull on it, he asked them to bring twelve jars of water and drench the altar and the sacrifice with it.

Elijah was not dismayed and prayed aloud to God. 'Lord God, let it be known today that you are the only God in Israel. Show these people your power.' As he spoke, fire flashed from the sky. It burnt up the bull, the wood, the stone altar and dried up the water in the trench. The watching crowds were stunned at the sight and they began to chant, 'The Lord is God! The Lord is God!'

The priests of Baal knew that they had failed and that Elijah had shown the power of his God. They tried to run away, but Elijah ordered the people to chase after them. When all the priests had been caught, they were put to death.

The Drought Ends

I Kings 18

King Ahab had watched Elijah's contest on Mount Carmel with the priests of Baal. When everything was over, Elijah went up to him and told him to get ready to race for home, because there was about to be a torrential downpour. While the king prepared his chariot and horses, Elijah climbed to the summit of the mountain with his servants to scan the horizon for rain clouds. At first they saw nothing and the sky was clear blue and cloudless, as it had been for nearly three years.

Suddenly the servant spotted a small cloud a long way in the west rising over the sea. 'Quickly,' Elijah told him, 'run to King Ahab and tell him to get into his chariot and to head at once for home before the rain stops him from travelling.'

Ahab followed Elijah's advice and set off just as the wind began to drive dark clouds across the sky and heavy rain started to fall. Elijah gathered his robe around his waist and, strengthened by God, he ran ahead of the chariot all the way to the city of Jezreel.

Ahab's wife, Jezebel, did not welcome Elijah when he arrived. She had heard how her priests of Baal had been made to look foolish by Elijah and then killed by the crowds. She sent a message to the prophet threatening to murder him. As soon as he received it he became afraid and left the city to hide in the desert for some time.

Elisha is Chosen

I Kings 19

While he was in hiding, Elijah became very depressed and could see no point in living. For years before the contest on Mount Carmel, he had led a lonely life, disliked by Ahab and Jezebel because he trusted the Lord God. He hoped everything would change in Israel after his victory over the priests of Baal, but Jezebel's hatred for him meant that again he was lonely and afraid. 'Take away my life,' he prayed to God. 'I might as well die.'

God's answer was to provide bread and water for Elijah so that he had the strength to survive in the desert. Then He told the prophet that he would no longer have to work alone. There was a young farmer called Elisha who also trusted God. The two would become companions, each helping the other to make God's name great in Israel once more. Elijah was to visit the city of Damascus to find him.

Elijah cheered up when he heard the news and he travelled as quickly as he could to Damascus. When he asked for Elisha, he was sent to a large field which was being ploughed by twelve teams of oxen, one behind the other. Elisha was driving the team at the back.

The old prophet went up to Elisha, took off his cloak and threw it over the young man's shoulders. This was a sign that one day Elisha would become God's prophet in Israel. After Elijah had explained why he had come to meet him, Elisha was determined to give up his work as a farmer there and then, in order to serve God with every moment of his time. He killed his oxen to show that he did not want them any more, and when he had said goodbye to his family, he set off with Elijah.

Naboth's Vineyard

I Kings 21

Elijah became bolder now that he had Elisha to help him. He even began to visit King Ahab more often to tell him what God thought about the way he was ruling Israel.

Next to Ahab's palace in Jezreel there was a vineyard owned by a man called Naboth. One day Ahab went to ask if he could buy the land. 'I want to use it for a vegetable garden,' the king explained. 'I'll give you a better vineyard in exchange or pay you a generous amount for it. What do you say?'

'Your majesty, I could not let you have it at any price,' Naboth replied. 'It's belonged to my family for years.'

King Ahab went back to the palace angry at Naboth's answer. He turned the matter over and over in his mind and then wearily went to bed after having had nothing to eat. When Jezebel, his queen, found him in this mood, she asked him what was wrong. He told her about Naboth's vineyard. 'Are you the king of Israel or not?' she shouted at him. 'Don't just lie there. Get up and have some food. You can cheer up because I'm going to get that vineyard for you.'

Later on she put her plan into action. She wrote several letters to important citizens in Jezreel using the king's name and seal at the end of each, asking them to kill Naboth. She even told them how to do it.

What they did was to hold a great feast to which Naboth was invited as the guest of honour. Then, in the middle of the banquet, two men were paid to stand up and, in front of everyone, they pointed at Naboth, accusing him of being an enemy of God and the king. People believed their lies and Naboth was taken at once out of the city to be stoned to death.

Jezebel waited at the palace until a message came from the feast to say that Naboth had been killed. She went straight to Ahab with the news. 'I told you I would get you that vineyard,' she told him. 'You can go and take it over now: Naboth is dead.'

Ahab was delighted and went immediately to claim the land as his own. While he was at the vineyard, the prophet Elijah arrived and spoke harsh words to the king because he knew that God was displeased at Naboth's murder. 'Your majesty,' said Elijah sternly, 'all your life has been spent in doing things which are wrong. God wants me to tell you that the future holds trouble for you and your family. When your wife Jezebel dies, her body will be thrown to the dogs of the city. None of your family will have a proper burial.'

When he heard this, King Ahab was full of sorrow for what he had done and he begged God to forgive him. God heard his cries and because He had pity for him, He promised that most of the disasters which Elijah foretold would not happen until after the king had died.

Three years later Ahab was killed in a fierce battle against the king of Syria, but Jezebel lived on several years after his death.

The Chariot of Fire

II Kings 2

The time came for Elijah's life to end. The prophet himself realized this, so one day, when he and his companion Elisha were travelling from a town called Gilgal, he asked the young man to let him go on alone. 'Wait here, Elisha, God wants me to go on to Bethel.'

'I won't leave you,' he replied. 'As long as you live, I will stay with you.'

They finished the 32 kilometre walk to Bethel together. Again Elijah asked his friend to let him carry on by himself. 'Look, Elisha,' he pleaded, 'God wants me to go on to Jericho. Don't you come. Wait here.'

God had made it clear to Elisha that this was the last day of his master's life, so he was determined not to desert him. 'No,' he insisted, 'wherever you go, I will come too.'

It was another 24 kilometres journey to Jericho. When they reached the city later in the day, they met about fifty men who were faithful servants of God. They all had great respect for Elijah and, as they too sensed that his life would soon end, they wanted to be with him as much as possible.

God told the old prophet to travel east for about eight kilometres to the River Jordan, so with Elisha he set out for the last time. The fifty men walked with them until they reached the river bank where Elijah made a request. 'I'd like you all to come no further with me,' he asked. 'Elisha and I will cross the river. I want no one else with me.'

The two men reached the opposite bank and walked on until they were out of sight of the men from Jericho. Elijah knew that these were his last moments and that Elisha was to carry on his work as God's special messenger or prophet in that land. 'Before I'm taken from you,' the old man said, 'ask anything you like from me.'

Elisha thought carefully and, knowing how hard it would be to lead God's people without Elijah, he asked for the strength to be able to do it. 'Whatever power God has given to you,' Elisha replied, 'I would like to have a large share of it.'

'You ask a great deal,' Elijah told him, 'but I hope that God can give you your wish. I am now going to be taken from you. If you see how I go, you will know that you have been granted double my power.'

As they talked together, a whirlwind moved towards them across the barren desert. Suddenly a chariot of fire appeared, drawn by horses of fire. It drove between the two men, keeping Elisha at a distance. Elijah seemed to be gathered up into the chariot, which was then caught up by the spiralling wind. The force of the whirling wind lifted Elijah and the fiery chariot up into the sky. Elisha stood and watched until they disappeared into the clouds and he could see them no longer.

He buried his head in his hands and tore his outer robe as a sign of his sorrow. When he opened his eyes, he noticed Elijah's cloak on the ground in front of him. He put it on to show that he meant to carry on Elijah's work by helping people to serve and obey the Lord God.

Then he went back over the River Jordan and rejoined the fifty men from Jericho. As soon as they saw him coming towards them, they realized that he was to be God's prophet in the land and they bowed to him. 'The Spirit of Elijah now rests on Elisha,' they declared with certainty.

111

Elisha and the Shunamite Boy

II Kings 4

Elisha travelled with Gehazi, his servant, throughout the kingdoms of Judah and Israel giving advice and help wherever he could. He went into palaces and ordinary houses, telling everyone, whether they were kings or poor people, how they ought to serve the Lord God.

One day he visited the town of Shunem, which was in the northern kingdom of Israel. He often used to call for a meal at the home of a wealthy farmer who lived there. The farmer's wife felt sorry that Elisha had to move continually from place to place without a house of his own, so she had a small room built for him on their flat roof. Inside she put a bed, a table, a chair and a lamp; everything he needed for resting and sleeping when he arrived.

Elisha was so thankful to her that he wanted to do something in return. 'Tell me what you'd like me to do for you,' he said.

'There's nothing sir,' she answered. 'I'm happy as I am.'

Elisha still wanted to show his appreciation and he learnt from Gehazi that the woman longed to have a son. He felt sure that God would give her a baby boy, and told her that before long her wish would come true.

'No, sir,' she protested. 'It won't. You're making it up.'

'I'm not,' he reassured her. 'God will provide a son for you.'

Sure enough, nine months later, in the following spring she was very pleased when she gave birth to a baby boy. The years went by and one summer morning the boy was out in the fields helping his father with the harvest, when he fell to the ground and lay groaning and holding his head. The farm workers carried him back to the house where his mother, who was heartbroken, held him on her lap until, at midday, he died. She carried him up the outside staircase and put him on the bed in Elisha's little room.

Although she was very upset, she took one of the servants and a donkey and rode off at once to find Elisha, who had gone to Mount Carmel. As soon as

she met the prophet, she told him, with tears in her eyes, about her son. He then gave his stick to Gehazi and ordered him to run back straight away and place the stick on the child's body. Elisha followed more slowly with the mother.

Gehazi did as his master asked, but it had no effect on the boy. He came back and told Elisha, who quickly entered the house and went alone into the room on the roof. He prayed for God's strength to enter the child and then he stretched himself out on top of the boy's body. He did this twice and the second time the cold limbs began to become warm again. Suddenly the boy sneezed seven times and opened his eyes. He was alive again!

Elisha opened the door and called the boy's mother upstairs. She ran up the steps and stopped at the door of the room, looking nervously in. 'Go on,' said Elisha, 'pick up your son!' She was overjoyed as she held him in her arms. She praised God and thanked the prophet with all her heart.

Elisha did many wonderful things because he was filled with the wisdom and power of God, and news of them spread throughout the kingdom of Israel and further beyond.

The General's Leprosy

II Kings 5

To the north of the kingdom of Israel lay the kingdom of Syria, whose army was commanded by a man called Naaman. Although he was a great soldier and had led his men in many successful campaigns, he was unhappy because he suffered from leprosy, a terrible skin disease.

One of his servant girls had been brought up in Israel, but had then been captured by a Syrian raiding party and taken to work for Naaman. She was upset to see her master always unhappy, so she plucked up courage and talked to Naaman's wife about the disease. 'When I lived in Israel, my lady, I heard about a man of God called Elisha. They said he healed many people. If my master, Naaman, could only meet him, I know everything would be all right.'

Naaman was so desperate to be cured that when he heard about the prophet, he made up his mind to go to Israel at once to meet him. The king of Syria gave him permission to make the journey and he wrote a letter to the king of Israel asking for his help. Naaman set off as soon as he could with the letter and gifts of gold, silver and expensive clothing.

When he arrived, he visited the king of Israel to present him with a letter. The king was puzzled and

suspicious at what he read. 'How does he expect me to help? Am I supposed to be God? Perhaps it's a trick. Maybe the king of Syria wants to quarrel with me because I can't help him; then maybe he plans to invade Israel.'

Elisha heard about Naaman's visit and asked the king to let him meet the Syrian. 'Don't be anxious, your majesty,' the prophet assured him. 'I may be able to show these people that the God of Israel has great power.'

The king agreed and he sent Naaman to Elisha's house. The prophet refused to come out to meet the Syrian commander, but instead he sent him a message. 'If you want your skin made completely well, you must go to the river Jordan and wash in it seven times. Only then will you be healed.'

Naaman stood in his chariot and shook with anger. 'Who does this Elisha think he is?' he shouted. 'The least he might have done is to come out to meet me. He could have prayed to his God and healed me here and now. Besides, if I've got to bathe anywhere, why make it the Jordan: it's nothing but a filthy stream. We've better rivers in Syria.' He turned his horses and drove off in a fury.

His servants galloped after him and persuaded him to stop to listen to them. 'Sir,' they pleaded, 'you're upset because Elisha has not asked you to do anything grand. If washing in the Jordan will heal you, what's the harm in that?'

Naaman knew that being well meant more to him than anything, so he swallowed his pride and went to the banks of the Jordan. With his servants watching, he took off his outer robes and went down into the water. He did it six times, but the white blotches of the disease were still on his skin. The seventh time, as he came out and the water ran off his body, to his amazement the marks had all gone: he had been completely cured. It must have been the happiest moment of his life, and he realized the power of the God of Israel.

Naaman returned to thank Elisha and to offer him gifts, but the prophet would not accept anything at all. Gehazi, Elisha's servant, could not understand this, so, after Naaman had set out, he followed them and lied in order to have some of the gifts for himself. He was given silver and clothing which he hid in his house. Elisha found out about it and was so angry that he sent Gehazi away, telling him that he would always have the very disease from which Naaman had just been healed.

Jehu and Queen Jezebel

II Kings 9

Some years later, when Ahaziah was king of Judah and Joram was king of Israel, the Syrians kept attacking them, so their two armies joined forces to fight off the invaders. In one very fierce battle at Ramoth King Joram was so badly wounded that he had to return to his palace at Jezreel to recover. Ahaziah went with him. Joram was the son of King Ahab and he ruled his country as badly as his father had done. His mother, Queen Jezebel, was still alive, encouraging the people to worship Baal instead of the Lord God of Israel. From the time that Ahab and Jezebel had killed Naboth and taken his vineyard, God had declared that a new king would one day take the throne from Ahab's family.

One of Joram's best soldiers was Jehu, an army commander. He was at Ramoth resting with his friends after the battle, when a messenger arrived from the prophet Elisha. He was shown into a room full of officers and asked to speak privately with Jehu.

The two men went together into a nearby room. When the messenger had shut the door, to Jehu's surprise he took out a jar of oil and poured a little on his head.

'Jehu,' he said, 'I do this on the instructions of the prophet Elisha. In the name of the Lord God of Israel, I anoint you king of Israel. You are to take the throne from King Joram and all Ahab's family must die. Their evil influence must not remain in the land.'

The messenger did not give Jehu a chance to say anything, but rushed out of the building, leaving the stunned commander to rejoin the other officers.

'Are you all right?' they asked when he walked in. 'What did he want?'

'I daresay you all know,' he replied.

'We don't know. Tell us what happened.'

'Well,' Jehu explained. 'He anointed me in the name of the Lord God as king of Israel.'

Jehu was popular with the army, so his fellow

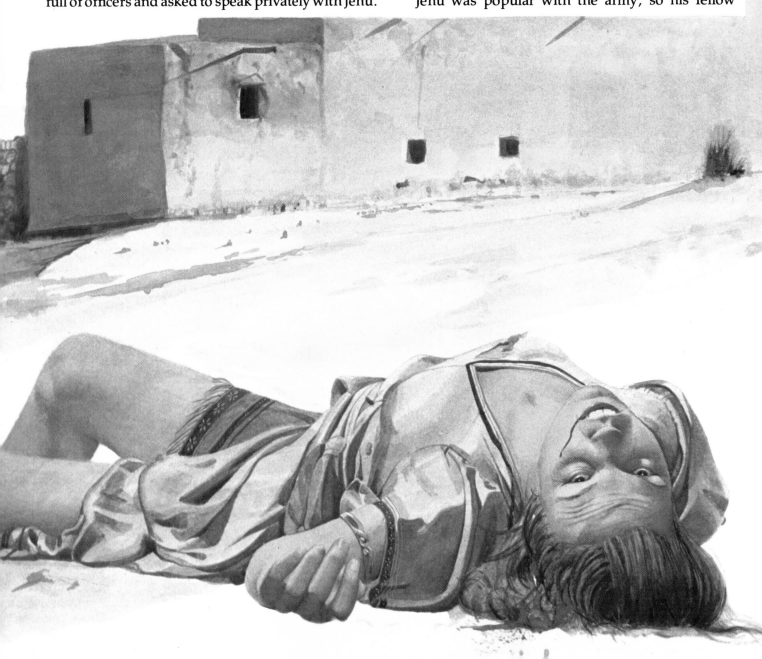

officers were delighted. 'Long live King Jehu!' they shouted. 'Jehu is king!' They spread out their cloaks for him to stand on and ordered a trumpet fanfare to be played.

Jehu now had to deal with King Joram, so he made sure that Ramoth was sealed off by soldiers to stop word of his plan getting out. Then, with a detachment of soldiers, he mounted his chariot and drove the 64 kilometres to Jezreel as quickly as he could.

A sentry there saw a dust cloud moving fast along the desert road to the city, so he reported it to King Joram, who sent out two messengers to see who it could be. Jehu refused to let them return, in order to keep Joram puzzling.

The sentry on the city wall realized how furiously the leading chariot was being driven and guessed that it must be Jehu, who was famous as a reckless charioteer. When King Joram heard this, in spite of his battle injuries, he mounted his own chariot and rode out with King Ahaziah of Judah to meet the approaching soldiers.

They met Jehu on land once owned by Naboth and as soon as both kings discovered that the soldiers had not come in peace, they were frightened and tried to escape. As Joram wheeled his chariot around, Jehu drew his bow and killed him with the one arrow. 'God has punished you, Joram,' he cried out, 'in return for the murder of Naboth by your family.' As King Ahaziah drove off, he too was shot, but he managed to reach the land of Judah before he died from the wound.

Jehu then drove into Jezreel and went straight to the palace. Queen Jezebel, who had done so much harm to Israel, was with some palace officials looking out of an upstairs window. She knew that she would be killed, so in scorn for Jehu she had arranged her hair specially and put on her make-up.

'If you are on my side,' Jehu shouted to the officials, 'throw her down.' They seized Jezebel and hurled her out of the window. The fall killed her, and as her body lay on the ground, Jehu drove his chariot over it. Then he entered the palace as the new king of Israel. To begin with he ruled well and encouraged his people to worship only the Lord God.

Amos, the Farmer

The Book of Amos

After Jehu's death the kingdom of Israel was ruled by his family for many years until his great-grandson Jeroboam became king and was named Jeroboam the Second. He was a great leader, whose army recaptured land which had belonged to Israel many years before, and made the kingdom so peaceful that it grew more and more prosperous. He rebuilt the cities, using the best craftsmen to make them into splendid places with beautiful buildings.

Unfortunately all was not well. First, the people began to depend on the army for their safety and not on the Lord God; second, although many people enjoyed great riches, there were others who were very poor. Someone who noticed these problems was a farmer called Amos. He grew figs and reared sheep in the kingdom of Judah, but twice a year he travelled to Israel to sell his fruit and wool in the

markets there. He became so angry at the way the people had forgotten God's laws, that he decided to say what he thought about it.

He used to wait until a crowd had gathered to examine his goods, then he would speak out.

'Listen to the Lord God,' he told them. 'The people of Israel have done wrong and He will punish them. Poor people have their money and goods taken from them by those who are rich already. If they have nothing left, they are sold as slaves for the wealthy. The Lord led you out of the land of Egypt and has protected you in the past, but you break His laws and stop His prophets from speaking. A disaster will happen to this kingdom: no one will escape, not even the swiftest charioteers or the strongest soldiers. You are God's people, that is why it is terrible that you ignore Him. Oh yes, you have great festivals when you worship Him, but what use are they when the poor suffer so much. Let justice flow like a stream and goodness like a river which never runs dry. Return to God and you will live. If not, this nation of Israel will be destroyed.'

To show his listeners how they had abandoned the Lord God, he told them about a dream he had had. 'I saw God standing next to a wall which was straight and upright. In His hand was a weighted cord, a plumb-line, which builders use to see if a building is upright. God said that He was holding it to show that His people in Israel were not leading straight, upright lives. Israel will be destroyed and the holy places will be left in ruins.'

When the king heard what Amos was saying in the market places, he was furious and sent a priest called Amaziah to speak to him. 'You've said enough, Amos,' he told him. 'Get back to Judah where you came from.'

'I'm just an ordinary farmer,' Amos answered. 'I'm not saying what I think. It was the Lord God who told me to come here. He gave me the words I spoke. I beg you, listen to Him. He is the Lord.'

Amos was forced to pack up what he had not sold and return south to Judah. Although very few people thought any more about him then, years later they remembered his words and realized that he was right.

119

Jonah and the Great Fish

The Book of Jonah

God often spoke to His people by using ordinary men and women as messengers of His word, and through the laws, songs and stories which parents have passed on to children from the earliest times.

One such story which has been told for many hundreds of years is about a man called Jonah. God wanted him to travel by sea to Nineveh, the capital city of Assyria, where he was to tell the people that their way of life was not pleasing to God and that unless they changed their behaviour, they would be destroyed.

Jonah was afraid to go, because Assyria was Israel's deadliest enemy, so he went on board a ship about to sail in the opposite direction to Nineveh. They had not been at sea long when a fierce storm broke. The wind and waves battered the ship until it seemed in danger of sinking. The crew threw the cargo overboard and prayed desperately to their gods for help. When the captain went below deck, he found Jonah there fast asleep. 'Get on deck and start praying to your God,' the captain shouted. 'We need His help.'

The sailors were sure that someone on board was to blame for the storm, so they tried to find out who it was by drawing lots. They picked out Jonah's name. He then told them that he was running away from God and that they had better throw him into the sea if they wanted to stay alive. No one wanted to throw him overboard, so they all tried to row the ship towards land. As they did, the gale howled even more, making the vessel pitch and roll like a bucking horse. They had to give up and decided to do as Jonah said. Several men picked him up and hurled him into the mountainous waves. Almost at once the storm died down and the sea became calmer.

That might have been the end of Jonah, but God did not want him to drown. Instead, He caused a huge fish to swim up to him and swallow him whole. For three days Jonah stayed inside the huge sea creature, praising God that he was still alive.

'The water covered me and I choked for breath; the
    seaweed entwined my hair;
But You, O Lord my God, rescued me from the
    deep waters.
I will sing praises to You, because You are the
    God who saves.'

On the fourth day the fish made its way to a sea
coast and coughed Jonah out on to the beach.

Now that Jonah was on dry land again, God told
him to go to Nineveh with the message. This time he
obeyed. When he reached the city, he warned
everyone that unless they put an end to all the wrong
in their lives, Nineveh would be destroyed in forty
days.

He was amazed to find that the citizens listened to
him. They all decided to change their ways. The king
of Nineveh himself prayed to God asking for His
forgiveness. When God saw how sorry they all were,
He was filled with love for them and forgave them all.

This didn't please Jonah, who felt that God had
made him look foolish, so he left the city and sat
down to see whether God would destroy it after all.
But God now wanted to teach Jonah a lesson. First,
He made a tree grow quickly to give him some shade
as he sat in the hot sun; then, the following day, He
made the plant wither and die. In the heat Jonah
nearly fainted from sunstroke and he became furious
that the tree had died.

'Jonah,' God said, 'you are upset about a dead
plant and you did not even plant it yourself.
Shouldn't I be upset about a city where the people
were destroying themselves with evil? One hundred
and twenty thousand children live there. I made
them all. Why shouldn't I care for them? I would
rather save them than a plant.'

Jonah learnt that God loves and cares for all people
in all countries of the world.

Isaiah

The Book of Isaiah

During Amos' lifetime the southern kingdom of Judah became very prosperous. This continued throughout the reign of a king named Uzziah. Although the Assyrians were threatening to invade the land, few people were worried, because Uzziah had strengthened the walls of Jerusalem and had a large army ready for battle. He encouraged farmers to plough new fields and plant new vineyards.

When Uzziah died, many people in Judah wondered what the future might hold for them. One day a young nobleman named Isaiah was in the great temple at Jerusalem when he had a dream which changed his life. He pictured God seated on a throne in the temple, His robes filling the building. Around the throne hovered some majestic six-winged creatures. Each one used two wings to cover its face, two to hide its body and two for flying. Smoke filled the temple which shook from their echoing voices. 'Holy, holy, holy!' they cried. 'The Lord God is holy! The whole earth is full of His glory!'

What Isaiah saw and heard made him very unhappy. When he thought about God, who was free from all wrong, he felt ashamed of his own life. 'What hope is there for me! I am unclean and so is the world I live in. Even so, I have seen God!'

At this, one of the creatures flew towards him carrying in a pair of tongs a burning coal from the altar. The coal touched his lips and he heard the creature speak to him: 'God has forgiven you and burned all the wrong from your life.'

Then God's words rang out clearly. 'Whom shall I send as My messenger into the world?'

'I will go! Send me!' Isaiah replied at once, and from that moment he became God's prophet in Judah. Through him God gave messages to the people. He told Isaiah that it would not be long before Judah was invaded and the people sent away into exile. God wanted Isaiah to warn everyone and to urge them to begin to serve God with new devotion. Few people listened to Isaiah at first when he told them God's words:

'Listen to my song about a friend who had a
   vineyard.
He dug the soil and planted the finest vines.
He even built a tower to protect them,
But the grapes ripened and were sour.

'My people are like that. Their lives are spoiled and because of this I will let their vineyard be destroyed. The wall around it will be broken down and wild animals will trample on the vines. Everywhere will become overgrown with weeds and thorns.' By this God meant that the land of Judah would be destroyed like the vineyard.

Sixteen years later Ahaz became king and was one of Judah's worst rulers. When the country was attacked by the Syrians, instead of trusting God he asked for help from the Assyrians and this led to Judah having to obey them for many years. During his reign the people turned away even more from the Lord God.

Even though Isaiah was distressed at what was happening, God told him that the day would come when things would be different. He would bring peace and prosperity again to the land:

'The desert will rejoice and be filled with flowers;
Everyone will see God's glory and greatness;
Let everyone who is discouraged hear this:
Don't be afraid: God will save you.
The blind will see; the deaf will hear.
Streams of clear water will flow through the desert.
Jerusalem will ring with joy and gladness;
Sorrow and grief will be gone for ever.'

These words gave Isaiah hope for the future and in addition God explained that one day He would send someone into the world who would bring peace and joy. The Jews called this special person 'the Messiah' or 'the Christ' and later Christians came to realize that Jesus was the person Isaiah was writing about.

All this was in the future. Meanwhile, things did not improve in Judah until King Ahaz died and his son, Hezekiah, began to reign.

King Hezekiah and the Assyrians

II Kings 18

Hezekiah, who was the great-grandson of Uzziah, became king of Judah when he was twenty-five years old. He served God faithfully throughout his reign and under him the country became more and more prosperous. During this time both Judah and Israel were constantly threatened by another country called Assyria, whose well-trained and well-equipped army was very successful when Sennacherib was their emperor. Their army advanced right into Judah and captured Israel on their way south. King Hezekiah became worried when the enemy seemed determined to attack Jerusalem itself. He ordered the citizens to make spears and swords, but he also sent Sennacherib gifts of gold and silver, hoping in that way to stop the advance. The emperor replied by instructing a large force to move straight to Jerusalem.

When they reached the city walls, the Assyrians called King Hezekiah out to meet them. He refused and instead sent three of his officials. Hundreds of people crowded onto the walls to watch.

An Assyrian commander came forward and began to mock the three men and their fellow citizens. 'Who are you to resist the might of Assyria?' he scoffed. 'You have no strength, only empty words. Don't rely on Egypt for help: that's like leaning on a piece of straw! Your God hasn't stopped us so far; He's not likely to from now on.'

Hezekiah's officials did not want the citizens of Jerusalem to hear the commander's discouraging words, but he raised his voice to make sure that everyone on the walls caught his message. 'Hezekiah can't save you,' he shouted. 'Don't trust the Lord your God. You can't win, so why not surrender? If you do, you will be able to eat and drink all you need. No one can stop us: no one can save Jerusalem.'

He did not know that Hezekiah had opened up an underground tunnel, through which enough water flowed into Jerusalem for everyone.

The people heard the commander in silence and then the three officials went back inside the walls to report to King Hezekiah. He was very distressed at the news and dispatched someone at once to tell Isaiah, the prophet of God. Isaiah was not at all disheartened and encouraged the king by the message he sent back. 'Do not be afraid,' he wrote. 'The Lord God will make Sennacherib return to his country, where he will die.'

The Assyrians heard a report that the Egyptians were sending an army to help defend Jerusalem, so Sennacherib wrote to Hezekiah, warning him again that no one would halt his army's advance.

Hezekiah took the letter into the Temple and prayed for help. 'O Lord our God,' he cried, 'rescue me from our enemies, so that the world may know that you are the only true God.' Again Isaiah brought hope to the king. 'God has shown me,' he told him, 'Sennacherib will not enter the city: The Lord God will defend us.'

That night, as the Assyrian army was sleeping, the power of the Lord God swept through the camp, and at dawn the next day thousands of soldiers were found dead in their tents. Sennacherib was stunned by this disaster and he was forced to return to the Assyrian city of Nineveh, where he died not long afterwards. Hezekiah led the citizens of Jerusalem in praising the Lord God, who had saved them.

Josiah's Discovery

II Kings 22 & 23

When Hezekiah's son, Manasseh, became king, he overturned all the good things that his father had done. He encouraged the people of Judah to stop worshipping the Lord God by building altars for other gods in the Temple at Jerusalem. He not only killed hundreds of innocent men and women, but he even killed one of his own children as an offering to one of these gods. God was so greatly offended by all the wrong things that people were doing that He vowed to punish Jerusalem. 'I will wipe away the wicked from the city like dirt off a dish. The citizens who survive will become the slaves of others. I will let them be captured and taken away by their enemies.'

It was not very long until Jerusalem was destroyed just as God foretold, but before this happened there were several other kings in Judah. Manasseh's son, Amon, was as cruel and evil as his father. He had ruled for only two years when he was murdered and his eight-year-old son, Josiah, became king.

When Josiah was twenty-six, he decided to repair the great Temple in Jerusalem. As one of the officials was collecting money from the Temple storeroom, he found a dusty roll of old parchment which made him curious. He opened the dry material very carefully and found that written on it were the laws which God had given to Moses and the Israelites. He sent it at once to King Josiah, who asked for it to be read to him.

As neither his father nor his grandfather had served the Lord God, Josiah had never heard God's law before. The scroll had been in the storeroom since the days of Hezekiah. Listening to the words, Josiah realized how much the people of Judah were disobeying the Lord God and breaking His commandments. He was so dismayed that he ordered everyone in Jerusalem and the rest of Judah to assemble in and around the Temple.

The young king stood in the crowded courtyard and read the scroll aloud from beginning to end.

Then he made a solemn promise to the Lord God that he would obey and serve Him for the rest of his life, and that all the people of Judah would do the same.

Next he commanded the temple to be cleared of the objects which had been used to worship Baal and the other gods. Statues and altars were torn down and were taken out of the Temple with everything else to a place in the bottom of the valley adjoining it. They were smashed to pieces and burned, along with the remains of shrines from all over the land.

Once all the destruction had finished, the people began to worship the Lord God in the way that their ancestors had done, following the instructions written in the scroll they had found. For the rest of his life Josiah dedicated himself completely to serving and obeying God, as he had promised during the great gathering in the Temple. Although he did so much good, it did not change God's solemn vow that the day would soon come when Jerusalem would be destroyed and its citizens taken as slaves to another land. What it did mean was that when that time came, many of the people were faithful followers of the Lord God and continued to worship Him wherever they went.

Jeremiah

The Book of Jeremiah

One of King Josiah's subjects was a prophet called Jeremiah. He was about thirty years old when the king discovered the scroll of the law and was delighted when Judah began to worship the Lord God once again.

Some years before, God had asked Jeremiah to be His special messenger to the nation. This made him feel very afraid, but God promised to strengthen him for the task. 'If I ask you to speak to anyone for me,' God told him, 'do it and tell them exactly what I tell you. Don't be afraid, because I, the Lord God, will be protecting you.'

After King Josiah's death many people in Judah began to ignore God, and the whole country was also in danger of being invaded by Nebuchadnezzar, king of Babylon. His powerful army had already defeated the Assyrians and captured Nineveh, their capital city.

Jeremiah spoke out bravely, telling everyone that unless they started to worship God again, the nation of Judah would be destroyed. God gave a similar message for the northern kingdom of Israel, but the people of both nations refused to listen and many of them hated Jeremiah for the things he said.

Jeremiah was filled with sorrow at this, because he

knew that God loved Israel and Judah, and that he longed for them to follow him again.

'My sorrow is impossible to heal,' he said. 'My heart is sick. I am wounded because my country is wounded. I am filled with sadness and dismay.'

One day Jeremiah went to a potter's house and, as he watched the man shaping the wet clay on his wheel, he realized that God was teaching him something from what he saw. When anything spoiled the clay, the potter broke it up and started again. This was what God would do to Israel and Judah which had been spoiled by the way people lived. God would bring the two kingdoms to an end.

When Josiah's son, Jehoiakim, became king, Jeremiah was beaten and put in chains for a while to prevent him from speaking about disasters to come.

Jeremiah was forbidden to teach in the Temple, but he wrote down his thoughts on a piece of parchment and gave it to his servant, Baruch, to read for him. When the king heard what was happening, he sent for the parchment. When he read it he was so furious that he cut it into little pieces and burnt it.

While Jeremiah was locked up, a relative visited him and asked him if he would like to buy a field which was for sale. Jeremiah bought it to show everyone that, although he was sure that the Babylonians would capture the city, one day the people of Judah would return to their land again and all their property would once more be theirs. Jeremiah was all the more certain of this because God had spoken to him about it. 'I will lead the people back,' he told the prophet. 'One day they will be safe here. They will again be my people and I will be their God.' Soon Jehoiakim died and his young son Jehoiachin began to rule Judah. Early in his reign the Babylonian army of King Nebuchadnezzar marched to Jerusalem and after a two months' siege, they broke into the city and took the king and many of his officials back to Babylon with them.

King Nebuchadnezzar appointed another of Josiah's sons, Zedekiah, to rule instead of Jehoiachin. He did not lead Judah well and ignored Jeremiah's words of advice and warning. Then Nebuchadnezzar heard that the new king was asking the Egyptians for help, so he sent the Babylonian army straight to Jerusalem to attack it again.

The city was surrounded by soldiers for eighteen months, but still Zedekiah would not listen to Jeremiah, who knew that Jerusalem would soon be destroyed. He was accused of siding with the enemy by telling the citizens that the Babylonians would win, so the king, to silence him, had him thrown into a deep waterless well with mud at the bottom.

Then they realized that it was pointless keeping him there, so they pulled him out with long ropes. By this time food was running out and, for the first time, King Zedekiah asked Jeremiah to advise him.

The Destruction of Jerusalem

Jeremiah 52; Lamentations 5; Psalm 42 & 137; Ezekiel 37

The citizens of Jerusalem became weaker and weaker, through lack of food, until they were no longer strong enough to fight off the Babylonians. Nebuchadnezzar concentrated all his soldiers on the city when he realized this. They launched a fierce attack and broke down the walls. King Zedekiah tried to escape, but was captured and taken to King Nebuchadnezzar. He was made blind, put into heavy chains and escorted to Babylon.

The invaders were determined that Jerusalem would no longer be a threat to them, so they flattened the walls completely, tore down the buildings and set fire to everything that would burn. Everything was destroyed including the great temple and the royal palace. As the dust settled on the rubble-filled streets and the smoke rose above the ruins, it was hard to believe that once this city had been the home of kings like David, Solomon and Josiah, and that here the Lord God had been worshipped for so many hundreds of years.

Nebuchadnezzar ordered all except the poorest citizens to be marched in chains to Babylon, where they would begin a new life. Among those who were taken there was Jeremiah, whose words of warning

130

had been ignored for so long. Like everyone else, Jeremiah was heartbroken to see Jerusalem in ruins and was not looking forward to life in exile in a foreign land, but he never lost hope. He encouraged the people to believe that one day Babylon would be defeated, as God had promised, and Jerusalem given back to those who served the Lord God.

When the long column of refugees reached the city of Babylon, they were amazed at its beauty. The huge buildings with their magnificent carvings reminded them of what Jerusalem had been like and they showed their sadness in their songs:

'By the waters of Babylon we sat down and wept,
    when we thought of Jerusalem.
We hung our harps on the branches of the willow
    trees,
For how can we sing the Lord's song in a foreign
    land?'

Many of the people were ashamed at what had happened and they asked God to allow them to return one day.

'Look at our disgrace, O Lord: our dancing has
    turned to sorrow,
Because Jerusalem is in ruins; only wild dogs prowl
    in its streets.
You, Lord, reign for ever: make us Your children
    again;
We long to start again the life we knew before.'

Although they decided to work hard and make the most of their new surroundings, they often thought of home and they began to think of the Lord far more than when they were in Jerusalem. They longed to worship Him again in the Temple:

'Just as a deer gasps for cooling stream water,
In the same way I long for You, O God.
I thirst for God with all my being;
I thirst for the living God.
I remember how I mingled in the crowd
I remember proceeding to the Temple of God.
I will hope in God. One day I will praise Him
    again.'

Someone who felt sure that one day they would return to Jerusalem was a prophet called Ezekiel, who was told by God that this would happen. God often showed him the future through dreams and visions.

Once Ezekiel pictured a whole valley full of dry human bones and as he looked they began to join together into skeletons. Next they were covered in flesh and skin. Then finally the bodies began to breathe and stand up. The vision was God's message to His people. 'I will make you breathe again and give you back the life you once had. Then you will be sure that I am the Lord your God.'

The people from Judah came to be known as Jews and Ezekiel helped them to look forward to the day when they would return to Jerusalem.

131

Daniel and the King's Dreams

Daniel 1 & 2

One day King Nebuchadnezzar decided that some of the Jews exiled in Babylon should become part of his royal court. 'Find a few outstanding young men,' he ordered his officials. 'They must be healthy and handsome, clever and well-educated.'

Among the people they chose were four friends: Daniel, Shadrach, Meshach and Abednego, who were to be trained for three years. They fitted in quickly with their new life at court, but they all refused to give up their worship of the Lord God. The only problem they found was about the meat they were offered at meal times: Jews had strict rules about the kind of meat they could eat, so Daniel and his friends asked Ashpenaz, their guardian, to be allowed to eat vegetables instead. At first he was uncertain, but then he agreed, which meant that the young men remained faithful to their Jewish laws.

No sooner had Daniel finished his training at court, than he was able to help the king. For some time Nebuchadnezzar had been troubled by a strange dream. He felt sure that it had a meaning which he did not understand. This worried him so much that he could not sleep: he kept thinking about the dream.

In the end he called all his magicians and fortune-tellers to see him. When they were all standing in front of him, he gave them his orders.

'Tell me what my dream means!'

'May the king live for ever!' they replied nervously bowing to him. 'If you will tell us what you dreamt, we will explain it.'

'I will not,' thundered Nebuchadnezzar. 'You must tell me what I dreamt and explain it. If you cannot, you will be put to death; if you can, I will reward you with great riches.'

'But, your majesty, no one could do that. It is impossible.'

The king was so enraged that he ordered all the courtiers, including Daniel, Shadrach, Meshach and Abednego, to be killed. When Daniel heard this, he prayed for God's help to be able to work out the meaning. That night, Daniel himself had a dream and through it God showed him what the king's dream meant. When Daniel woke, he felt certain that he knew the answer and gave thanks to God. 'I give you praise, O Lord God,' he said, 'for my wisdom comes from you. You have answered my prayer.'

Then, summoning up his courage, Daniel asked to see the king.

'Can you do what I ask?' asked Nebuchadnezzar.

'I can't, your majesty,' answered Daniel, 'but God can. He has already shown me your dream. What you saw was a huge statue, dazzling in its brightness. Its head was gold, its chest and arms silver, its waist and hips bronze, its legs and its feet a mixture of iron and clay. As you were looking at it, a huge stone smashed into the feet, shattering them and making the statue crash to the ground and crumble into dust, which the wind blew away.'

The king was speechless at Daniel's description, because it was exactly right. 'Your majesty, let me explain what it means. You are a great emperor—the golden head of the statue is a picture of your power. Just as silver and bronze are not as splendid as gold, so, after you, will come two empires not as splendid as yours. Later will come an empire which will crush everything which has gone before it. Although at first it will have the strength of iron, later it will be divided and finally destroyed by God, who will make a new kingdom which will last for ever.'

Daniel impressed all the courtiers who heard what he said, but no one was more amazed than the king. He rose from his throne and bowed low in front of Daniel. 'Your God is the greatest of all gods,' he said. 'I promised to reward the man who explained my dream. I will see that it is done.'

The king made Daniel a very important person in his empire and gave him many magnificent gifts. Shadrach, Meshach and Abednego also became leaders in Babylon.

The Fiery Furnace

Daniel 3

Later on, King Nebuchadnezzar ordered a gold statue to be made and set up near Babylon. It was 27 metres high and glinted in the sun. When it was in position, all the leading officials of the area travelled to see it being dedicated.

It was a splendid ceremony, with everyone assembled in their finest robes. To begin it, the royal herald made an announcement. 'Listen to the king's command!' he shouted. 'In a moment you will hear the music of trumpets, oboes, zithers and harps. As soon as it starts, you must bow down and worship this golden statue. Anyone who does not obey, will be hurled at once into a blazing furnace. You must do this today and whenever the music sounds in the future.'

He then gave a signal and the music rang out. Everyone present bowed themselves low to the ground and worshipped the statue, but Daniel's three friends, Shadrach, Meshach and Abednego, refused to bow down, because they thought that they should only worship their own God.

Several courtiers had been jealous of the three men ever since they had become important people in Babylon. They realized that the royal command was being disobeyed and went directly to the king with the news. 'Your majesty has ordered everyone to bow down and worship the golden statue as soon as the music is played. Three Jews—Shadrach, Meshach and Abednego—refuse to obey you.'

King Nebuchadnezzar was very angry and sent at once for the men to appear before him. 'Next time the music sounds,' he told them, 'you will bow down, otherwise I will have you thrown into the furnace.'

They would not change their minds. 'If our God can protect us, your majesty, then He will. Even if He cannot, we will not worship any other god.'

The king's face went red with rage. 'I've heard enough!' he boomed. 'Make the furnace seven times hotter than usual. Tie their arms and throw them into the flames. See that it is done without fail.'

The soldiers bound them with strong ropes and led them away. As they neared the furnace the heat became unbearable. The guards managed to push the three down into it, but then were themselves overcome and killed by the fumes and flames.

After a while, there was no sign of the guards, so the king himself went to the furnace to see what had happened. He found the dead men and then looked into the furnace, which by now had cooled a little. What he saw amazed him. 'How many did we send into the furnace?' he demanded.

'Three, your majesty,' his officials answered.

'Then why can I see four men? They're all alive and walking about in the flames. One of them looks different, like a god. Shadrach, Meshach and Abednego, come out! Your God is the greatest of all!'

Slowly all three walked through the door of the furnace. Their hair was not singed, their clothes were not burned and they did not even smell of smoke.

'I say this to everyone in my empire,' proclaimed the king. 'Praise the God of the Jews. He rescued these men, because they trusted Him. No one is to insult their God. I will punish anyone who does. There is no other God like their God.'.

Everyone had to obey the king and the three friends were made more important and powerful than they had been before.

The Writing on the Wall

Daniel 5

Twenty-three years after King Nebuchadnezzar had died, his son Belshazzar was ruling in Babylon. One day he held a magnificent banquet with over a thousand guests. They sat at long tables in one of the huge halls of the royal palace talking and listening to music, while hundreds of servants served them with wine. They drank from beautiful cups, but in the storerooms Belshazzar had some which were even more splendid and he wanted to show them off to everyone who was there.

The king called over one of his servants. 'You know all the cups and bowls which my father, King Nebuchadnezzar, brought from the Temple in Jerusalem. Bring them at once. We will use them today.'

The servants went at once and carried in hundreds of exquisite cups and dishes made of gold and silver, which were handed to all the guests. They drank their wine from them and gave thanks to the gods whose statues were made of gold and silver and other materials.

It must have been a beautiful and dazzling sight, with everyone in their finest robes and the light from the flickering wall lamps glinting on the shining metal throughout the hall.

Belshazzar was laughing and enjoying himself like everyone else, when suddenly he went silent and stared across the room. One by one people realized that something was wrong, so they stopped talking and drinking and their eyes followed those of the king's.

What they saw terrified them. A human hand, unconnected to any body, seemed to appear from nowhere and began to write words near one of the lamps on the wall which faced the king. Belshazzar went white with fear and began to tremble. 'Bring in my magicians and fortune tellers,' he cried out, his voice shaking.

The servants rushed to find them at once. When they arrived, they were puzzled by the writing. The king then made an announcement in front of everyone in the hall. 'If someone can read the words and tell me what they mean, I will give him great power and honour in Babylon.'

Nobody could do it and the king became more upset. Just then, his mother, who had heard the commotion, came into the hall. At once she had an idea. 'Your majesty, a man called Daniel once explained one of your father's dreams to him. Send for him and see what he says.'

Daniel, now about eighty years old, was escorted immediately to the banqueting hall where the king spoke to him. 'Daniel, I have heard that you can explain dreams and other mysterious things. You will see some strange writing on that wall. Tell me what it means and I will reward you generously.'

'Your majesty,' Daniel answered. 'I do not want gifts, but I will do as you ask. Your father, King Nebuchadnezzar, was a great king, but at the end of his life he lost all his power and realized that God was even greater and controls all things. You know this, but you act as if you are more important than God.

Even tonight at this banquet, you have offended God by drinking from the cups and bowls which were made for His Temple at Jerusalem and by using them to worship your Babylonian gods. It is God who caused the hand to write on the wall. The words are "Numbered, Weighed, Divided". "Numbered" means that God has decided the number of days you will stay as king: your reign is about to end. "Weighed" means that God has weighed up and judged how good a king you are and He is disappointed in you. "Divided" means that your kingdom will be split up and given to the Medes and the Persians.'

The king heard Daniel's bad news in silence, then he kept his promise and, in front of all the guests, he rewarded him by dressing him in a royal robe, hanging a heavy gold chain around his neck and appointing him to be the next most powerful man in Babylon to himself.

Belshazzar's days were indeed numbered, for that very night God's words came true. Some soldiers from the land of Media stole into the palace, killed him and made their own leader, Darius, the king of all Babylon.

Daniel in the Lion Pit

Daniel 6

King Darius allowed Daniel to keep his important position in Babylon, and along with two others he was put in charge of the governors of the different parts of the empire. Daniel's work was so outstanding that his two colleagues and the governors became jealous of his success. They began to look for ways of finding fault with him, but they were not able to, because Daniel did everything well. 'The only way we're likely to catch him,' they thought, 'is through the way he worships his Jewish God.'

They plotted together for a while and when they had formed a cunning plan they asked to see King Darius. 'Your majesty,' they said, 'we have all agreed that you should issue a command throughout the empire, saying that for thirty days no one should be allowed to make a request to any god or man except you, your majesty. Anyone who disobeys your order will be thrown into a pit full of lions.'

The king was flattered and very pleased by their idea. He signed the order straight away and put on it the seal of the Medes and Persians, which meant that it had become a decree which no one could change.

When Daniel heard about it, he guessed at once that it had been done to trap him. His enemies knew that three times a day he knelt at his open window and prayed to God. If he did this any more, he would be breaking the king's decree. Nothing could stop Daniel worshipping God, so he carried on as he had always done.

His enemies kept a close watch on his house and as soon as they saw him open his window and kneel down, they went directly to the king and asked him if his command was still in force.

'It is,' replied Darius. 'The laws of the Medes and Persians cannot be altered.'

'Then your majesty should know that Daniel has broken your decree and prays three times a day to his God.'

The king was distressed to hear this, because he liked Daniel and trusted him. All day he tried to find some way to save him, but he couldn't: the law was unchangeable.

Finally he had to send soldiers to Daniel's house with instructions to arrest him and throw him into one of the lion pits. Darius himself went with Daniel to the pit. 'I'm sorry, Daniel,' he told him sadly. 'I had hoped so much that your God would save you.'

The guards pushed Daniel down into the pit and rolled a huge stone across the entrance, which the king marked with the royal seal, so that no one could open it. He then returned to the palace and spent all night awake, tossing and turning in his bed, unable to sleep at all.

As dawn broke, Darius got up and went quickly to the pit in the hope that somehow his friend Daniel might still be alive. He stood at the entrance and shouted as loudly as he could. 'Daniel! Daniel! Has your God saved you?'

He was overjoyed to hear Daniel's voice replying from the other side of the rock. 'Your majesty! God kept the jaws of the lions closed. They have not harmed me. He has saved me because I am innocent and have done you no wrong.'

Darius ordered the guards to break the seal and roll back the stone. They threw a rope to Daniel and pulled him out. The king was pleased to see that he had not been hurt at all. He was glad that Daniel was still alive, but furious at the people who had tried to have him killed.

Without further delay he issued another order that all the conspirators and their families should themselves be hurled into the lion pit. This was done and not one survived. The king then sent this message to every citizen in every part of his vast empire:

'Everyone will respect the God of Daniel. He is the living God, who rules for ever. His Kingdom will never end and His power will last for ever. He protects and rescues His people: He saved Daniel from the lions.'

Rebuilding the Temple in Jerusalem

Ezra 5, Psalm 122

During the last years of Daniel's life Cyrus of Persia became the emperor, and through him some of the Jews were allowed to leave Babylon and return to Jerusalem. Jeremiah and Ezekiel had foretold that this would happen many years earlier when Jerusalem was destroyed, but at the time, although people hoped it might be true, not many believed it.

The return of the Jews came about because the Persian empire believed that the people they conquered should be allowed to carry on living in their own lands worshipping in their own way. Cyrus ordered this decree to be read out throughout his empire:

'This is the command of Cyrus, Emperor of Persia. The Lord God has made me responsible for building a new Temple for Him in Jerusalem. May God be with His people, the Jews. Go to Jerusalem and rebuild the temple. If you need help for your work, it must be given to you.'

Led by a man named Zerubbabel, about 50,000 Jews set off, taking with them many of the valuable cups and bowls which Nebuchadnezzar had taken to Babylon. The new Temple could not be as grand as the one that was destroyed, because the Jews had very little money to use for it. In spite of this, they were delighted that once more they could worship God in the city of their ancestors. They worked hard, cheerfully praising God as the new foundations were laid: 'The Lord God is good and His love will last for ever.'

Unfortunately they soon began to face difficulties. During the time the Jews had been in Babylon, other people had settled in and around Jerusalem. They objected to the Jews returning and taking over the land where they lived, so they tried to persuade one Persian emperor after another to make them leave. At last they succeeded and the rebuilding had to stop. For several years nothing happened until Darius became emperor.

Two men, Haggai and Zechariah, felt sure that the time was right to begin work on the Temple again. One day Haggai gave the people a message he had received from God. 'My people, why do you live in well-built homes while my Temple is in ruins? Has no one told you how splendid it once was? Now it is nothing. Don't be disheartened. Start work again, because I am with you. The new temple will be more glorious than the old one. I promise that you will live in prosperity and peace.'

Encouraged by Haggai and Zechariah, they started work on the temple again. Some Persian officials in Jerusalem wrote to Darius asking him if it was to be allowed or not. They told him that the Jews were claiming that the emperor Cyrus had given them permission.

When he received the message, Darius checked through the records of the empire and discovered that it was correct: Cyrus had not only given permission, he had even suggested that they do it. Darius replied to his officials ordering them not to stop the rebuilding and to help the Jews all they could.

It was not long before the Temple was finished and a ceremony was held to dedicate it for the worship of God. They made sure that all the services and festivals were carried out just as Moses had instructed their ancestors. They were able to sing the great songs of King David with a new joy in their hearts:

'I was glad when they said to me,
We will go into the house of the Lord;
We are now standing inside the gates of Jerusalem.
Pray for peace in the city;
Let everyone who loves this place be prosperous.
For the sake of the house of the Lord,
I will give myself for you, Jerusalem.'

Nehemiah Rebuilds the City Walls

Nehemiah 4

The Jewish families who had returned to Jerusalem spent so much time working on the temple and their own homes that they had not been able to rebuild the city walls. This meant that they would be unable to defend themselves properly if anyone attacked them.

The news reached Susa, the capital of the great Persian empire, that Jerusalem was in danger from a people who lived near the city. A Jew named Nehemiah was very distressed to hear this and made up his mind to go there at once to help put up new buildings and walled defences. He was in charge of the wine in the palace of Artaxerxes, the emperor, so he had to ask for permission to travel to Jerusalem.

The emperor let him leave immediately and gave him an escort of horsemen to protect him on the journey. When Nehemiah arrived, he inspected the damage to the city walls. In places there was so much rubble that the donkey he was riding could not find a path through it all. He encouraged the local officials to begin work at once on the defences.

As soon as the people who lived near Jerusalem heard that the gaps in the walls were being filled in,

they were very angry and plotted to attack the city to stop the work going ahead. Because of the danger, Nehemiah ordered half the men to do the actual building, while the other half stood guard with spears, shields and bows at the ready. Everyone, even the builders, hung a sword from his belt all day.

Stone by stone the walls were restored and strengthened until Nehemiah's enemies realized that they had no chance of a full attack on the city. They decided instead to ask him to meet them outside where they could kill him. Nehemiah refused. 'What I am doing is too important to leave,' he told them. 'I won't stop just to talk to you.' Then they tried threats, but Nehemiah was not afraid.

At last after only fifty-two days, the great wall was finished and they all knew that it had been achieved with God's help. Now that the city was safe from attack, they were able to rebuild more of the houses, so that more families could live there.

The people held special services when the wall was finished. They listened to God's law being read and then promised that they would all serve Him faithfully in the future. Here is one of the songs they made up to celebrate the occasion:

'When the Lord restored Jerusalem,
  we felt like people in a dream;
Our lips were filled with laughter,
  and our mouths shouted for joy.
All the nations heard of it and knew
  that the Lord had done great things.
The Lord has done great things for us,
And it makes our hearts rejoice.'

Esther, the Young Queen

The Book of Esther

Although a large number of Jews returned with Nehemiah to Jerusalem, a great many stayed in the lands where they had by now become settled. In Susa, the capital city of the great Persian empire, several of them held important positions. At this time the king of the Medes and Persians was Xerxes, or Ahasueras, as he is sometimes called.

One day his queen, whose name was Vashti, offended him by refusing to attend a banquet, because he planned to make a special show of her in front of the guests. Xerxes was so angry that he said that she would no longer be his queen and that he would search for another one.

Among the Jewish families living in Susa was a very attractive girl called Esther. Her parents had both died, so she was looked after by her cousin, a man named Mordecai. Along with several other girls she was taken to the royal palace when Xerxes was looking for a new queen. As soon as the king met her, he liked her more than any of the others and he decided to give her the crown once worn by Vashti. A great celebration banquet was held and she was proclaimed queen of the Medes and Persians. One thing the king did not know about her was that she was a Jew: that was a secret she kept from him.

Not long after this Mordecai, who had become a royal official, uncovered a plot to kill the king. He told Esther to inform Xerxes, who found that it was true, and the people responsible were put to death. Xerxes was so grateful that Mordecai's loyalty was noted down in the records of the empire.

Years later a man called Haman became the most important official in Persia, and Xerxes ordered everyone to bow to him in respect. Mordecai refused to do this and, as a result, Haman hated him and decided to punish not only him, but also every other Jew in the Persian empire. He persuaded the king to issue a decree ordering that all the Jews be killed on a chosen day. Mordecai was bitterly distressed when he heard this and he sent a message to Queen Esther asking her to plead with the king for the Jews to be spared.

Esther was afraid because the king had not wanted to see her for a month and no one could go to him

without first being asked; also, the king still had no idea that she too was a Jew. Mordecai pleaded with her again. 'You're as much in danger as any other Jew. Go to the king. Who knows? God may have let you become queen to do just that.'

Esther asked all the Jews to pray for her and three days later she nervously entered the throne room. King Xerxes saw her at the door and, to her relief, he pointed his sceptre towards her as a sign that he welcomed her. She went forward, and as she knelt in front of him he asked her what she wanted. She replied by inviting the king and Haman to a banquet which she was going to prepare that very night.

Xerxes accepted her invitation and went along with Haman, who was pleased to be the queen's special guest. She invited them to another banquet the next evening. They both agreed to return and, as they were leaving, Haman spotted Mordecai near the palace gate still refusing to bow to him. In his rage Haman had a tall gallows built the next day, hoping to have Mordecai hanged on it.

That night King Xerxes was unable to sleep, so he asked for some of the official records to be read to him. To his surprise he heard Mordecai's name read out: he had forgotten that Mordecai had saved his life some years earlier. Xerxes decided to reward him, so in the morning he told Haman to dress Mordecai in royal robes and let him ride through the city on the king's horse. Haman was angry and humiliated, but had to carry out the king's orders.

The king and Haman went to Esther's second banquet as planned and during the meal Xerxes asked her to make a request. He promised to give her anything. 'Your majesty,' she courageously replied, 'my request is that I and my people, should be allowed to live! We are about to be destroyed!'

'Who dares to do such a thing?' Xerxes asked.

'There is the man, your majesty,' Esther said, pointing at Haman. 'He is our enemy!'

Haman went pale with terror as the king stormed out of the room in a rage. Soon he returned and commanded that Haman should die on the very gallows that had been built for Mordecai.

Unfortunately the order had already gone out,

signed with the king's seal, to kill all the Jews in the empire. The laws of the Medes and Persians could not be altered, but the king issued another decree telling Jews everywhere to defend themselves against anyone who attacked them. That is what happened and the Jews managed to destroy all their enemies.

So God used a young girl to save His people, the Jews, and each year, to this day, Jewish families remember Esther's courage at the festival of Purim.

The Maccabees

I Maccabees 3 & 4

The Persian Empire lasted for about two centuries until a new power took control. This was the Greek army led by Alexander the Great. In only thirteen years he managed to become the ruler of all the land between the Mediterranean Sea and the river Indus in India. When Alexander died, his generals fought each other to decide who should rule. The vast empire was divided up and most areas had one new king after another for many years.

Wherever the Greeks were in control, they influenced the way the people lived: new buildings were built in Greek styles, people dressed in Greek clothes and Greek gods were worshipped. This had even happened in Jerusalem, although the Jewish leaders there managed to live and worship as their ancestors had done.

Then King Antiochus the Fourth became the ruler of Jerusalem and the surrounding territory and he had different ideas. He decided to stop the Jews worshipping God as they had always done and he insisted that all the people must begin to live exactly as the Greeks lived. He angered the Jews by raiding the temple and putting in it a statue of the Greek god Zeus.

Some Jews went along with his plans and became like Greeks, but most Jews were furious and in Jerusalem there were riots which Antiochus crushed with great cruelty.

A group of people led by a man called Mattathias were opposed to Antiochus and his ideas. They

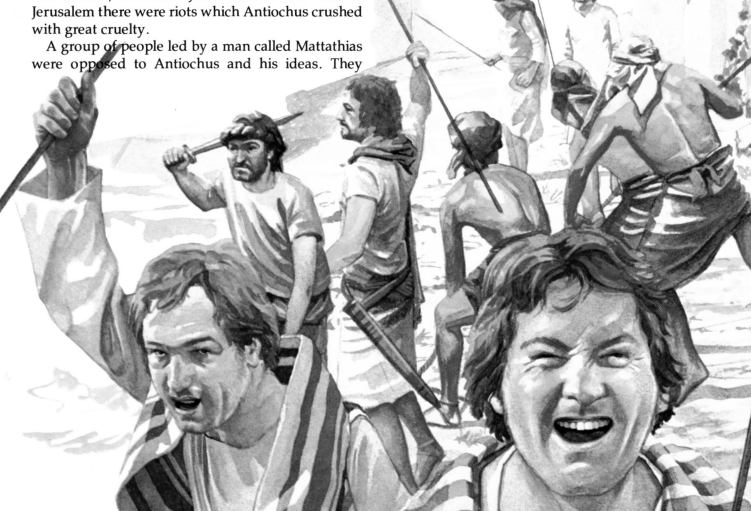

began to form themselves into a small army and they hid in the hills, waiting for a chance to attack Jerusalem to win it back for the Jews. Before this chance came they made raids throughout the countryside, tearing down any Greek altars or statues they found. When Mattathias died, his son, Judas Maccabeus, took over as leader.

Judas learnt that Antiochus planned to wipe out all the Jews in Judea and Jerusalem, and he decided that the time had come to attack the Greeks. His army of four thousand men was so determined that they had many successes. In spite of its strength, the Greek army was not able to stop Judas from reaching Jerusalem and marching right into the city. The Jewish soldiers were distressed to see the temple courtyards overgrown and Greek statues in the building. Judas ordered his men to pull down the Greek altar and to replace it with a new one. They made the temple fit once more for the worship of the Lord God. There was tremendous rejoicing when the great lampstand was lit: everyone sang hymns of praise and thanked God for helping them to restore the temple. Each year, to this day, in the festival of Hannukah, Jewish families remember the courage of Judas and his soldiers in bringing back true Jewish worship to Jerusalem.

Although Judas was later killed in battle, his brothers continued to fight for freedom until the area around Jerusalem became controlled by the Jews. It stayed like this for many years. Then, as the great Roman empire began to spread, Jerusalem came under the rule of the Romans.

It was in 37 BC that a new king was put in charge of the area. His name was Herod, and it was during his reign that Jesus was born.

The Promise of the Messiah

Isaiah 40 & 46; Micah 5

From the days of Abraham God remained faithful to his people, the Jews. At times they prospered, obeying Him in all that they did; all too often they ignored Him and had to live through years of great sadness and suffering.

God showed them in the sayings and writings of His prophets that one day a special person would be born who would bring peace to the world and give new hope to God's people. This person came to be known as the Messiah, and the Jews have always looked forward to the time when he would come.

Isaiah, who was one of the prophets, said that the Messiah would be a descendant of King David: 'From the stump of David's family tree, a new shoot will burst out. A new king will arise. God's spirit will be with him to give him wisdom, understanding, and strength. He will know and honour the Lord God. He will judge the poor with fairness and defend those who are helpless. He will stand up for all that is right and trustworthy.

'Through him, the wolf will live with the lamb and the leopard with the goat; lions will be tamed and babies will play safely near poisonous snakes. The earth will be full of the knowledge of God as the waters fill the sea.'

God told Isaiah that the Messiah would be outstanding even as a baby: 'A child will be born for us; a son will be given to us. He will rule over us and his names will be "Wonderful Helper", "Mighty God", "Prince of Peace". His power and peace will never end.'

Living at the same time as Isaiah was another prophet called Micah. God made it clear to him where this promised ruler would be born: 'Bethlehem, you may be one of the smallest towns in Judah, but from you will come the one who will rule my people. He will care for My people as a shepherd feeds his flock: they will live in safety because he is great and will bring them peace.'

Christians are certain that the Messiah, about whom Isaiah and Micah wrote, has already come. They believe that about 700 years later that special person was born in the town of Bethlehem and given the name of 'Jesus'.

The New Testament

God's Message to Mary

Luke 1

In the small town of Nazareth a young girl called Mary was looking forward to marrying a carpenter whose name was Joseph. One day she was busy in the house when she realized that someone else was in the room with her. She looked around and what she saw made her afraid; a person she did not know was standing looking at her.

It was an angel, a messenger from God. As soon as he saw that Mary was trembling with fear, the angel spoke to her. 'Don't be worried, Mary,' he said. 'The Lord God is with you and is going to bless you more than you can imagine.'

Mary was puzzled. She didn't understand the angel's words and she still felt afraid. 'Mary,' the angel reassured her, 'there really is nothing to be frightened of. God wants to honour you by blessing you with his love and his goodness. You are going to have a baby son and you must call him Jesus. He will become a great person and will be known as the Son of the Most High God. God will make him a king, like his ancestor David, but the Kingdom over which your son will rule will last for ever.'

Mary was astounded at what she heard and she was very puzzled. 'But I'm not married,' she protested, 'how can I have a baby?'

'Joseph will not be the father of your child,' the angel explained. 'The power of God's Holy Spirit will be with you and this special baby will be the Son of God. Remember, God can do anything.'

Mary knew that it was a great honour for God to choose her to become the mother of His son. She was quiet for a moment and then thanked the angel for his message. 'I will serve and obey the Lord as best I can,' she told him.

The angel listened to her and then left. Mary felt excited and overwhelmed by God's message to her, and she was bursting to tell someone about it. Not far away in a hilly part of Judaea lived her cousin Elizabeth with her husband Zechariah. Elizabeth was going to have a baby too: an angel had spoken to her husband about it. Mary knew that she would understand what had happened and would not think she had imagined it, so she decided to go to see her.

When Elizabeth heard the story, she knew that Mary was speaking the truth. 'God has honoured you more than any other woman,' she told her. 'He will give His blessing to your son, Mary. It's a privilege for me to be visited by the mother of God's son.' Mary was so happy that she made up a song of thanksgiving to God.

'My heart is full of praise for the Lord;
My spirit rejoices in God my Saviour.
He has chosen me, an ordinary girl.
From this day all generations will know
That the mighty Lord has done great things for me:
His name is holy.
He will give His mercy to everyone who honours
    Him.
God has shown that He is strong:
He removes proud rulers from their thrones;
He raises up the poor and the humble.
He sends rich people away with nothing in their
    hands;
He fills the hungry with good things.
He has remembered His promises to our fore-
    fathers;
He has shown His mercy to Israel.'

The Birth of John the Baptist

Luke 1

Some months before the angel came to give Mary the news that she was going to have a baby, something similar had happened to her cousin, Elizabeth. Her husband, Zechariah, had devoted his life to serving God, but, to their great sadness, they had never had any children. When they both became old, they gave up hope of ever becoming parents.

Zechariah was a priest and one day he was given the great honour of carrying out an important ceremony in the Temple at Jerusalem. As he was praying alone, an angel of God appeared and stood by him. 'Don't be afraid, Zechariah,' he said. 'God has heard your prayer. Your wife, Elizabeth, is going to have a son. When he is born you must call him John. He will be a great man who will help many people to begin to obey and honour God again.'

'But I'm a very old man,' protested Zechariah. 'My wife is too old! That's impossible!'

'My name is Gabriel,' answered the angel. 'God Himself sent me as His messenger with this good news. Because you have not believed my words, you will be unable to speak at all until after the child is born.' Gabriel then left him.

To Zechariah's horror he found he could not say a word. From then on, in order to tell people what he thought, he had to write or use signs. After he had finished his period of duties at Jerusalem, he returned to the hill town where he lived to be with Elizabeth. As the angel had foretold, she soon found that she was going to have a baby. Nine months later their son was born.

A week later, at the baby's naming ceremony, their relatives and friends said that he ought to be called Zechariah, like his father.

'No!' Elizabeth insisted. 'His name is to be John.'

'You can't call him that,' they objected. 'It's not one of the family names! Look, Zechariah, we know you can't speak, but you must decide.'

Zechariah asked for a wax writing tablet and a pen. Everyone looked on as slowly and deliberately he spelt out the name: JOHN. His choice amazed them

all, but they were even more astounded when he suddenly started to speak again. With his first words he gave thanks to God:

'May the Lord God be praised! He has come to set His people free!
As He promised in days gone by, He has raised up someone to save us,
To deliver us from our enemies and those who hate us.
All this He has done so that we may serve Him without fear.
You, my child, will be called the messenger of Almighty God;
You will go before the Lord to prepare the way for Him;
To tell the people that they can be set free and forgiven;
Through God's mercy, you will be the messenger of hope and peace.'

News about what had happened soon spread through the country, and people began to wonder what sort of man John would become.

Jesus is Born

Luke 2

Mary stayed with her cousin Elizabeth for about three months. As God's son grew inside her, other people would begin to notice that she was going to have a baby. People might have started saying unkind things about Mary, because she had no husband, so Joseph decided to marry her. By doing this he was able to care for her and stop people gossiping.

Joseph and Mary had been living for several months in a house at Nazareth when news came that the Emperor Augustus had ordered everyone to go to the town from which their families came. Officials would then make a note of their names and decide how much money they would have to pay as a tax. They both had to travel over one hundred kilometres to Bethlehem, which was known as 'the town of David' because, hundreds of years before, King David had lived there.

The journey was hard for Mary. She knew that the baby could be born at any time and it must have been uncomfortable for her to ride so far along the bumpy roads on the back of a donkey.

At last they caught sight of Bethlehem on a distant hilltop. As they made their way up the slope towards the houses, they were looking forward to being able to rest for a while. They called at the house where they were hoping to stay, but it was completely full. So many other people had also come to Bethlehem that there was no room left for Mary and Joseph.

Mary then suddenly realized that the baby would probably be born that very night; they had to find some shelter. Joseph managed to persuade someone to let them rest in a stable where the animals were kept. It was not very comfortable, but at least it was somewhere to go.

During the night Mary's special baby was born and his crying filled the stable. They had no cradle for him, but then they thought of the manger where the animals used to feed. After Joseph had filled it with soft hay, Mary wrapped her new son in strips of cloth and laid him in it. They were both thrilled with the baby and praised God for His goodness to them.

That same night, on a hillside near Bethlehem, some shepherds were looking after their flocks when, suddenly, an angel of God stood close to them and the field seemed to be filled with light. The shepherds cowered in terror until the angel spoke to them. 'Don't be afraid! I have brought you good news which will make all the people rejoice. Just now, a Saviour, who is Christ the Lord, has been born in the town of David. If you go to Bethlehem, you will find him in a manger.'

As the angel finished speaking, the whole sky was filled with light and the sound of singing. The praises of countless angels seemed to be echoing around the universe:

'Glory to God in the highest heaven and on earth peace to all men.'

The angels were suddenly gone and the shepherds left their sheep and made their way at once to Bethlehem. They soon found the stable, and there, just as the angel had described, was a baby asleep in a manger. To the amazement of Mary and Joseph the shepherds reported what had happened out on the hillside. Then they left, singing praises to God, and returned to guard their flocks.

Mary treasured these things in her heart and she thought a great deal about them in years to come.

Jesus is Taken to the Temple

Luke 2

Mary and Joseph moved to a house in Bethlehem for a short time, until the baby and his mother were strong enough to go to Nazareth. Soon after he was born, a special ceremony was held, when he was given the name Jesus. About a month later, another ceremony had to be performed when the parents showed their thanks to God by dedicating their new baby to Him.

Mary and Joseph went to the great Temple in Jerusalem for the service. They had only been in the busy Temple courtyard for a few minutes when an old man came up to them and asked to hold the child. Mary let him.

When he had Jesus in his arms, the old man, whose name was Simeon, amazed them both by saying some very surprising things. 'I have lived here in Jerusalem for many years,' he explained. 'All the time I have served God faithfully and I have longed for the day when someone would come to help God's people, Israel. God promised me that I would see this Saviour in my lifetime.

156

'Lord, now you can let me die in peace as you
    promised;
With my own eyes I have seen your Saviour,
The one through whom all people will be set free.
He will be a light to bring understanding to the
    whole world;
He will bring glory to Your people Israel.'

As Mary and Joseph listened, they were
astonished at the way Simeon was describing Jesus.
He then turned to Mary and warned her that the
future held much sadness for her. 'Through this child
many people will find hope; but many will speak
against him; sorrow will stab your own heart like a
sharp sword.'

It wasn't until many years later that Mary understood what Simeon meant. He knew that one day
many people would turn against Jesus and would kill
him.

Simeon handed the baby back to Mary and, as they
were talking together, they were then joined by a
lady called Anna, who spent a great deal of time at
the Temple. She was 84 years old and, like Simeon,
she had served God faithfully for many years. As
soon as she saw Jesus, she too gave thanks to God. 'I
know,' she said, 'that through this child God will set
His people free.'

Mary and Joseph must have wondered what
would happen to Jesus in the future. One thing they
were certain about: God had a special plan for him.

It was in this very place that Jesus, when he was
twelve, amazed the Jewish teachers by his wisdom
and intelligence so that even in his childhood, he
showed himself to be an outstanding person, as
Simeon had foretold.

157

King Herod and the Wise Travellers

Matthew 2

While Mary and Joseph were at Bethlehem they had some unexpected and unusual visitors, who had travelled from far-distant lands. The men who came to see them were interested in studying the stars and had become puzzled by one star in particular which seemed to be shining very brightly and moving across the night sky. They believed that this star meant that a new king had been born, so they had decided to follow it in the hope that it could lead them to him.

After a long, tiring journey by camel, they arrived in Jerusalem and went to King Herod, who was the ruler of that area. 'Your Majesty,' the travellers asked, 'where is the newborn baby who is going to become a king? We would like to worship him and offer him gifts.'

Herod was puzzled, for he knew of no baby king. He was also worried in case a child had been born who would one day take his throne away from him. He asked the travellers to wait in another part of the palace, while he found out for them.

The king lost no time in asking the cleverest people in Jerusalem to come to see him at once. 'Tell me,' he asked, 'we Jews think that someone will come one day to set our people free. The Messiah we call him. Where will he be born?'

'Not far from here, your majesty,' they replied. 'In the town of Bethlehem.'

Herod then asked for the travellers to be brought in. 'The child you look for may be in a town called Bethlehem. I suggest that you go there, make a careful search and let me know if you find him. After all, I too would wish to worship a new king.'

That same night they followed the star again and, to their delight, it seemed to stop over the town of Bethlehem and to be shining on one house in particular. They knocked on the door.

Joseph opened it and, after he had recovered from the surprise of having such visitors in the middle of the night, he took the men inside where they saw Mary and her baby. Then the noble travellers knelt down on the floor of the house and worshipped Jesus. They asked their servants to unload some special gifts for him and they handed Joseph gold, frankincense and myrrh, which were presents worthy of a king.

When they left, instead of going back to Jerusalem, they followed a sense of danger that they had had, and went back to their own country by a different road. Joseph, too, had a warning dream that night. God told him to take Mary and Jesus south to Egypt until it was safe for them to return.

Herod waited for some time for the travellers to return with their news. When he realized that they had tricked him, he became very angry and called for the commander of his soldiers. 'You are to take a detachment of men to Bethlehem. Go without delay and search each house. You are to kill every boy two years old and under.'

Jesus was by this time safely on his way to Egypt. Mary and Joseph stayed there some time until they learned of Herod's death. They decided to return not to Bethlehem but to Nazareth, the town where Mary had grown up.

John Baptizes Jesus

Matthew 3

About thirty years later another King Herod was the ruler of Galilee, the area where John and Jesus grew up. John left home and lived on his own in the desert, where he could think and pray to God uninterrupted by other people. He wore rough animal-hair clothes, fastened around the waist with a leather belt. He found his own food in the desert, which often consisted of such poor and simple things as locusts and wild honey.

He became certain that God wanted him to travel throughout the area around the River Jordan, encouraging everyone to worship and serve God. He believed that they needed to be prepared for the time when God would send the Messiah into the world. This would be someone who would bring hope to God's people.

As he went from place to place, John urged people to be baptized by him as a sign that they were sorry for the way they had lived in the past and that they now wanted God's forgiveness. Because of this, he became known as John the Baptist. Crowds used to come from Jerusalem and from all around the River Jordan. Many people were then baptized by John. He told them not only to follow God faithfully, but also to alter the way they lived: they must start being fair and honest in their dealings and they must share their possessions with those who were poor. He upset many people by the blunt way he spoke and later he even became unpopular with King Herod.

Some Jews began to wonder if John himself was God's promised Messiah, but he quickly denied it. 'Someone is going to come who is far greater than I am,' he said. 'I am not worthy enough even to unfasten his sandals.'

One day Jesus decided to be baptized by John, so he travelled from Galilee to the place on the banks of the River Jordan where he knew he would find him.

John had probably heard from his parents, Elizabeth and Zechariah, about the wonderful thing which had happened to Jesus when he was born. When at last, the cousins met, John became embarrassed that he had come. 'I can't baptize you,' he protested. 'You ought to baptize me instead!'

'Baptize me, John,' Jesus replied. 'That is what God wants.'

John agreed to do it, so the two men waded into the river. As soon as Jesus had been baptized, a dove flew down from the sky towards him. John knew that this was a sign from God to show that the power of His Holy Spirit was with Jesus. Then it seemed as if a voice rang out. 'This is my Son, whom I love. I am well pleased with him.'

John knew from the dove and from the voice that Jesus was the person chosen by God to bring hope and joy to the world. From this moment, Jesus spent the rest of his life travelling from place to place, like John, but his message was different. He told everyone about a new kingdom which he called the Kingdom of God. His mission was not to overthrow the Roman rulers of the time but to urge people to let God rule their lives and to serve Him wholeheartedly. Only in this way could the world begin to change for the better.

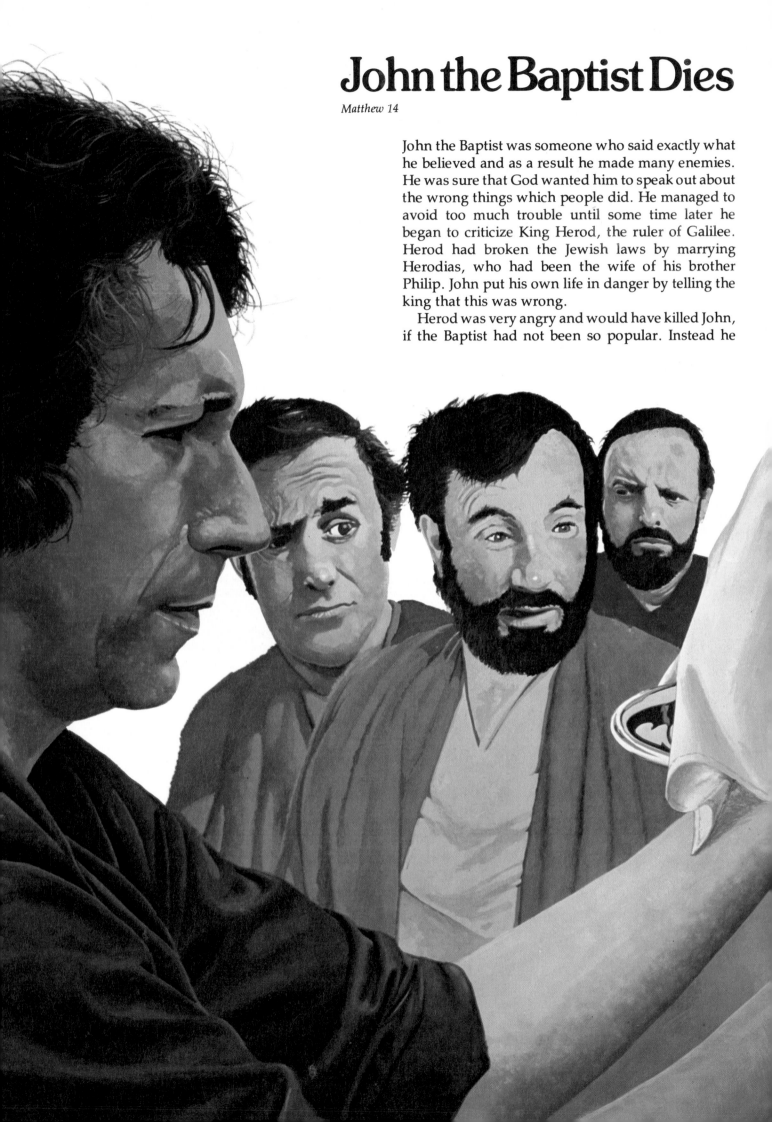

John the Baptist Dies

Matthew 14

John the Baptist was someone who said exactly what he believed and as a result he made many enemies. He was sure that God wanted him to speak out about the wrong things which people did. He managed to avoid too much trouble until some time later he began to criticize King Herod, the ruler of Galilee. Herod had broken the Jewish laws by marrying Herodias, who had been the wife of his brother Philip. John put his own life in danger by telling the king that this was wrong.

Herod was very angry and would have killed John, if the Baptist had not been so popular. Instead he threw him in prison. Herodias was not at all worried about what people thought and she made up her mind to have John put to death. She worked out a plan and put it into action on the king's birthday.

Herod held a magnificent banquet and he invited all the important people from the Galilee area.

Herodias had a beautiful daughter called Salome, who was an excellent dancer. During the entertainment her mother asked the king if he would like her daughter to dance for him. He was delighted with the idea and so Salome was brought into the room. Everyone was entranced to see how gracefully she danced. 'Salome,' Herod said to her, when she had finished, 'tell me what you want. I'm so pleased, I would even give you half my kingdom!'

The girl went to her mother and asked her what she ought to say. Then she returned to the king. 'I would like one thing,' she told him. 'Give me now on a dish the head of John the Baptist.'

There was a stunned silence in the hall and everyone's eyes were on Herod to see what he would do. He did not want to kill John, but he had made a promise to Salome which he had to keep. 'Very well.'

The order was obeyed immediately and a short while later, to the horror of the guests, the soldier came back carrying a large dish on which was John's head. He gave it to Salome.

When John's friends heard the news, they came to the palace and the king allowed them to take away the body in order to bury it.

The Temptation in the Desert

Matthew 4

Jesus knew that it would be hard to spend all his time travelling and meeting people. It would be even more difficult to convince them to dedicate their lives to God's service. Before he could do this, he had to be sure that he himself was willing to serve God, no matter what might happen. He decided to go alone into the desert and spend forty days thinking and praying about the future.

He realized that he must rely completely on God and that he must want nothing for himself, if he was going to put God's wishes before his own. Three times while he was in the desert, the Devil put thoughts into his mind which tempted him to think more about himself than about God. He went through agony as the thoughts turned over and over in his mind. Each time he had to decide, 'What shall I think? What shall I do?' The Devil began by testing him where he was weakest.

Jesus had not eaten for several days and he was very hungry. 'Look at all the rocks and stones around you,' the Devil said. 'If you are the Son of God, you could change them into bread, and then you could eat as much as you like.' 'No,' thought Jesus. 'The scripture says that man cannot live on bread alone; he needs God's words even more.' Jesus felt sure that whatever lay ahead, God would provide for his needs.

Then the Devil tempted him again. 'Imagine all the kingdoms of the world. See them stretched out before you. If you were prepared to use evil and wickedness as your weapons, you could be the ruler of it all. Worship me and you shall have power and wealth.'

'I will not,' Jesus replied. 'The scripture says that we are to worship and serve only the Lord our God.' Jesus knew then that more than anything else he wanted God to rule in the world.

The Devil would not give up. 'Why don't you come with me to the city of Jerusalem, to the very top of the Temple? Below you there is a drop of hundreds of metres. Test God's love and power. Throw yourself off. He won't let you die. He will send his angels to catch you. You'll come to no harm.'

Jesus put the thoughts right out of his head. 'The scripture says that we must not put the Lord our God to the test.'

The Devil saw that Jesus would only use God's power in order to bring honour to God's name. He would never use it selfishly.

In these ways Jesus overcame temptation and, as a result, he felt closer to God. He was certain that, whatever happened to him, he would be able to put God's will first, and that God would give him the strength to bear any hardship which came from serving Him.

Jesus and the Fishermen

Matthew 4; Luke 5

Nazareth, the town where Jesus grew up, was in Galilee, an area which gave its name to a great inland lake called the Sea of Galilee. After his forty days alone in the desert, Jesus travelled with his new friends to as many places as they could in the area around the Sea of Galilee. He taught people about God and as often as possible, he healed those who were sick. As the news about him spread, larger and larger crowds gathered wherever he went. Some just came to listen to his words, but others came to ask him to heal either their friends or themselves.

Most towns had a synagogue, a building where Jewish families met to learn and to worship. Jesus took every chance to teach in the synagogue meetings and soon his reputation as a wise and clever speaker spread throughout Galilee. In some towns a great number of people used to come to listen to him, and on occasions he was glad to get away from them all to be alone.

This happened once at Capernaum, a town on the northern shore of the Sea of Galilee. A crowd had followed him to the lakeside, where he noticed two fishing boats drawn up on the beach. Nearby were the fishermen washing their nets. Jesus went up to one of them, a man named Simon Peter, and asked if he would row him out from the shore. 'I want to talk to them all from the boat,' Jesus explained. 'They won't be able to push me then and they'll hear me better too.'

Peter did as he asked, taking some of the other fishermen with him. Jesus spoke to the people by calling to them from the bows. After a while he finished and sat down, so the crowd began to go away.

'Peter,' said Jesus, turning to the burly fisherman, 'head for deeper water and throw out your nets. You might catch something.' Although Peter knew that Jesus was no fisherman, he had been impressed by everything he had heard him tell the crowd. 'Sir, we've been fishing all night and we didn't catch a thing. But if you say so, I'll do it.' When they were further out on the lake, they cast the nets and before long the water around them was breaking with the threshing of hundreds of fish.

There were so many that the nets began to strain with the weight. Peter quickly shouted to his friends on the shore. 'Hurry up and get here!' he called. 'We can't manage.' With the extra help they hauled the nets on board and filled both boats until they lay so low in the water that they were afraid they might sink. The fishermen were astonished and didn't know what to say. They had never seen so many fish in one catch. It was Peter who spoke first. 'Lord, I'm not worthy to be in the same boat as someone as great as you.'

'Listen,' Jesus said to them. 'If you'll all follow me, I'll help you to catch more important things than fish.

I'll make you fishers of men!' He explained how he needed some companions to help him to teach as many people as possible about God. These people became known as the disciples.

As soon as they had landed the boats, the fishermen made up their minds to give up their work and to travel from place to place with this amazing person they had met. They left everything and followed him. Among those who went with Jesus to become his first disciples were Andrew, who was Peter's brother, and two other brothers named James and John. On the next day they were joined by a further two men: Philip, a friend of Peter's, and a man called Nathanael.

The Wedding in Cana

John 2; Matthew 22

Two days later Jesus and his disciples were invited to a friend's wedding at a village called Cana. Mary, the mother of Jesus, was also there and during the feasting she came over to him. 'You must do something to help,' she said. 'They've run out of wine.'

Jesus knew how embarrassing this was for the bride and bridegroom: the wedding wouldn't be over for a long time, and they had nothing left to drink. 'Don't worry,' he reassured his mother. 'I'll do something at the right time.'

Mary then asked the servants to do whatever her son said. In the room there were six huge jars con-

taining water. 'Fill these again to the brim with water,' Jesus told them. The servants filled some waterskins from a nearby well and topped up all the large jars. 'Now, it may seem a strange thing to ask,' Jesus said, 'but I want you to fill a small jug from the jars and take it to the man in charge of the feast.'

Looking puzzled, they carried out Jesus' instructions. The man tasted the liquid in the jug and was amazed. 'This is wonderful!' he exclaimed to the bridegroom. 'It's the finest wine that's ever passed my lips! Most people have the best to begin with: you've kept it till the end!'

Jesus had used the power which God had given to him to change the water into wine. This was the first of his many miracles and it made his disciples trust him even more.

Once Jesus was trying to teach people something about God's Kingdom when he remembered the weddings he had been to. So he told a story about one in order to help everyone to understand what he meant.

'A king gave a magnificent wedding feast for his son. He sent his servants to call for the guests who had been invited, but they all refused to come. Then he sent some more servants with yet another message. "The feast is ready for you."

'Nobody took any notice, and the people who had been invited carried on as if nothing had happened: one worked on his farm, another in his business and some of the others attacked and killed the servants.

'The king was furious and ordered his soldiers to kill the murderers. He then asked the servants who were left to invite anyone they could find to the feast. They invited everyone they saw.

'It was the custom in those days for each guest to be given a special robe to wear at a wedding. It was an insult to the kindness of the host not to put it on. Soon the hall was full and the king entered.

'He looked around and was deeply offended that one man was not wearing the special robe. "Tie his hands and feet, and throw him outside into the darkness," he ordered. "Let him stay there, for many people are invited, but few are chosen."'

Jesus told the story to show that although God, like the king, invites people to serve Him, not everyone wants to do so and even among those who accept His invitation, some still let Him down.

The Teaching of Jesus

Matthew 5 & 6

Jesus wanted to find a quiet place to talk to his disciples, away from the crowds who had begun to gather wherever he went. They decided to climb one of the hills which bordered the Sea of Galilee.

After a short walk they sat down on the hillside and as Jesus taught his friends about the Kingdom of God. As time went by they were joined by more and more people who had found out where Jesus was.

He began by telling them about the sorts of people who would receive God's love and blessing:

'Happy are those who know that they need God; the Kingdom of Heaven belongs to them.
Happy are those who mourn; God will strengthen them.
Happy are those who are humble; God will give them all they need.

Happy are those who are hungry to do what is right; they will be satisfied.
Happy are those who are kind; God will show kindness to them.
Happy are those who have pure thoughts; they will see God.
Happy are those who work for peace; they will be God's children.
Happy are those who have suffered for doing right; the Kingdom of Heaven belongs to them.'

All the disciples knew the laws of Moses very well. Jesus also taught them that to have wrong thoughts was as bad as actually doing wrong.

'You have all learned,' said Jesus, 'that it is wrong to murder anyone. What I say is that it is wrong even to be angry with someone else. Here's another

170

example: the law of Moses says that if someone hurts or offends you, you have the right to pay them back—an eye for an eye, a tooth for a tooth. On no account must you ever take revenge: if someone hits you on one side of your face, turn the other cheek towards him and let him hit that too. If someone forces you to walk a distance with him, willingly do it and go an extra distance as well. We were brought up to believe we should love our friends and hate our enemies. Well, this is not enough. You should love your enemies and care for those who make you suffer. Treat other people as you would like them to treat you. You will in that way become the sort of people God wants to have in his Kingdom.

'One thing is very important,' Jesus continued. 'I have not come to do away with the old laws and rules. I want us to think about them and what they are for, then we'll be able to obey them in a new way.'

'But, master,' interrupted one of the disciples, 'now that we've given up our jobs, how are we going to manage for money as we travel around with you?'

Jesus then replied by telling the disciples how riches could stop someone from serving God wholeheartedly. He wasn't saying that money is wrong, but that, like anything else, it can easily become more important to us than God.

'Don't collect great wealth for yourselves on earth; it might be stolen from you anyway! Store up your treasure in heaven; no one can take from you the riches that God can give. The things you love most of all are the things that are most valuable to you.'

'I see that,' the disciple said, 'but we've got to eat.'

'Don't be too worried about the everyday things in your lives, like the food you eat or the clothes you wear. There are more important things in life. Look at the birds around us. They don't grow food for themselves and yet your Heavenly Father cares for them, and you are worth even more to Him. And those flowers over there. They don't know about spinning or sewing and yet even King Solomon with all his riches was not as well dressed as one of them! So don't worry! Trust God. He knows what you need. If you make His Kingdom the most important thing in your life, He will look after everything else.'

The Lord's Prayer

Matthew 5, 6 & 7

Jesus spent the whole day on the hillside explaining his ideas to everybody. As the sun began to set, most of the people from nearby towns made their way back down to the lake, leaving Jesus with his disciples.

As dusk faded to darkness, they could see the lights of towns where one by one oil lamps were being lit in every home.

'You know,' said Jesus to his friends, 'you have to be like lights shining in a dark world. It's impossible to hide a hilltop town at night; the lights are seen by everyone. That's how it should be with you. Who's ever heard of putting an oil lamp under a bowl? You make sure it's high enough up in the room, so that the whole room is lit up. Your lives must be like that; as your goodness shines in the world, other people will see it and give thanks to God for you.'

'But, master,' said one of the disciples, 'it's hard to lead good lives when there's so much wrong in the world.'

'Don't judge other people like that,' Jesus replied.

'You're probably as bad, if not worse yourself. It's like going up to someone and saying, "Excuse me, there's a speck of dust in your eye," when all the time there's a massive plank in yours and you've done nothing about it! First take the plank out of your own eye and you'll be able to see clearly to help others!'

Jesus then told them how important it was for them to pray to God in the right way. When some people talk to God they think more about themselves and what they want. He said that real prayer is finding out what God wants us to do.

'When you pray,' Jesus explained, 'don't use lots of words which mean nothing. God knows what you need even before you ask Him. This is how you should pray:

'Our Father in heaven,
may Your name be honoured;
may Your Kingdom come;
may Your will be done on earth as it is in heaven:
give us today our daily bread.
Forgive us our wrongs
as we forgive those who wrong us.
Do not test us too hard,
but protect us from evil.'

Jesus made it clear that God loves those who serve Him as a father loves his children, so no one need be afraid of praying to Him. 'Ask and you will receive;' he said, 'seek and you will find; knock and the door will open for you. Everyone who asks will receive something; everyone who seeks will find something; and everyone who knocks will have a door opened. After all, if you had children of your own and they asked you for some bread, you wouldn't give them a stone, would you? If they wanted some fish, you wouldn't hand them a poisonous snake! Be sure of this, God will give good gifts to His children too!

'Before we find somewhere to sleep tonight,' Jesus continued, 'I've one last thing to mention. Try to remember my words. Anyone who takes notice of what I say is like a man who builds his house on solid rock; even if it is battered by rain and wind and floods, it will not be in danger because it is safe on the rock. Anyone who ignores my words is like a foolish man who builds his house on sand; rain and wind and floods will easily destroy it. Build your lives on my teachings and you will be able stand as firm as a rock amid the troubles of the world.'

When Jesus had finished talking to his friends, they all got up and began to walk down the hillside.

The Centurion's Servant

Matthew 8

During the lifetime of Jesus the whole of Galilee and beyond was part of the Roman Empire, and so there were Roman soldiers living in most of the towns. Many Jews hated them and would have nothing to do with them. Not all the Roman soldiers, however, were hostile to the Jews. Some of them sympathised with their beliefs and customs, and gradually won the trust of the people they ruled.

A Roman centurion living in Capernaum was very upset because a servant, who was very dear to him, was dying from a serious illness. The officer had heard about the wonderful things which Jesus had been doing in Galilee, so when he discovered that he was in the town, he had an idea. He asked some of the Jewish leaders there to see if Jesus would heal the servant; he thought that Jesus would be more willing to do it for them. 'Please come,' they told him. 'This centurion isn't our enemy. He is a friend to us all and has even built a synagogue for us out of his own money.'

Jesus agreed to go with them. They were nearly at the house, when the centurion sent a servant with a message which said, 'Sir, I don't deserve the honour of having you in my house. I'm not even worthy to meet you myself. I am a man with authority over the soldiers in my charge. I order one to go and he goes; I order another to come and he comes. You have authority too. Just say the word and I know my servant will be healed.'

Jesus was amazed at how much the centurion trusted him and he turned to the crowd which had followed him. 'I have never found anyone with a faith like this officer's.' He then told the servant to return to the house. 'When you get there,' Jesus called after him, 'the sick man will be well.'

It happened just as he said, and the servant began to get better at once. Jesus healed many more people, among whom was Peter's mother-in-law, who lived with him in Capernaum. She had a very high temperature, which went down as soon as Jesus touched her hand.

As evening fell, many people were brought to Jesus to be healed. He cured those who were sick in their minds, and healed the ill and lame. This explained the words of the prophet Isaiah many hundreds of years before, 'He took our sicknesses away and carried our diseases for us.'

Because of all that they saw him doing, many people wanted to become Jesus' followers. Unfortunately not all of them were willing to sacrifice everything in order to live the sort of life he lived. For example, a Jewish teacher came up and offered to become a disciple. 'I'm prepared to go with you wherever you go,' he said, and he was very sincere in his wishes.

'Listen,' Jesus told him, 'if you follow me, you will have no home. Foxes have holes in the ground and birds have nests in the trees, but I have nowhere of my own to rest and sleep.'

When the man heard this, he realized that he had not thought deeply enough about what being a disciple really involved, so he changed his mind.

Jesus asked his disciples to give up their belongings, homes and families in order to follow him.

A Paralysed Man is Healed

Luke 5

On another occasion people in Capernaum learned that Jesus had come to the town again and was spending the day at a friend's house. It wasn't long before a stream of uninvited visitors started going inside to meet him. Soon the main room was completely full: there was nowhere to sit down with the crowd packed in as tightly as possible, making the place hot and stuffy. There were faces at all the doors and windows, as everyone eagerly strained to catch a glimpse of Jesus and to hear what he was saying.

There was a man living nearby who had been paralysed for some time and spent the whole of his time lying on his bed. His friends heard that Jesus had returned, so four of them decided to take the invalid along to the house in the hope that Jesus might be able to heal him. Each of the men held on to a corner of the mattress and set off with their friend through the streets.

As soon as they reached the house, their faces fell. It was obvious that they had no chance at all of getting into the building, let alone of taking their friend to Jesus. They put the mattress down on the ground and wondered what to do. Then one of them had an idea. 'Look,' he said excitedly, pointing at the house. 'It's got an outside staircase going up on to the roof.'

'So?' said one of the others.

'Well, why don't we take him up there? When we're on the roof, we can take off some of the tiles and lower him down through the hole to Jesus.'

'Do what?' said the paralysed man.

They all agreed it was worth trying, so they fetched some long ropes and went up the steps on to the flat roof area and began removing the tiles.

Jesus and the people in the house stopped talking and looked up as pieces of plaster fell down on to their heads and shoulders. They must have thought the roof was collapsing. Next a gaping hole appeared and through it the faces of four men. Then to everyone's amazement a mattress was swung through the big gap and lowered into the room. The crowd had to push back to make a space and Jesus looked down at the paralysed man now lying at his feet. 'Your friends trust me a great deal,' he told him. 'I want you to know that all the wrong and sinful things in your life have been forgiven.'

When some of the Jewish leaders heard Jesus say this, they became very angry. 'It's an insult to God,' they muttered. 'Only God can forgive someone's sins.'

'Listen,' Jesus answered, 'it's harder to change what people are like than it is to heal them. I can't show you that this man's sins have been forgiven, but I will show you that I have the power to do that and many other things.'

He looked straight at the man on the mattress. 'I want you to get up, collect your mattress and go back home.' To the amazement of everyone who could see, the man stood up shakily, bent down to pick up his bedding and pushed his way through all the people into the fresh air outside. He and his four friends returned home praising God. All the onlookers gave thanks to God for what had happened in the house. None of them had ever met anyone like Jesus.

175

The Storm on the Lake

Mark 4 & 5

One evening after Jesus had spent a busy day mixing with large numbers of people, he suggested to his disciples that they should all borrow a fishing boat and sail across the Sea of Galilee to find a peaceful place on the other side.

There was a good breeze which soon took them out into the middle of the lake. Jesus was so exhausted that he lay down in the stern and fell soundly asleep.

It can be dangerous on the Sea of Galilee because strong winds can suddenly sweep down from the surrounding hills and whip up the water into lashing waves.

Those among the disciples who had been fishermen knew what was going to happen when the breeze turned into a gusty wind and the boat began to pitch about more and more. They had no time to reach the shore before even stronger winds howled around the rigging and great waves pounded the small boat. They dropped the sail but, as water started coming in over the sides, the disciples all knew that there was a risk of sinking and they became very afraid.

The only person who was not worried was Jesus, who was still fast asleep with no idea of the danger at all. One of the disciples made his way to the stern hanging on to the side of the lurching boat as he did so. When he reached Jesus, he shook him to wake him and shouted in his ear. 'Master,' he bellowed. 'Wake up! We're going to drown! Don't you care?'

Jesus sat up and called out to them, 'Don't be afraid. Trust me!' He looked at the darkened sky and the waves beating against the boat. 'Peace, be still!' he cried. 'Peace, be still!' Almost at once the raging wind died down and the water became calmer, until soon a new stillness settled over the lake and the boat again moved gently on the lapping swell.

The disciples were silent. 'What sort of person is this?' they thought. 'Even the wind and waves obey him.'

'You haven't much faith yet,' Jesus told them. 'Remember: trust me. Well, let's not stay here! We were on our way to the other side of the lake, so why don't we carry on?'

They all agreed and after they had baled out the water, they headed across to the shore. The part of the coast where they landed was an isolated area. One or two farmers kept pigs and sheep on the cliff tops, but that was all. The disciples got out of the boat and clambered among the rocks which came down to the lakeside. Several tombs had been cut out of the rocks and the whole place seemed desolate and unfriendly.

As they walked about the shore, they suddenly heard strange cries and a banging noise. They went to see what it was and found a man crouched down near a tomb. He was very sick and from time to time he would run in all directions, screaming and cutting himself with sharp stones. There was an evil power in him which he could not control.

As soon as he saw Jesus, instead of running away, the man went up to him and knelt at his feet. He said that his name was Legion. Jesus began to talk to him and, as he did so, Legion's face became gentler and all the wildness seemed to go from his eyes. Jesus had calmed another storm, Legion's mind.

The man knew that he was better and Jesus told him to go back to his friends and tell them all how God had healed him. Then Jesus and the disciples returned to their boat and sailed back across the lake.

Jairus' Daughter

Mark 5

Jesus then made his way to Nazareth, where his home was. His friends went with him. The people who lived there were surprised when he began to teach about God: they couldn't believe that such wise words were coming from the lips of Mary's son, the one whom they had seen growing up and playing the streets with the other children.

Later on Jesus was sitting in a lakeside town in Galilee, surrounded by the crowds who always gathered to hear him, when a Jewish leader named Jairus pushed through the people and knelt in front of him. The man was so upset that it was hard to hear the words he blurted out. 'It's my daughter,' he cried out. 'She's dying. Come with me to my house. Please. She's only twelve and she's the only daughter I've got. If you come, she'll get better.'

'Of course I'll come,' Jesus said. 'You lead the way.' Jairus then led him and the disciples through the streets to his home. The crowd went as well.

Before they reached the house, Jesus suddenly stopped in his tracks, and stared around him at all the people. 'Who touched my clothes?' he called out.

'What do you mean?' asked one of his disciples. 'People are pushing and jostling you all the time.'

'I don't mean like that,' Jesus answered. 'No, someone touched me for a special reason; someone who wanted to be healed.' He looked around again to see who had done it. A woman then fell at his feet, sobbing and begging his forgiveness. 'I'm sorry, master. I've had a blood disease for twelve years. No one could help me, but I knew that I only had to touch the hem of your clothing and I would be well. And I am; I know I'm better already: I can feel the strength in my body.'

'That's all right,' Jesus told her. 'You trusted me, so you have recovered. May God's peace go with you.'

Jairus had been standing near Jesus and had been becoming more and more impatient with the woman. Every moment Jesus delayed meant that his daughter's sickness grew worse. Just then one of his servants broke through the crowd and went up to him. Jairus could see that the man had brought bad news. 'It's your daughter, sir. It's too late. She's just died. There's no need for Jesus to come.'

Jesus heard the servant, but paid no attention to him. 'Don't be afraid, Jairus. Just trust me,' he told him. He then walked quickly to the house and went in, taking Peter, James and John with him. The house was full of relatives and friends of the family who were all crying loudly. 'Why all the noise?' Jesus asked them. 'She's not dead—she's only sleeping!'

'Don't be ridiculous!' they scoffed at him. 'Of course she's dead.'

Jesus insisted that he was right and he asked everyone to leave except for the girl's parents and his three disciples. When the house had been cleared, the six of them went into the girl's bedroom. Jesus went up to the bed on which she was lying and he took her hand in his. 'Come on, little girl,' he said, 'get up!'

To everyone's delight, she opened her eyes and sat up immediately. Then she got out of bed and began to walk across the room to her parents. They hugged her and thanked God that she was alive and well. 'I expect she's hungry!' Jesus laughed. 'Why not give her something to eat!' And with that, he left the house with Peter, James and John.

Matthew's Call

Matthew 9; Luke 9

One by one, more men decided to give up their jobs in order to travel with Jesus wherever he went. Among these was someone named Matthew. He was a tax collector, which made him very unpopular, because he collected money from everyone for the Romans.

Few people would speak to him at all, except on business, so he was surprised when one day Jesus came up to his roadside table and began to talk to him. Matthew was so impressed by him that when Jesus asked him if he would be prepared to become one of his followers, he agreed.

Some people criticized Jesus for mixing with tax collectors and other outcasts, but he would not stop. 'They need my help,' he said. 'After all, healthy bodies don't need a doctor, but sick bodies do.'

It wasn't long before Jesus had chosen twelve men to be his closest friends and helpers. He knew that on his own he could not possibly travel everywhere in Galilee, let alone to areas further away. He decided to send them out in twos to put into practice the things he had taught them. They were to tell people about the Kingdom of God and care for people's needs, especially by healing those who were sick. 'You must trust God,' Jesus told them. 'Take nothing with you. God will provide for you.' The twelve men then set out and for a while they went from town to town in the same way that Jesus did.

The Sower

Matthew 13

When he was teaching people about God, Jesus often told them stories with a special meaning, called parables. One day he wanted to tell those gathered around him that they must listen carefully to his words and keep them in their minds. The story he told was about a farmer who was sowing his seed.

As the sower walked up and down the field, he scattered handfuls of seed on the ground around him. The trouble was that not all of it grew. Some fell on a path, and straightway birds swooped down and ate it up; some dropped among nearby rocks and took root, but the shoots withered in the heat of the sun; some lodged where there were thistles and weeds and had no chance to sprout at all. The grain only did well and grew into strong, healthy plants when it fell on good soil, which had been well prepared by ploughing, hoeing and watering.

The disciples wondered what the story meant, so Jesus explained it to them. What he said was something like this: God's word ought to grow in our lives, as the seed grew in the good ground, but all too often it doesn't. Many things happen to stop us doing what God wants: sometimes evil thoughts make us forget what God has said and His word is snatched out of our minds, just as the birds snatched away the seed; sometimes we serve God for a while, but, like the plant in the rocky soil, when things become hard, we give up; sometimes other things such as our wealth or our jobs become more important to us than God's words and they stop us from following Him, just as the weeds stopped the seed from growing. God wants us to be like the seed growing in the good soil. He wants us to be people who hear His words; then when we understand them, He wants us to put them into practice by serving Him in the world.

Jesus Tells More Stories

Matthew 13 & 25

Jesus wanted more and more people to put God before everything else in their lives: to be ready to serve and obey God at all times. Only in this way could God make the world a better place. God's Kingdom is not restricted to one particular place: it is made up of people everywhere who let God rule their lives.

Jesus was sure that being a member of God's Kingdom was the most important thing that could happen to anyone and that it was worth giving up everything to serve God. To fix this idea in people's minds he told them this story.

There was a merchant who collected pearls. He was only interested in the finest and he travelled everywhere to find them. One day he came across a magnificent pearl, the best he had ever seen. It was so expensive that he didn't have enough money to buy it, but he wanted to have it more than anything else. This special pearl was so important to him that he decided to sell his whole collection to pay for it.

Although crowds of people came to meet Jesus and to listen to him, only his twelve disciples were ready to give up all their time to being with him. He didn't mind that there were so few of them, because he believed that God's Kingdom would begin to spread throughout the world. 'It's like mustard seed,' he told his friends. 'It's so tiny that you can hardly see it, but if a farmer sows it in a field, it will grow and grow until it's taller than most other plants—so tall that birds think it's a tree and start nesting in the branches!'

Jesus realized that as God's Kingdom began to spread throughout the world there would be difficulties. Even though some people tried to stop others from serving God, His Kingdom would never be destroyed. In the end God would destroy everything which tried to spoil His Kingdom. 'It's rather like a man who sowed some very good wheat seed in a field,' Jesus explained. 'During the night, while he was asleep, one of his enemies sowed weeds there as well. Weeks later the two sorts of seeds produced shoots and soon the plants were quite tall. When the farmer found out that there were weeds in the field spoiling the wheat, he wondered what to do. He decided to let both carry on growing and then, at harvest time, he pulled up all the weeds, bundled them up and burnt them. The wheat was carefully cut and stored in his barn. So in the end, what was harmful was destroyed and he kept what was good.'

Jesus taught the disciples that God expects those who serve Him to make the most of their lives and not to waste their opportunities. He told a story about someone who had to go on a journey. While he

182

was away, he asked three of his servants to take care of his money. Two of the men put the money to good use and managed to increase the amount they had in the first place; the third man did nothing with his share except to bury it for safe keeping. After a long time the man they worked for returned. He was very pleased with the two who had used the money well and gained some more; he was angry with the one who had wasted his opportunity. 'Well done!' he said to the two who were hardworking. 'You served me faithfully and I will reward you for it!' Jesus made it clear that God expects His followers to be like the first two men and to make good use of all His gifts.

Feeding the Five Thousand

John 6

When the disciples came back to Jesus after travelling throughout the countryside, they all decided to go by boat away from the lakeside towns to somewhere quiet. They had much to talk about and Jesus wanted to hear how they had all got on. Unfortunately, as they were getting into the boat, they were spotted by someone who guessed where they were going. The word spread quickly and soon people left the towns and walked as fast as they could to the same place.

As Jesus stepped out of the boat and saw that the crowd had already gathered, he knew that he could not ignore them. They were like sheep without a shepherd and he had to help them. They walked up a hillside and after they had found somewhere to sit down, he taught them for most of the day.

They had been there for a long time when Jesus

184

realized that they must all have been hungry. 'Philip,' he called out to one of his disciples, 'where can we buy food for everyone?'

'We can't do it, master.' he answered. 'Just to give them a morsel of bread each it would cost at least 200 pieces of silver. Anyway, we're a long way from anywhere. Where could we buy it?'

'See if anyone here has brought bread,' Jesus suggested.

The disciples moved from person to person, asking what food each had. It seemed that no one had any. Then Andrew found someone. 'There's a young boy here,' he told Jesus. 'He's got five barley loaves and two small fish. But what good is that with so many mouths to feed.'

'Make them all sit down in rows,' Jesus said. 'I'd like them in separate groups of about a hundred people each.'

As soon as this had been done, they were able to count the crowd. There were over 5,000 men, women and children. The little boy then gave his food to Jesus who held it in his hands and thanked God for it. He then broke up the bread and fish and asked the

disciples to share it out. To their amazement they didn't run out of food. The more they gave out, the more there seemed to be. The huge crowd was fed on this small amount. When the people had eaten what they wanted, the disciples collected any pieces which were left over into baskets. They filled twelve baskets with the remains. As evening drew near the crowds went back home, but on the next day they came out to look for Jesus again. When they found him, he had some important things to say to them.

'You came to find me today,' he said, 'because of the bread I gave you to eat. The food you had yesterday isn't important: it always goes mouldy after a while. The most important food is the sort which lasts for ever.'

'Give us some of that bread,' they asked him.

'I am the bread of life,' he explained. 'Anyone who comes to me will never be hungry; anyone who trusts me will never be thirsty. What I mean is that if you trust me, God will give you a new sort of life, which will satisfy you now and go on even after you have died. We need the life which God can give us even more than the bread we eat each day.'

The Good Samaritan

Luke 10

A Jewish teacher was once talking to Jesus in order to try to catch him out with difficult questions. The man knew that in order to please God he had to serve Him with his whole life and to show concern for his neighbour. 'Who is my neighbour?' he asked Jesus. 'Whom should I care for?'

'Let me tell you a story,' Jesus replied. 'A man was travelling along the desert road from Jerusalem to Jericho. Suddenly, a band of robbers jumped out on him from behind some rocks. They punched and kicked him, tearing the clothes off his body, and then they left him lying injured by the roadside.

'He lay there some time until another traveller came along. It was a priest, but instead of stopping to help, he took one look and went straight past on the other side of the road. The next to approach was a man known as a Levite, who helped at services in the Temple at Jerusalem. He did the same as the priest and took no notice of the dying man. Soon a third person came down the road riding a donkey. This was someone from Samaria and no one would have expected him to help because the Jews never had anything to do with the Samaritans. When he reached the injured man, he felt very sorry for him and dismounted to examine his injuries. When he saw how serious they were, he took some wine and a jar of olive oil from the panniers on the donkey and poured the soothing liquids on to the wounds. He then tore up some clothing into long strips and bandaged the cuts.

'When the Samaritan was sure that the injured man was strong enough, he lifted him on to his own donkey and took him to the nearest inn, where he found him a bed and cared for him. The next day the Samaritan had to travel on, so he gave the innkeeper two silver coins. "Look after him," he said. "If it costs you any more to do it, I'll pay you in a few days when I return."'

Jesus looked hard at the Jewish teacher. 'Well, tell me what you think: which of those three men behaved as a neighbour should towards the man who was attacked?'

'The one who helped him,' he replied grudgingly. He didn't like to admit it was the Samaritan.

'You're right,' Jesus told him. 'You should go and do the same yourself.'

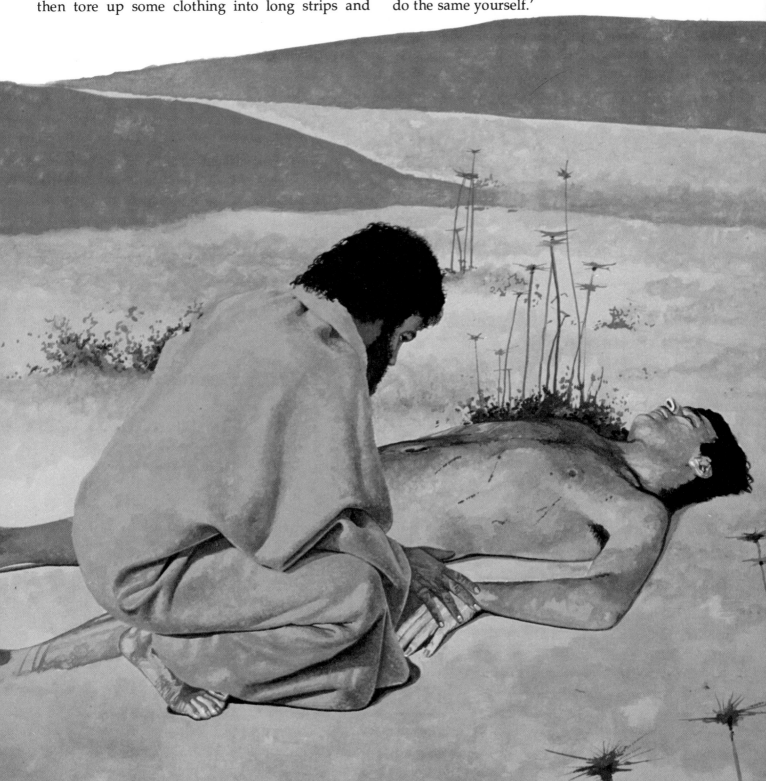

The Woman at the Well

John 4

Jesus and his disciples were once travelling through Samaria when at about noon they arrived at a town called Sychar. The midday sun blazed fiercely, so he was glad to find a well just outside the town where he could sit and have a drink of water. He didn't expect to see anyone about, because most people stayed indoors at that time of day to avoid the heat.

He was surprised to see a woman coming towards him carrying a water jar on her head. When she reached the well, she dipped the jar into it. As she did so, Jesus spoke to her. 'Please give me a drink of water,' he said.

'But you're a Jew and I'm a Samaritan,' she replied. 'You're not supposed to talk to us or touch anything of ours, so how can you ask me that?'

'If you knew who I am,' Jesus told her, 'you'd ask me for some water yourself.'

'How could you give me any water?' said the puzzled woman. 'It's a deep well and you haven't even got a container of your own.'

'If you drink this well-water,' he explained, 'it will satisfy you now, but then in a while you'll be thirsty again. Whoever drinks my water will never be thirsty again. The water I give will last forever.'

'Give me some then,' she said. 'I won't ever have to come here again.'

The woman didn't understand what Jesus was saying. He meant that if she put her trust in him, then God would make something new out of her life and that this new life from God would always satisfy her like a drink quenching your thirst for ever. Jesus knew why she had come to the well in the midday heat: she didn't want to meet anyone else. She was too ashamed to face them and Jesus guessed why.

'Go and bring your husband to meet me,' he said.

'Sir, I have no husband,' she answered, embarrassed at his words.

'Of course you haven't,' Jesus went on. 'You have had five husbands and you're not married to the man you're living with at the moment. You know it's wrong, so that's why you came here at midday.'

'Sir, you are a man of God; I can see that. You know all about me. I have heard that when the Messiah comes, he will be able to tell us everything.'

'I am the Messiah,' Jesus answered.

Just then the disciples returned and were shocked to find Jesus talking to a Samaritan woman. She was so excited at having met Jesus that she took no notice of them and rushed into the town to tell everyone.

All the people she talked to saw at once that somehow she was different and they too came to meet Jesus. They begged him to stay there for a few days to teach them. Many of them believed that he was the Messiah and when he left they told the woman what they felt. 'We believe him now. We have listened to him and we are sure that he is the Saviour God promised to send into the world for all mankind.'

The Lost Sheep

Luke 15

Jesus was happy to talk to anyone; it didn't matter who they were or what sorts of lives they had led. He was especially friendly towards those who were outcasts in their town or village: the ones whom respectable people refused to go near, because of something they had done or simply because they were poor. Jesus insisted that God cares for everyone. He told them three stories to explain what he meant. The first was about a lost sheep.

'Imagine that a farmer owns a flock of a hundred sheep. What does he do if he loses one? He doesn't ignore it. He leaves the ninety-nine which are grazing safely in his field and he sets off to look for the one which is missing. He searches until he finds it. As soon as he sees it, he's overjoyed and he carries it on his shoulders back to the farm. Then he sends a message to his friends and neighbours. "Come and join me for a celebration! I've found the lost sheep!"'

Jesus was saying that God wants everyone to serve Him. He doesn't want to lose anyone and He is more pleased when one person is sorry for the life he led than He is to see ninety-nine respectable people who think they have never done any wrong.

The Lost Coin

Luke 15

In the second story which Jesus told about God's love a woman loses something very precious to her. When girls were married in those days, they were often given some coins as a present by their parents. These became as important as a wedding ring.

'One day,' he explained, 'a woman lost one of the ten silver coins she had. It meant so much to her that she refused to rest until she found it. She swept the house and looked everywhere. Suddenly she spotted it and was so happy that she asked all her friends to join her for a celebration. "I'm so pleased! I've found the lost coin!" Each person is as precious to God as the lost coin was to the woman. He is even more pleased when someone He thought He had lost begins to follow Him.'

On another occasion Jesus reminded his disciples that if God loves us and is willing to forgive us, then we should show the same love and forgiveness to other people. 'Be ready to forgive someone time and time again,' he said to Peter. He then told a story about a king whose servant owed him a lot of money.

The man couldn't pay it back and admitted it to the king. He should have been punished, but the man fell on his knees and asked for more time to find the money. The king felt sorry for him and told him he needn't pay back the money.

The man left the throne room and met another servant who owed him a small amount. He seized him by the throat and shook him hard. 'Pay me my money!' he bellowed. The other man couldn't and he begged to be given more time. Instead of showing forgiveness as the king had done to him, he threw the other servant into prison. When the king heard about it, he was very angry with the first man. 'You should have shown him the same kindness I showed you!' he shouted, and sent him to prison at once.

Jesus then explained that God expects His followers to forgive other people in the same way that God is willing to forgive them.

The Lost Son

Luke 15

Jesus told a third parable about God's love. Many people take no notice of God, so Jesus reminded his listeners that God is willing to forgive those who tell Him that they are sorry for this.

In this story a farmer had two sons. The younger one decided that he was fed up with living at home and he wanted to leave to make his own way in the world. 'When you die,' he said to his father, 'you will leave some land to me. I'd like it now before I go.'

His father didn't think it was a good idea, but he did as his son asked. The young man then sold the land, and to his father's sorrow he left home with the money, vowing never to return again. He travelled to a distant country where no one would know him, but instead of being sensible with his money, he wasted it all by spending it foolishly.

It wasn't very long before he had none left and became very miserable. To make matters worse, there was a food shortage in the area, so it was hard to find anything to eat. In the end he became so desperate that he took a job looking after some pigs and he even ate their bean pods to stay alive. Then one day he realized what he had to do. He would go home and ask his father to forgive him. So he set off at once on the long journey.

His father still loved him very much and had never given up hope that he would come back. Imagine his excitement when he saw his son coming up the road to the farm. He ran to meet him and hugged him with joy. 'Father,' the young man sobbed, 'I have done wrong to you and to God. I'm not fit to be your son.'

His father was so happy to have him back that he forgave him and arranged a splendid party to celebrate his son's return. His elder brother was working in the fields at the time, but when he arrived back he found that a party was being given. He was furious because his father had welcomed his young brother back. 'All these years I've worked hard,' he complained. 'You've never given a party for me!'

'My son,' his father explained gently. 'You have always been close to me, but we thought your brother was dead, and look, he's alive! We thought we'd lost him for ever, but now he's been found again! That's something to be pleased about. It's something we have to celebrate!'

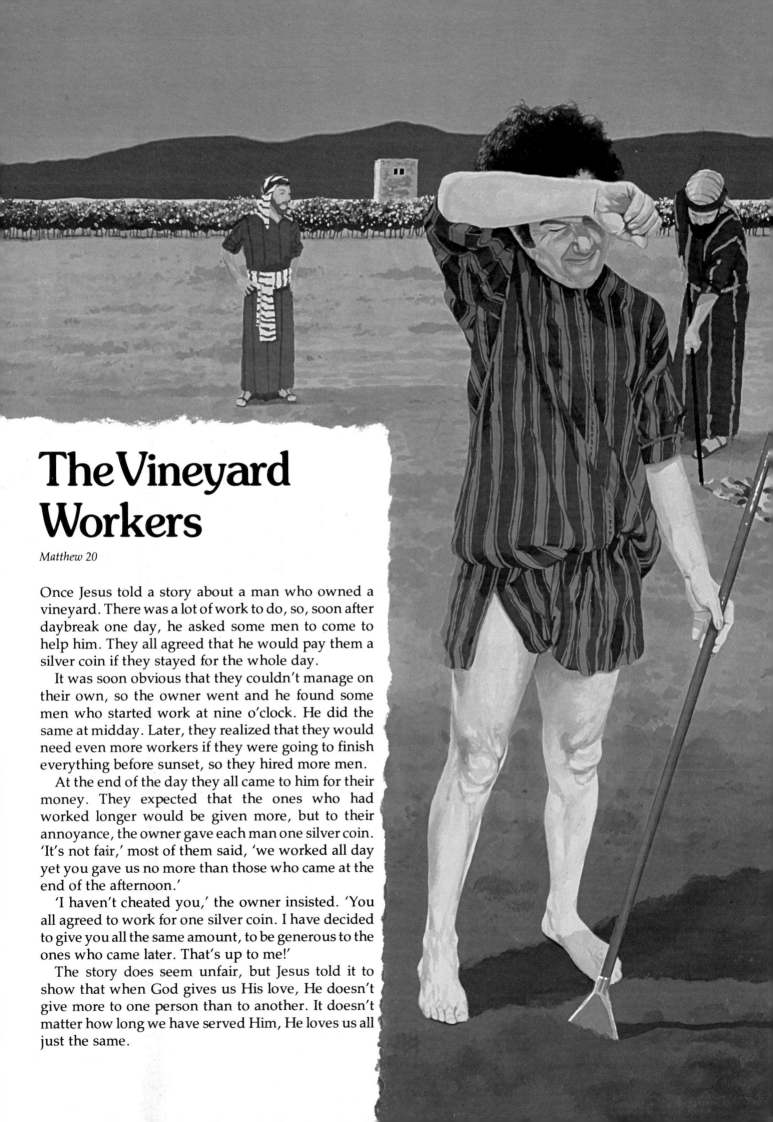

The Vineyard Workers

Matthew 20

Once Jesus told a story about a man who owned a vineyard. There was a lot of work to do, so, soon after daybreak one day, he asked some men to come to help him. They all agreed that he would pay them a silver coin if they stayed for the whole day.

It was soon obvious that they couldn't manage on their own, so the owner went and he found some men who started work at nine o'clock. He did the same at midday. Later, they realized that they would need even more workers if they were going to finish everything before sunset, so they hired more men.

At the end of the day they all came to him for their money. They expected that the ones who had worked longer would be given more, but to their annoyance, the owner gave each man one silver coin. 'It's not fair,' most of them said, 'we worked all day yet you gave us no more than those who came at the end of the afternoon.'

'I haven't cheated you,' the owner insisted. 'You all agreed to work for one silver coin. I have decided to give you all the same amount, to be generous to the ones who came later. That's up to me!'

The story does seem unfair, but Jesus told it to show that when God gives us His love, He doesn't give more to one person than to another. It doesn't matter how long we have served Him, He loves us all just the same.

Jesus Heals a Blind Man

John 9 & 12

Day after day, a blind man called Bartimaeus used to sit and beg in the streets of Jericho. One afternoon he heard a great commotion a few streets away and he realized that a large crowd of excited people was coming nearer. He asked someone what it was all about and he was told that they were all following Jesus who was walking through the town. This made him sit up and take more notice, because he had heard how Jesus could heal people. 'Perhaps, this may be my chance of having my eyes healed.'

To his delight the jostling crowd turned into the very street where he was. He made up his mind to try to attract the attention of Jesus as he went by. It seemed impossible, because Jesus was surrounded by hundreds of people all talking and shouting as they walked. As the noise approached, Bartimaeus shouted as loudly as he could. 'Jesus! Son of David! Have pity on me! Have pity on me!'

'Save your breath,' someone told him. 'He'll never hear you.'

'Jesus! Have mercy on me!' he kept calling.

Then to his surprise the footsteps seemed to stop. The people in the crowd were still talking to one another; but the noise was becoming much quieter, as if they were waiting for someone to do something. Bartimaeus heard a voice say, 'There's a blind beggar over there. Bring him here to me.' Then he felt two men bend down on either side of him. Holding his arms gently, they helped him to his feet. 'Cheer up!' they said. 'Jesus wants to talk to you.'

Just then the same voice, which he now knew belonged to Jesus, spoke to him. 'Tell me, what would you like me to do for you?'

'Sir, I want to be able to see.'

'Of course you do,' said Jesus gently. 'Because you trust me I will give you your sight!'

Immediately light seemed to flood through Bartimaeus' eyes. He blinked and rubbed them and realized that he saw the face of Jesus. 'Praise God!' he shouted. 'Praise God! I can see! I can see!' Everyone else was excited too and the streets of Jericho were filled with the sound of people's praises.

Some time later when Jesus was in Jerusalem, he healed another blind man. The Jewish leaders refused to believe the man's story. His parents came and told them that he had been born blind. They were still not convinced and so they talked again to the man himself. 'I'm only sure of one thing,' he told them. 'Once I was blind, but now I can see.'

The man had definitely received his sight, but all the Jewish leaders could do was to criticize and question what had happened. In a way, they were now the blind ones. They were like the people Isaiah once wrote about: 'Their eyes would not see, their minds would not understand.'

'Whoever sees me,' Jesus once said, 'also sees God, who sent me into the world. I am the Light of the World. Everyone who believes in me will live in light, not in darkness.'

WhoWasJesus?

Matthew 16; Luke 9

One day, Jesus went with his disciples to the countryside near a town called Caesarea Philippi. He wanted them to be absolutely certain why they were travelling with him, so, when they were sitting and talking, he asked them a direct question. 'Who do people say that I am?' he asked.

'Well, some think you're John the Baptist or a prophet like Elijah come back from the dead,' they told him.

'What do you all think? Who am I?'

There was a silence for a moment, then Peter answered without a trace of doubt in his voice. 'You are the promised Messiah, the Son of the living God!'

'That is so Peter,' Jesus said. 'My Father in Heaven has helped you to understand this. Listen, Peter. You are like a rock—that's what your name means. The words you have spoken will be the solid rock on which I build my church. It will last for ever and no power will be able to destroy it. I will give to you the keys of God's Kingdom, and God will bless everything you do.'

Peter was certain that Jesus was the Son of God because, together with the other disciples, he had been close to him for a long time. He had been able to listen to his wise teaching and often seen him per-

form miracles to help all sorts of people. He knew that Jesus must be this special person that the Jews had been waiting for.

From that moment on Jesus began to talk much more about the future. He kept telling his disciples that he had soon to travel south to Jerusalem, where he would have to face suffering. The Jewish leaders would oppose him and he would then be killed.

Although at the time his friends did not understand what he meant, he told them that three days after his death he would be raised from the dead to new life.

Peter was upset by this talk about dying and he tried to stop Jesus saying such things. 'Lord, that can't be true!' he protested. 'Nothing like that's going to happen to you.'

'Don't say things like that, Peter,' Jesus answered. 'You are thinking like a man. It has to happen because that is what God has planned. Nothing must get in the way. I have to say this to you all. If anyone wants to follow me, he must forget about himself and be prepared to suffer as well.

'You could own the whole world and life would still not be worth living; if you give up everything to follow me, God will give you a new sort of life which no one can take from you.'

Jesus knew that the next months would be hard both for him and the disciples, but he trusted God to give him the strength to endure whatever was to happen.

197

The Vision on the Mountain

Matthew 17

About a week later Jesus asked Peter, James and John
to go with him to find a quiet place where they could
pray together. In order to be quite alone, they
climbed right to the top of a hill. Jesus knew that he
could no longer stay in Galilee and he wanted to
prepare himself for the suffering which lay ahead at
Jerusalem.

As Jesus began to pray, the three disciples fell
asleep. Soon afterwards they woke and saw an amazing vision. They saw a change come over Jesus. His
face seemed to radiate with strong light and his
clothes seemed to shine and glisten. Just then they
saw the figures of two more people standing by
Jesus. Their appearance was also radiant and they
started to talk to him about his death in Jerusalem. As
they talked, it became clear that they were Moses and
Elijah who had lived hundreds of years before. As
these two great leaders honoured Jesus, the disciples
realized that people would still respect the words of
people like Moses and Elijah, but it would be Jesus,
above all, who would show God's glory in the world.
Peter thought he had to say or do something. 'Lord',
he blurted out, 'let me build a shelter for each of you.
We must honour you somehow.'

Before he could do anything, a bright cloud
enveloped the three and a voice spoke clearly from
the cloud. 'This is my Son, whom I love dearly. I am

very pleased with him. Listen to all he says.' The disciples were afraid, because they knew that it was God speaking to them and they turned their heads away. Then Jesus came up to them and touched them one by one. They looked around and to their surprise the two figures had gone. They could only see Jesus and his appearance was normal once more. He then made them promise never to tell anyone about the vision until after his death.

The vision showed Jesus that God would be with him as he went to Jerusalem and that God wanted him to be prepared to suffer. This was how God's name would become glorious.

Jesus and his friends walked down the hillside to join the other disciples who were waiting for them. They found that a large crowd had gathered and, as they approached, a man rushed up to Jesus.

'It's my son,' he explained. 'He has an illness which makes him do dangerous things. He has fallen into fire and water without realising it. I asked your disciples to heal him, but they couldn't.'

Jesus was disappointed when he heard this. 'Will you never learn?' he said to the disciples. 'Let me see the boy.' The father quickly led his son to Jesus, who made him well at once. The disciples asked him why they hadn't been able to do anything.

'Because you didn't have enough faith,' Jesus told them. 'You didn't really believe that he would be healed. You only need a tiny amount of faith, as tiny as a mustard seed.'

They went on to Capernaum. On the way Jesus again warned them that soon he would have to die, but that after three days he would rise again. They were still puzzled by this talk about his rising again, but they did not like to ask him what he meant.

Jesus and the Children

Matthew 18 & 19

Jesus was in a house at Capernaum with his disciples when he heard them discussing something among themselves. 'What's the matter?' he asked them. There was a silence, but Jesus knew that some of them had been arguing about who was the most important person of them all. 'Listen carefully,' Jesus told them. 'The greatest person is the one who is prepared to think of others before he thinks of himself.'

A little boy was playing in the house at the time, so Jesus called him over and put his arm round him. 'Unless you become like little children,' he explained, 'you cannot enter the Kingdom of Heaven. Whoever

humbles himself like a child will become great in the Kingdom. If anyone shows love to a child like this, he is showing love to me and to God my Father.'

The disciples soon forgot what Jesus had said about showing love to children. They had left Capernaum and were making their way south along the valley of the River Jordan towards Jerusalem. At one town some mothers brought their small children to Jesus. They wanted him to pray with them and ask God to bless their lives in the future.

Jesus was talking to a crowd of people when the mothers walked up. The disciples knew that he was busy so they stopped the women. 'Don't bother

him,' they said. 'He hasn't got time to see you.'

The women insisted that they should be allowed through and it wasn't long before Jesus noticed the commotion. He called out severely to the disciples. 'Don't stop them! Let the little children come to me. The Kingdom of God is made up of people like them.'

The disciples moved out of the way of the women, who went up to Jesus. He put his arms around the children and prayed, asking God to bless their lives.

After he had done this, he was about to move on, when a wealthy young man, who was an important person in the town, ran up and knelt in front of him. 'Master,' he asked, 'what do I have to do to receive life which lasts for ever?' He was talking about the new life which only God can give.

'You know God's laws about stealing, killing and so on,' Jesus answered. 'The Ten Commandments.'

'I've never broken any of them,' he replied.

Jesus looked at him for a moment and he was certain that only one thing could stop the young man from putting God first in his life: his riches. 'There's one thing you must do. Sell everything you own and give the money away to the poor. Then come and follow me. God will give you treasure in heaven.'

The young man's face fell. Jesus' words upset him, because he was very rich and he wasn't willing to part with any of his possessions. The man slowly stood up and went home feeling sad.

Jesus did not believe that it was wrong either to have money or to own things: they only became an obstacle when they stopped a person from serving God wholeheartedly.

'It can be very hard for wealthy people to enter the Kingdom of God,' He told the disciples. 'It is easier for a camel to go through the eye of a needle than it is for a rich man to serve God.'

201

Jesus and Nicodemus

John 3

Many of the Jewish leaders were against Jesus because he claimed to be the Son of God. One important official called Nicodemus had heard a great deal about Jesus and he wanted to find out more for himself. He was afraid to go to see him in the daytime in case anyone spotted him, so he decided to call secretly after dark at the house where Jesus was staying.

Jesus invited him inside and they talked together for a long time. 'I know that God is with you,' Nicodemus said. 'No one could teach or heal people as you do without God's help.'

'Nicodemus,' Jesus replied, 'what I am about to say is the truth: if someone wants to belong to the Kingdom of God, he must be born again.'

This completely baffled Nicodemus. 'How can an adult be born again?' he asked. 'He can't go back inside his mother!'

'I don't mean like that,' Jesus explained. 'No one can enter the Kingdom unless God's spirit first changes his life. God gives a new life which is like being born all over again.'

The two men talked well into the night and then Nicodemus left as stealthily as he had come, but with much to think about.

Zacchaeus Comes to Jesus

Luke 19

On his way to Jerusalem Jesus went through Jericho, where the usual crowds gathered to listen to him. The chief tax collector in the town was a man named Zacchaeus, who had become very rich by cheating people out of their money.

He was curious to see Jesus, but because he was not very tall, it was impossible for him to get even a glimpse of him. The street in which Jesus was walking was lined with fig trees, so Zacchaeus ran ahead of the crowd and climbed up one of these to get a better view. When Jesus reached the place, he stopped and looked up. Jesus found out his name and called, 'Do hurry up and come down, Zacchaeus. I'd like to go with you to your house.'

Zacchaeus was astonished and scrambled down to the ground. He eagerly led the way and welcomed Jesus to his house. Some onlookers were very angry that Jesus had gone there. 'Fancy going to eat with a man like that!' they grumbled. 'What has he done to deserve it?'

Jesus didn't think like that at all: he longed to share God's love with everyone and especially those whom no one else loved. As they talked together, Zacchaeus was impressed by the things Jesus said, but most of all by the fact that Jesus had wanted to meet him in the first place. During the meal he stood up and made a promise. 'I know that I have done wrong. I will give half of everything I own to the poor and I will repay everyone I've cheated, four times over.'

'That's good,' replied Jesus. 'Today God has begun to change you. It's like starting your life again. God sent me into the world to help people such as you.'

It was soon time for Jesus to be on his way again, because he knew that the moment had come for him to complete his journey to Jerusalem.

Jesus and Lazarus

John 11

Not far from Jerusalem was a village called Bethany, where Jesus had often been to visit three friends who were members of the same family. These were two sisters, Mary and Martha, who lived with their brother, Lazarus. Jesus was very fond of them all and he always looked forward to staying with them.

One day Lazarus became seriously ill and the two anxious sisters sent an urgent message to Jesus, asking him to come at once. Jesus was sad to hear the news, but he didn't rush immediately to Bethany. He was not anxious about Lazarus and he felt sure that through the illness God would be honoured.

Two days later Jesus set out and walked for several days to reach the house. When he was near to Bethany he heard that Mary and Martha were very upset, because Lazarus had died four days earlier and he had already been buried. The house was full of people who had come to comfort the two sisters.

Word reached them that Jesus was on his way, so Martha rushed out to meet him: she didn't want to talk to him in front of everyone else. Mary was too distressed to move from the house.

Martha saw Jesus just outside the village and she ran up to him with tears in her eyes. 'Lord,' she cried, 'if you had been here, Lazarus wouldn't have died!' She knew about all the wonderful things Jesus had done and that he had even brought people back to life, so she had a little hope that he might do the same for her brother. 'I'm sure,' she went on, 'God will give you whatever you ask for.'

Jesus saw that she was depending on him. 'Don't be worried,' he reassured her. 'Your brother will rise to life again.'

'We all will one day,' Martha replied, now a little uncertain.

'I am the resurrection and the life,' Jesus told her. 'Whoever believes me will live, even though he dies. Those who trust me will never die. Do you believe this?' he asked her.

'Yes, Lord,' she answered. 'I believe that you are the Messiah, the Son of God, who was going to come into the world one day.'

'Martha, why not go and fetch Mary,' Jesus suggested. 'She should be here too.'

Martha went back and whispered to Mary to come at once. She got up straight away and left the house, without a word to anyone else. The others who were there thought she was going to the grave, so they followed her.

When Mary found Jesus, she fell at his feet weeping. 'Lord,' she sobbed, 'if you had been here, Lazarus would still be alive.' When Jesus saw her tears and realized how upset all the others were as well, he knew that he had to do something to help them. 'Take me to the grave,' he asked them.

'Come with us,' Mary and Martha told him.

As they walked along, Jesus could not hold back his own tears. Everyone then realized how much he must have loved Lazarus.

When they reached the burial place, Jesus saw that it was a tomb cut into a rocky slope. A huge stone had been rolled across the entrance to seal it. 'Move the stone!' he ordered.

'But, Lord,' Martha said quietly to him. 'He's been buried for four days. It won't be very pleasant.'

'Listen to me, Martha,' he replied. 'I told you that you would see God honoured if you trusted me. Please do as I ask.'

She nodded and the heavy stone was rolled away. Everyone then watched Jesus to see what he would do. Some were afraid because they didn't know what might happen.

Jesus bowed his head and prayed to God. Then he looked towards the tomb and called out loudly. 'Lazarus, come out of there!' Everyone waited with bated breath. Then they caught sight of a movement in the tomb. They saw a figure come to the entrance still wearing burial clothes. It was Lazarus and he was alive!

'Take the burial clothes off him,' Jesus said as he went forward with Mary and Martha to throw his arms around his friend. Everyone was overjoyed and praised God that his power was so great.

Jesus Rides into Jerusalem

Matthew 21; John 12

Jesus and the disciples travelled on to Jerusalem, which was at that time crowded with Jews who had arrived from near and far for the great Passover festival. They had reached a hill called the Mount of Olives, when Jesus pointed to a village nearby.

'I'd like two of you to do something for me,' he told his friends. 'If you go to the village you'll find a donkey and her colt tied up by the first house. Untie the colt and bring it to me.'

'But what if anyone stops us?' they asked him.

'Tell them that the master needs it,' he answered, 'and there'll be no problem.'

The two disciples went at once and found the colt as Jesus had described. They were just about to take it when a bystander demanded to know what they were doing. When they said that the master needed it, the man nodded and let them carry on.

They led the colt to the place where Jesus and the other disciples were waiting. First, they threw some clothes over its back and then Jesus sat on it. Although no one had ridden it before, it stood calmly and was not at all restless. The words that the prophet Isaiah had written about the Messiah hundreds of years before were coming true: 'Jerusalem, your king is coming humbly to you, riding on a colt.'

Many of the people who were in Jerusalem for the Passover festival had heard about Jesus. The word quickly spread that he was approaching the city and would soon be arriving. It wasn't long before crowds gathered in the streets along which they thought he would enter the city. They believed that he was coming as their king, the Messiah, so they cut palm branches and prepared to welcome him.

As soon as they saw Jesus riding up the street, a great cheer went up. 'Praise God!' they shouted. Son of David, save us! Long live the King of Israel! Long live the one who comes in God's name!'

They waved the palm branches and spread them on the ground, together with clothing, to make a carpet for their king to ride over. The sound of their rejoicing echoed around the streets and buildings of Jerusalem. People who had never heard of Jesus began to ask questions about him, and those who knew him talked about the wonderful things he had said and done. Only the religious leaders of the city were unhappy, because they did not believe that he was the Son of God, the Messiah, and they didn't want the people following him. 'Tell them to stop shouting those things,' they asked Jesus.

'I cannot do a thing,' he told them. 'If they stopped, even the stones of the city would cry out!'

Jesus was thankful for the welcome the people gave him, but he knew that within a week another crowd would be shouting for his death. With these mixed feelings Jesus rode right into the centre of the city and spent some time looking around the great Temple. Towards evening he and the disciples left and returned to Bethany where they were staying.

Later on, Jesus' friends remembered some words written many years before by the prophet Zechariah:

'People of Jerusalem, rejoice and shout for joy!
See how your King comes to you:
He is great, yet he is humble,
For he rides on a donkey to meet you.'

Jesus in the Temple

Matthew 21 & 22; Mark 12

The next day Jesus and the disciples went into the city again and walked straight to the Temple. When Jesus had looked around it the day before, he had been very upset at what he saw.

In the outer courtyard there were large numbers of traders doing their business with the travellers who were in Jerusalem for the Passover. The traders sold pigeons and other animals which people needed for the sacrifices they made in the Temple services. The trouble was that the traders charged more than they should have done. When people paid money to the Temple officials, they had to use special Jewish coins instead of the usual Roman ones, so there were several stalls where Roman money could be exchanged for these special coins. Many of the traders cheated people by not giving them enough for their money. All this angered Jesus so much that he stormed into the courtyard, shouting at the traders to get out at once.

There was a great commotion as he turned over the tables and seats used by the swindlers, scattering their money all over the ground. The traders knew that Jesus was popular with many people, so they left quickly with Jesus calling after them. 'God said, "My house should be a house of prayer;" you have made it nothing but a den of robbers.'

When he had cleared the Temple of all the dishonest traders, Jesus began to teach the people who had gathered around him about God. The Jewish leaders became afraid that they might lose their power, as Jesus was so popular; they were also angry that Jesus claimed to be speaking in God's name. They made up their minds to get rid of him. First of all they tried to make him look foolish by asking him difficult questions, then they tried to trap him into saying something wrong.

On one occasion they came to Jesus, hoping that they could catch him out. 'We'd like to know,' they said, 'whether it is right for us to pay tax to the Roman Emperor.'

This was a hard thing to answer: if Jesus said 'Yes', then the Jewish people, who hated the Romans, would turn against him; if, on the other hand, he said 'No', then the Jewish leaders could report him to Pontius Pilate, the Roman Governor of Jerusalem, who might have been willing to arrest him. Either way, they felt sure that they had trapped him, but Jesus knew what they were trying to do.

'Bring me a Roman coin,' he said to them. Somebody handed one to him. 'Whose head is on this coin?' he asked.

'Caesar's, of course,' they replied.

'Very well. Give to Caesar what belongs to Caesar and give to God the things that belong to Him.'

No one could find fault with the answer Jesus gave and they were so amazed at his wisdom that they said nothing and left him alone for a while.

One day Jesus sat down not far from the Temple money chests where people made their offerings to God. The chests had funnels on top into which the coins could be thrown. Jesus noticed that the rich often made a big show of the amount they were giving. They would hurl their coins down the funnel to make a great rattling noise, which drew everyone's attention to them. Just then a widow, who was obviously very poor, came along and put two tiny coins into one of the chests.

'Do you see that woman over there?' Jesus told the disciples. 'She has given far more to God than all the wealthy people have done. What they gave was nothing to them, but this woman has given away everything she had.'

Jesus continued teaching and healing people in Jerusalem and he put into practice the two commandments which he told the people were the greatest of all: 'Love God with your whole being and love your neighbour as much as you love yourself.'

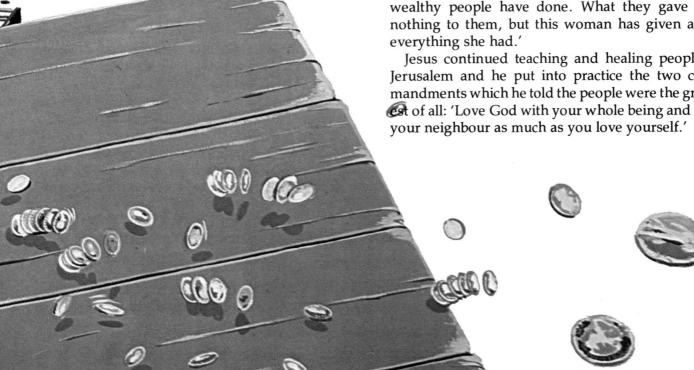

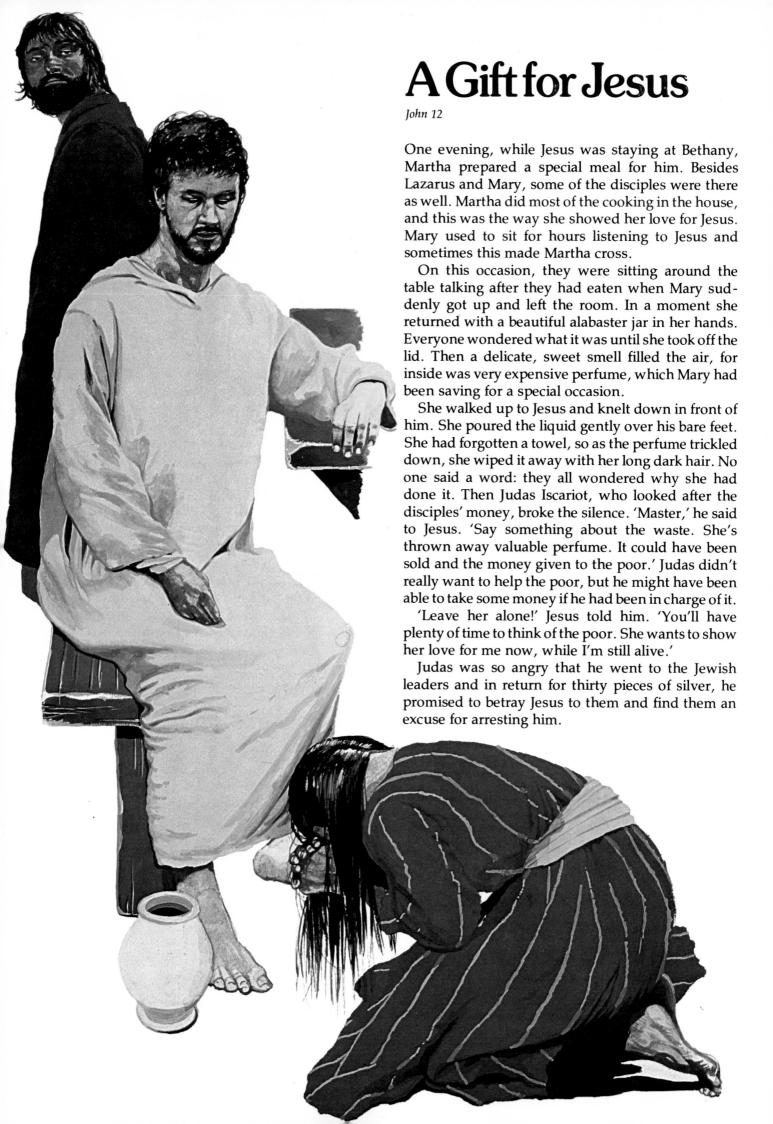

A Gift for Jesus

John 12

One evening, while Jesus was staying at Bethany, Martha prepared a special meal for him. Besides Lazarus and Mary, some of the disciples were there as well. Martha did most of the cooking in the house, and this was the way she showed her love for Jesus. Mary used to sit for hours listening to Jesus and sometimes this made Martha cross.

On this occasion, they were sitting around the table talking after they had eaten when Mary suddenly got up and left the room. In a moment she returned with a beautiful alabaster jar in her hands. Everyone wondered what it was until she took off the lid. Then a delicate, sweet smell filled the air, for inside was very expensive perfume, which Mary had been saving for a special occasion.

She walked up to Jesus and knelt down in front of him. She poured the liquid gently over his bare feet. She had forgotten a towel, so as the perfume trickled down, she wiped it away with her long dark hair. No one said a word: they all wondered why she had done it. Then Judas Iscariot, who looked after the disciples' money, broke the silence. 'Master,' he said to Jesus. 'Say something about the waste. She's thrown away valuable perfume. It could have been sold and the money given to the poor.' Judas didn't really want to help the poor, but he might have been able to take some money if he had been in charge of it.

'Leave her alone!' Jesus told him. 'You'll have plenty of time to think of the poor. She wants to show her love for me now, while I'm still alive.'

Judas was so angry that he went to the Jewish leaders and in return for thirty pieces of silver, he promised to betray Jesus to them and find them an excuse for arresting him.

Jesus Washes the Disciples' Feet

John 13

Jesus had arranged to use a large upstairs room in Jerusalem where he and the disciples could stay during the Passover festival. On the day before it began, he sent two of his friends into the city to get it ready and to prepare a meal for when they all arrived.

They did as he said and in the evening Jesus and the others arrived. They were all seated around the table when Jesus walked across the room and returned holding a jug, a basin and a towel. It was the custom in those days for servants to wash the feet of anyone visiting a house, but as the disciples had no servants, no one had done this.

Jesus decided to show his love for them all by doing the servant's job himself. He took off his outer robe and then with a towel tucked around his waist, he knelt down and poured some of the water into the bowl.

'You can't do that, Lord,' Peter protested.

'I'll explain in a moment what it's all about,' Jesus told him. Then one by one, he washed the feet of each person in the room. When he had finished, he put his outer robe back on and joined the disciples at the table. 'What I have done is an example to you all. You respect me by calling me "Lord", yet I was prepared to do the job of a servant and wash your feet. I want you to follow my example and wash one another's feet.'

They then understood what he meant; they were always to think of others before they thought of themselves.

The Last Supper

Matthew 26; John 13, 14 & 15

As Jesus sat at the table with his disciples, he knew that this would be the last supper they would eat together before he died, although at the time they did not realize this.

While they were eating, Jesus became quiet for a moment. 'I have to tell you this,' he said. 'One of you is going to betray me.' There was a shocked silence and the disciples looked at one another and wondered who it could possibly be. They were upset and horrified at the idea. 'Lord, is it I?' one of them asked. Then they all began to ask the same thing.

'It will be one of you,' Jesus continued. 'Someone who has been sharing this food with me tonight.' Jesus was looking at Judas Iscariot who was sitting near him. As Judas looked after the money and bought all the provisions for the disciples, it didn't seem odd that he should get up from the table and walk towards the door. They probably thought he was going to get more food. As he was going, Jesus called him over and whispered to him. 'I know what you have to do, my friend. Go and do it quickly.' That night Judas went to Caiaphas, one of the Jewish leaders to betray Jesus.

Then, Jesus asked for their attention. He took some bread and in front of them all he said a prayer of thanksgiving. Then he broke it and shared it among them all. 'Take some and eat it,' he said. 'This is my body which is going to be broken for you.' They passed the bread around the table and each took a piece and ate it. Later in the meal Jesus asked them to watch him again. He picked up a cup of wine. He said another prayer and passed it to each one in turn. 'This wine is my blood which I will shed for you,' he

told them. 'Drink some, all of you.'

Jesus then told them how they would soon be on their own without him. 'Where are you going, Lord?' Peter asked him, not realizing that he meant he would soon have to die.

'You can't come with me now, but later you will all tread the same path,' Jesus told them. 'Don't be worried. Trust God and trust me.'

'But, Lord,' said Thomas, still puzzled. 'If we don't know where you're going, how can we come with you?'

'I am the way, the truth and the life,' Jesus replied. 'No one can go to God the Father except through me.'

'Help us to know God,' interrupted Philip. 'That's what we all want.'

'Philip, have you been with me for so long and still don't understand? Whoever has seen me has seen God. If you will all love me and carry out all that I have said, God will send you His Spirit to give you strength. Let me give you this new commandment: you must love one another as I have loved you. This is the greatest love a person can show: to be ready to give up his life for his friends.

'In a way,' he continued, 'I am like a vine and you are like branches that have grown from me and are attached to me. If you stay attached to me and my words, you will continue to grow and your lives will produce wonderful fruit. God's name will be honoured. If you become separated from me and my words, you will stop growing and nothing good will come from your life. I want you to produce the sort of fruit that will last for ever. Stay close to me and I will stay close to you.'

With these encouraging words filling them all with hope, the disciples ended their meal and joined together in a song of praise to God. Then they got up from the table and followed Jesus downstairs into the darkness of the night.

The Garden of Gethsemane

Matthew 26

Jesus took the disciples out of the city and in the moonlight they made their way down a steep path into the Kidron Valley. As they went along, he surprised them by saying that soon they would all desert him. 'No, Lord. I'm ready to die for you,' Peter blurted out indignantly.

Jesus looked at him sadly. 'Are you, Peter?' He asked. 'Listen. Sometime tonight you will hear a cock crowing. Before it crows, you will have told people three times that you never even met me.'

'No, Lord I wouldn't,' he protested, and all the other disciples joined in, saying that they too would never let Jesus down.

They walked on a little further until they reached a hillside where wealthy people from Jerusalem had their olive gardens. They made their way among the shadows of the twisted tree trunks until Jesus stopped and turned to talk to them. 'I want you all to sit here and wait for a while. I want to pray on my own.' He went a little way ahead of them and knelt down.

As he began to pray, he was thinking about the pain he would soon have to go through when his enemies killed him. He began to wonder if he could carry on and bear such suffering. As his mind became full of the horrors he would have to face, he also remembered that this was what God wanted him to do. He felt torn one way by his own wishes and torn another way by God's. So great was the torment of his thoughts, that sweat streamed from his body on to the ground. 'Father,' he prayed; 'if you are willing, take away my suffering. No, I should not ask that. It's what you want, not what I want that matters.'

Jesus got up and went over to the disciples who had by then fallen asleep. He woke them up. 'Couldn't you stay awake with me for an hour?' he asked disappointedly. He then walked away again to pray and twice more he came back and found them fast asleep. 'Don't worry,' he said the last time. 'Sleep on and take your rest.'

The Arrest

Matthew 26

While Jesus was talking to the tired disciples, they suddenly heard voices further down the hillside and they spotted flaming torches moving towards them through the olive trees. 'Get up,' Jesus told his friends. 'Here comes the person who is going to betray me.'

Just then a large group of men, armed with swords and sticks, burst into the clearing. They had been sent by the Jewish leaders in Jerusalem. At the head of the crowd was none other than Judas Iscariot. He had already told the guards that he would kiss the person they were to arrest. The flickering torchlight lit up the cold determination of his eyes as he stepped up to Jesus. 'Hello, master,' he said trembling slightly. Then he kissed him.

At that, the men moved forward and began to pin Jesus' arms behind his back. One of the disciples seized a sword and with one stroke struck off a guard's ear. 'Stop!' Jesus called out. 'Don't do anything. Stand still.' He healed the man's ear and then raised his voice so that everyone could hear. 'Why have you come to arrest me with swords and sticks as if I were a robber? I used to teach in the Temple every day, but you didn't touch me. But then, this is your moment. This is the time for the darkness to be stronger than the light.'

He had hardly finished speaking when they tied his arms behind him and marched him down through the trees back to Jerusalem. They made no attempt to arrest the disciples, most of whom ran off, instead of following to see what happened.

The Trial of Jesus

Matthew 26

The most important Jewish leader was Caiaphas, the High Priest. It was to Caiaphas' house that Jesus was dragged by the guards. All the members of the Jewish Council made their way to the same place and they had made up their minds to hold a trial for Jesus there and then. They wanted to find some way of having Jesus put to death, so they were going to ask him questions in the hope that he would incriminate himself.

Peter had followed some distance behind the guards when they took Jesus from the olive garden. On reaching Caiaphas' house he stayed outside in the half light of the courtyard with some servants and guards, warming himself by an open fire. From here he was able to see and hear all that was happening to Jesus without being noticed.

First some people stood up and claimed that Jesus had spoken falsely about God and about himself. When these witnesses were questioned, it became clear that they were lying, because they became mixed up about things they said. Jesus listened to all their accusations in complete silence.

Then Caiaphas rose to face him. 'Will you say nothing at all?'

Jesus looked at him without speaking. The eyes of the whole Council were on him.

'In the name of the living God,' Caiaphas said sternly, 'I order you to answer me. Are you the Messiah, the Son of God?'

'If I tell you, you won't believe me,' Jesus replied to Caiaphas.

'Tell us,' Caiaphas snapped back. 'Are you this Son of God?

'Yes, I am,' he answered.

For a moment the Council members were stunned.

Then cries of horror and anger shattered the silence. Caiaphas tore his outer robe as a sign of disgust and shouted above the uproar. 'We need no more evidence! You have heard his own words. They are an offence to the Lord God. Now tell me, what punishment does he deserve?'

'Death,' they bellowed back. 'He deserves to die!'

The Jews had no power to put anyone to death; only the Romans who ruled Jerusalem were able to do that. They knew that they would have to take Jesus to Pontius Pilate, the Roman Governor, so they agreed to meet again at dawn to see that this was done. The Council then dispersed for a few hours.

All through the trial Peter had been sitting out in the courtyard listening sadly to what was being said. When it was all over, a servant girl from the house came up to him. 'I've seen you before,' she told him. 'You're a friend of that man Jesus.'

'I'm what?' he replied, embarrassed. 'I don't know what you're talking about.' He moved away from her and tried to lose himself in a group of people standing under an archway. Just then he heard another girl's voice. 'This man used to go around with Jesus,' she called out, pointing at him.

'Clear off!' Peter yelled back. 'I tell you, I don't know him.'

Some of the servants began to talk about Peter among themselves and after a little while, they came up to him again. 'We can tell you're from Galilee by the way you speak. You can't deny it: you're one of his friends.'

At this, Peter lost his temper. 'I told you before, I don't know him.' As he was speaking, he clearly heard a cock crowing in the night air and he remembered what Jesus had said to him earlier. 'Before the cock crows, you will have told people three times that you never knew me.' The memory of the words hurt Peter like the stabbing of a cruel blade. Tears came to his eyes and he ran from the house into the lonely streets of the city.

Jesus Meets Pontius Pilate

Matthew 27

At dawn the Jewish Council reassembled at Caiaphas' house. Caiaphas knew that the Roman Governor, Pontius Pilate, would do almost anything to keep the peace on that day. Jerusalem was crowded for the Passover festival and Pilate had travelled there with extra soldiers in order to prevent any possible trouble. With this in mind, Caiaphas stood up and called for silence.

'Sirs,' he said. 'You know what we have to decide. If Jesus is to die, we must send him to Pilate. If we send him this morning. I'm sure that Pilate will listen to us and pass sentence of death.'

The plan was accepted and they decided to go straight away. The guards were ordered to fetch Jesus, who was then escorted to the palace of the Roman Governor.

Jews did not normally go into a Roman's house, so when they arrived, Caiaphas refused to enter the building to meet Pilate. To avoid offending the Jews, Pilate decided to go to meet them. In the courtyard outside he tried to find out why they had brought a prisoner to him. 'What are your charges against him?' he asked.

'Sir, this man stirs up trouble wherever he goes,' replied Caiaphas. 'He is against our paying taxes to Imperial Caesar and he even claims to be our king.'

'Then you had better deal with him yourselves,' snapped Pilate. 'He is no concern of mine. Take him away and try him in your own courts.'

'We already have. We consider that he deserves to die. Only you, sir, can pass the sentence.'

'Very well. I will speak to him alone.'

Pilate then took Jesus inside and made him stand in front of him. 'Are you the King of the Jews?' he asked.

Jesus stood motionless. 'Those words,' he said, 'are yours, not mine.'

Pilate was puzzled, and still continued asking questions. 'You heard what they said about you. Won't you defend yourself?'

Still Jesus stood in silence. Pilate looked at him in amazement and wondered what he should do. 'I can't believe that this man deserves to die,' he thought. 'But if I refuse to sentence him to death, it will enrage the Jewish leaders and might cause a riot. Wait, there may be a way out.' He had remembered

that at that time of year, at the Passover festival, he always set free one criminal from the prison. The people were able to choose whom it should be. Pilate decided to try to make them pick Jesus by offering only two prisoners to them: Jesus and a well-known murderer called Barabbas.

He was certain that they would choose Jesus. What he did not know was that the Jewish leaders had already persuaded the crowd to ask for Barabbas.

Pilate led Jesus outside and they both stood in front of the restless crowd. He then lifted his voice so that he could be heard. 'I am prepared to set free one of two prisoners. Either this Jesus, who stands before you, or the murderer Barabbas. Which one do you choose? Jesus or Barabbas?'

To Pilate's surprise a great shout went up.

'Barabbas! We want Barabbas!'

'Tell me then, what shall I do with this man Jesus?' The people roared their reply. 'Crucify him! Crucify him!'

'Why?' asked Pilate. 'He has done no wrong.'

The shout came back even louder. 'Crucify him!'

Pilate was afraid. He could do nothing to change their minds. At any moment they might become impossible to control, so he quickly agreed. Saddened by what he had to do, he called for a bowl of water. In front of everyone, he dipped his hands into it. 'This is a sign,' he called out. 'I am not to blame for the death of this good man.' Then, to the crowd's delight, he ordered Barabbas to be set free. They were still cheering wildly as he ordered the guards to take Jesus away to crucify him.

219

The Soldiers Mock Jesus

Matthew 27; Isaiah 53

When the soldiers led Jesus away, they took him to the guard house. They thought that they would have some fun with him, so they fetched all their friends to watch. 'What shall we do with him?' someone called out.

'He's supposed to be a king!' jeered another. 'Let's make him a king!'

All Jesus was aware of was the laughing mass of mocking faces, as they roughly tore his clothes from him. They then threw a scarlet cloak like a royal robe around his shoulders and made him hold a reed as if it were a sceptre. One of the soldiers had plaited a circle of sharp thorns which they rammed on to his head as a crown. 'Long live the King of the Jews!' they all mocked, kneeling in front of him. 'Long live the King!' They they all got up and, still laughing at him, they hit him and spat on him.

When they had finished their cruel games, they took off the scarlet robe and escorted Jesus to a courtyard where he was lashed with a whip. After all the insults and pain, he was taken to the place where he was to die.

Throughout the centuries, when people have heard about Jesus' sufferings, they have remembered the words which Isaiah had written hundreds of years earlier about the Messiah:

'He was despised and rejected by men;
He was wounded for our wrongs; He was bruised
    for our sins;
Yet through his injuries, we are healed.
He suffered, but he said nothing:
He was taken like a lamb to be killed.'
We are all like sheep which have gone astray;
We have each one gone our own way;
But God has given him the punishment which we
    deserve,
He suffered, but he said nothing:
He was taken like a lamb to be killed;
He was seized and condemned and taken away to
    die,
He deceived no-one;
He did no-one any harm.
And yet he was treated as a wicked man.'

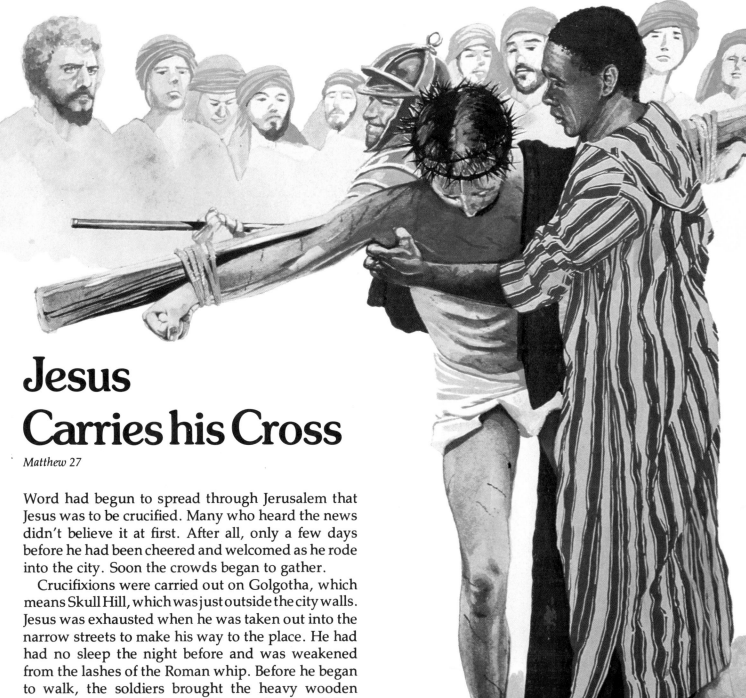

Jesus Carries his Cross

Matthew 27

Word had begun to spread through Jerusalem that Jesus was to be crucified. Many who heard the news didn't believe it at first. After all, only a few days before he had been cheered and welcomed as he rode into the city. Soon the crowds began to gather.

Crucifixions were carried out on Golgotha, which means Skull Hill, which was just outside the city walls. Jesus was exhausted when he was taken out into the narrow streets to make his way to the place. He had had no sleep the night before and was weakened from the lashes of the Roman whip. Before he began to walk, the soldiers brought the heavy wooden crosspiece on which he would have to hang and they made him drag it along. With weary step after weary step, he moved forward. His enemies were glad to see his pain, but many looked on with sorrow.

Several times he stumbled and fell under the weight of the beam. Then he would pick himself up slowly and carry on. The soldiers became annoyed at his slow pace, so they found in the crowd a man called Simon, who came from Africa, and they made him carry the beam for Jesus.

At last, after a walk which must have seemed like a never-ending journey, Jesus reached Golgotha. Two thieves were already hanging from crosses and between them both was the huge upright post on to which Jesus would be fastened.

The guards offered him wine mixed with myrrh to deaden the pain, but Jesus refused to taste it. Then they nailed him to the crossbeam and hauled it up until they could fasten it to the upright post far above the ground. As Jesus' body was pulled at every muscle and joint, he felt no anger. 'Father,' he prayed. 'Forgive them: they don't know what they're doing.'

Although the Jewish leaders objected, Pontius Pilate had ordered a notice to be fixed to the upright. Written in Hebrew, Latin and Greek, were the words 'Jesus of Nazareth, King of the Jews'.

The Crucifixion

Matthew 27; Mark 15; John 19

A large crowd came to Golgotha and stood around the crosses, looking up from time to time at the three men on them. Most of them were interested in the centre cross on which Jesus was hanging. Nearby, the Roman guards who had crucified him were sharing out his clothes by throwing dice for them. Many of his enemies had come to laugh at him. 'If you are the Son of God, come down from the cross. He helped other people; he can't help himself!'

One of the thieves who was hanging next to him also started to jeer. 'If you are the Messiah, save yourself and us.' His words made the other thief very angry. 'Don't you care what God thinks of you?' he asked him. 'We deserve to be here; this man has done

no wrong.' He then turned his head towards Jesus. 'Lord,' he said, 'remember me when you reach your Kingdom.'

'This very day you will be with me in Paradise.'

Just then three tearful women and a young man persuaded the guards to let them go right to the foot of Jesus' cross. When Jesus looked down, he saw that it was his mother, Mary, and she was being helped along by the young man, whose name was John. The other women were also called Mary: Mary Magdalene, and Mary, the wife of Clopas.

Jesus was heartbroken to see the distress of his mother and he called out to John. 'Look after her; treat her as your own mother.' Then he said to his mother, 'Look after him; treat him as your own son.'

The talking exhausted Jesus and his mouth was becoming parched in the heat. 'I'm thirsty,' he gasped. One of the women heard him and dipped a sponge in some cheap wine which was kept ready for

the purpose. She put it on a stick and held it up so that he could moisten his lips and drink a little of the wine.

At midday dark clouds seemed cover the sky, and for three hours it was as if the sun had gone for ever.

At three o'clock Jesus cried out loudly, 'My God, my God, why have you deserted me?' As a soldier rushed to give him more wine, some of his enemies thought he was praying to be rescued from the cross and laughed at him. Jesus knew that he had done all that he had set out to do: the love of God would not be defeated by the cross: his death would be a victory for the love of God.

'Father,' he called out triumphantly, 'I give myself into your hands. It is finished.'

With those words he died. At the same time a great earthquake seemed to shake the ground. A Roman centurion, who had watched it all, turned with amazement to his men. 'I am sure,' he told them confidently, 'that this man must have been the Son of God.'

One of the soldiers then made sure that Jesus was dead by piercing his side with a spear. Often bodies were left on crosses for several days, but two influential and wealthy men went to Pontius Pilate and asked for permission to take down the body of Jesus that very afternoon. Pilate agreed and so they went immediately to Golgotha. The two men were Nicodemus, and his friend Joseph of Arimathea, who was a secret admirer of Jesus.

Joseph owned a tomb in Jerusalem which had only recently been cut out of solid rock. It was in a private garden not far away, so the two men were able to carry the body there at once. As it was nearly the Sabbath they quickly anointed the body with oils and spices and then wrapped it in a linen cloth. Finally, they rolled the huge stone in to place across the entrance and went home.

The Empty Tomb

Matthew 28; John 20

The Jewish leaders had heard reports that Jesus had talked about being alive again three days after he died. They did not believe it, but in order to put paid to any wild rumours which might start, they went to see Pontius Pilate.

'Sir, we would like you to issue an order,' they said. 'Arrange for a guard to be sent to the tomb for the next three days. It will stop anyone from stealing the body and claiming that Jesus is alive again.'

'Very well,' Pilate answered. 'Take some soldiers now and make the tomb secure.'

They went straight away to Joseph of Arimathea's garden and sealed up the entrance of the tomb. Then guards were positioned around it.

When dawn broke on the morning of the third day, two women walked sadly into the garden carrying spices and oil. They were Mary Magdalene and Mary, the wife of Clopas. They had come to finish the annointing of the body of Jesus and they hadn't even thought about how they would be able to roll the huge stone aside. They knew nothing of the guards and the seal across the entrance of the tomb.

No one challenged them as they walked up to the place where Jesus was buried: for some reason the guards had gone. Then they remembered the size of the stone. 'How are we going to get inside?' they wondered. Suddenly they noticed something and stopped in their tracks. 'Look!' said one, 'It's been moved! Someone's been here before us! The stone has been rolled away!' They ran to the entrance and looked in. To their astonishment, they saw a young man seated inside, wearing a white robe. 'Don't be amazed!' he told them. 'I know you're looking for Jesus who was crucified three days ago. He is risen as he said he would. Here's the ledge where his body lay. You're looking among the dead for someone who's alive! Go quickly and tell the other disciples.'

The disciples had been stunned by the death of Jesus. It seemed to them that all hope had gone from their lives. To comfort one another most of them had spent the last three days together at a house in the city. It was here that the two women ran with their news. They themselves didn't really understand what had happened. 'They've taken the Lord from the tomb,' Mary Magdalene said, 'and we don't know where they've put him.' They then explained what they had seen and heard.

At first no one believed them, but Peter got up and ran out of the room followed by John. They ran all the

way to the garden and found the stone rolled aside,
as the women had described. John was the faster
runner so he got there first and looked in from the
entrance. Peter breathlessly pushed past him and
went right inside. They saw the linen clothes lying on
the stone ledge and, rolled up separately, the cloth
which had been around Jesus' head. They both knew
that the women's story was true and they began to
wonder what it could mean.

Later Mary Magdalene made her own way once
more to the garden and as she walked along sadness
seemed to weigh her down. She looked again at the
stone, her eyes reddened by the flow of tears. As she
stood and gazed at the tomb, she realized that there
was someone else in the garden too. She saw a man
standing in the shade of the trees and she ran to him
thinking that he was the gardener. 'Sir,' she pleaded,
bowing her head. 'If you've taken him, tell me where
you've put him, please.'

The man looked at her. 'Mary!' He said. She wiped
her eyes and saw that it was Jesus. He was indeed
alive! 'Lord! It is you!' she exclaimed. 'It is my Lord!'

Jesus spoke gently to her. 'Mary, I want you to go
back to the others and tell them that I am alive and
that soon I will have to return to God my Father. Just
tell them that.' Mary was filled with happiness and
left to do as he asked.

Jesus and Thomas

Luke 24; John 20

In the evening all the disciples except Thomas were still together at the same house, talking about the day's events. They were certain the Jewish leaders would be furious because the tomb was empty, so for safety they had barred all the doors.

After a while two more of Jesus' friends came in breathlessly and said that as they had been walking along the road to their home village of Emmaus, Jesus had joined them.

They explained how at first they had not recognised him and so they had told him about the way their friend, Jesus of Nazareth, had been killed. Jesus had replied by showing them how the scriptures had foretold the details of his life and death. When they had reached Emmaus, they had invited him into their house for a meal. He had gone in and sat down with them to eat. Suddenly, as he was sharing the bread with them, they had realised that it was Jesus. Afterwards they were so delighted that they ran all the way back to Jerusalem with their news.

No sooner had they told their story to the disciples than Jesus himself stood in the room with them.

'Peace be with you,' he said.

Many of them were terrified, thinking that he was some sort of ghost. 'Why are you afraid?' he asked them. 'Why don't you believe what you see?' He then showed them the marks which the nails and the spear had left in his body. 'Touch me if you like,' he continued. 'Then you'll be sure. Ghosts don't have flesh and bones, as I have!'

They were so overjoyed and amazed that they didn't know what to say. 'Come on,' said Jesus, breaking the silence. 'What have you got to eat?' They laughed together at this and one of the women found him a piece of cooked fish, which he ate as they watched him.

'I want to explain to you what has happened,' Jesus said as he finished his meal. 'When we were together before, I told you that I would die and rise again. Now all the things which refer to me in the writings of Moses, David and the prophets have come true.' He then showed them how the scriptures mentioned that the Messiah must suffer, but that he would rise to new life after three days. When Jesus finished explaining this, he left them as quickly as he had arrived. They were full of rejoicing and could not stop praising God because they had discovered that Jesus was alive.

When Thomas returned and they told him that Jesus had been there, he refused to believe them. 'Listen,' he insisted, 'unless I see and touch the nail marks in his hands, unless I feel the wound in his side, I will not believe a word of it.'

During the next days Thomas became infuriated that the others kept talking about having seen Jesus. A week after Jesus had spoken to them, they were all in the same place, this time with Thomas as well. To their delight, Jesus came into the room again. He greeted them in the same way, 'Peace be with you.' He then walked across to Thomas, who was completely taken aback. 'Here, Thomas,' he said. 'Look at my hands and touch them. Here's the wound in my side. Don't have any more doubts. Believe what you see!'

Thomas hung his head, ashamed at his own stubbornness. 'My Lord and my God!' he exclaimed.

'You only believed because you actually saw me,' Jesus told him. 'God will always bless those people who believe in me without seeing me.'

Jesus went on to visit a great many of those who had known him, including members of his own family. They all became even more certain that he was the Messiah, the Son of God.

Jesus at the Lakeside

John 21

After a few days seven of the disciples returned to Galilee. One evening they all decided to go fishing on the Sea of Galilee. They spent the whole night on the lake, but they didn't catch a thing.

Perhaps, when they heard the familiar creaking sounds as the boat moved in the water, Peter and the two brothers James and John might have remembered a similar night when they were fishing and caught nothing. That had been the start of a new way of life for them, for the next day they had met Jesus.

On this occasion too, as the rising sun began to touch the hilltops around the lake with a pink warmth, they felt that it had all been a waste of time.

As they headed for the shore, they heard a man shouting across the water to them.

'Haven't you caught anything?'

'No. Not a thing,' they called back.

'Throw your net out on the right side of the boat. You'll get some then,' the man told them.

Peter, James and John had heard those words before and they must have begun to wonder about the man on the shore. The disciples had nothing to lose, so they threw out the net again. Within moments it was straining from the weight of a mass

of wriggling fish that almost broke their net.

'It must be the Lord!' one of them said. Peter couldn't wait for the boat to reach the shore: he threw himself into the lake and swam ahead. Jesus was standing by a glowing charcoal fire on which he had been cooking some fish for them all.

He invited everyone to sit down and eat what he had cooked. He then handed them some bread.

After the meal Jesus took Peter to one side and talked to him. 'Peter,' he asked, 'do you love me more than these others do?'

'Yes, Lord,' he answered. 'You know I do.'

'Then take care of my lambs,' Jesus said. 'Are you sure you love me?'

'Yes, Lord, I've already told you that.'

'Then feed my sheep,' Jesus said. 'Peter, answer me again: do you love me?'

Peter was sad that Jesus asked him a third time.

'Lord, you know what I think: of course I do.'

'Peter,' Jesus said, 'I want you to take care of my sheep.'

Peter realized what Jesus meant. He wanted him to carry on his work in the world: to care not only for the other disciples, but for anyone who came to him.

Later on in Galilee Jesus talked again to all the disciples and told them to serve him whenever they could. 'God has given me the authority to say this to you,' he said. 'Go to every nation and help people to become my followers. Baptize them in the name of the Father and of the Son and of the Holy Spirit. You will teach them my words and commandments, and I will promise to be with you always until the end of time.'

The disciples then returned to Jerusalem, as Jesus had told them to wait there for a while.

The Ascension

Acts 1

Finally the moment came when the disciples were to see Jesus for the last time. It was forty days after he had risen from the tomb and in those weeks he taught them much more and they became even more certain that he was alive.

On the last day they were together, the eleven disciples who were the closest to him took the same steep path down from Jerusalem that they had taken the night Jesus had been betrayed. This time they did not stop in any of the olive gardens, but walked on up the hill which is called the Mount of Olives until they reached the top. No one else was in sight apart from themselves and Jesus, so they were able to talk freely.

He began by speaking of the Kingdom of God to them, but he soon realized that even after being with him for so long, they did not really understand what he meant by those words. Many of them still expected him to overthrow the Roman authorities somehow and make himself the new king. He tried to explain to them that God's Kingdom was made up of people who wanted to serve Him and were willing for Him to rule their lives. Jesus himself had shown them by his own life what obeying God might involve: it had led him to his death on the cross.

'You must not leave Jerusalem,' he told the eleven men. 'Soon, God will send you the gift of His Holy Spirit. When this happens, you will know a new power in your lives. You will be able to be my witnesses here in Jerusalem, then in Judaea and Samaria and later in every part of the world. This power will not be given to you until after I have gone.'

As he finished speaking to them, a cloud moved across the hilltop. It seemed to surround him and hide him from them. The cloud moved on and up higher into the sky. When the hilltop had cleared, Jesus was nowhere to be seen. They scanned the sky, but realized that he had left them. Just then they had a vision of two men in white clothes who stood near them to reassure them. 'Don't stand gazing up into the sky like that,' they said. 'This Jesus who has been taken from you will one day return in the same way as you saw him leave.'

The eleven men then walked down the hill and returned to their house in Jerusalem. These men came to be known as the apostles, the ones whom Jesus had chosen to be his closest companions. Their names were Peter, John, James, Andrew, Philip, Thomas, Bartholomew, Matthew, James the son of Alphaeus, Simon and Judas the son of James. Originally Judas Iscariot was one of them, but after betraying Jesus, he had killed himself in shame.

They decided to choose someone to take his place to make their number up to twelve again. A meeting was held which was attended by about 120 friends of Jesus. Peter, whom they all thought of as their leader, stood up and explained the sort of person it had to be. 'He must have seen the risen Lord,' he explained, 'and he must have travelled with us from the time we first began to follow Jesus.' They all prayed for God to guide them and then they chose a man called Matthias as the twelfth apostle.

The twelve gathered regularly for prayer together and often they were joined by Jesus' mother, Mary, his relatives and people who had been close to him.

Perhaps as they met, they remembered something which Jesus said the night before he died. 'It is better for you that I leave you,' he had told them. 'If I do not go, God's strength will not come to you. But if I do go away, I will send you the Holy Spirit so that you may know God's power in your lives.' They did not have long to wait before those words came true.

231

The Gift of the Holy Spirit

Acts 2

On the day the Jews were celebrating Pentecost, their harvest festival, the apostles were still in the same house at Jerusalem. All the followers of Jesus who lived nearby joined them to talk and pray.

They had been sitting there for a while when suddenly a strong wind seemed to blow through the whole house and the sound it made filled their ears. Then it seemed as if tongues of flame were flickering through the room, touching each person in turn. They felt a new power in their bodies and they discovered that they were speaking and praising God in languages that none of them had ever learned. God had sent His Holy Spirit to them and He was showing them that with His strength they would be able to do wonderful things in His name.

When the disciples left the house and went out into the streets, other people heard them talking in many different languages. There were Jews from many nations in Jerusalem for the festival.

'These are Galileans,' some of the travellers exclaimed in amazement. 'How is it then that they are speaking in our own languages?'

Some others who heard the disciples laughed at them and thought that they had been drinking too much wine. It wasn't like that at all. It is true that a change had come over them: this group of fearful men and women had suddenly become very bold and were going out into the public places of the city telling any who wanted to listen about Jesus. It had happened because God had filled their lives with His Holy Spirit and this had given them a new courage and a new feeling of joy and excitement.

Peter Preaches

Acts 2

A large curious crowd had begun to gather, to discover what had happened to the disciples. Peter went up some steps so that he could be seen by everyone and then, strengthened by God's Spirit, he began to talk to them all. 'Listen to me,' he called out. 'These people haven't had too much to drink. What you are seeing is something that the prophet Joel foretold many years ago. God told him that the day would come when He would pour out His Spirit on all people; they would boldly proclaim His message to the world; and at that time wonders and miracles would be seen.'

The crowd had grown quiet by now. It was a miracle in itself that this ordinary fisherman from Galilee should make a huge crowd listen to him.

'You remember the wonderful things which Jesus of Nazareth did in this city of Jerusalem. It was God who made those things happen. You killed him by letting wicked men crucify him. But that was not the end. God raised him from the dead and the twelve of us here saw him alive. He is now ruling in power with God and he has sent us the gift of His Holy Spirit. That is why we are able to speak to you like this today. Be sure of this: this Jesus who you crucified is none other than the Son of God, the Messiah!'

His words impressed many who were there. 'What should we do then?' they asked.

'You must put all wrongdoing out of your lives,' Peter explained, 'and be baptized in the name of Jesus. Then your wrongs will be forgiven and you too will receive God's Spirit.'

Many of the crowd believed what Peter had said and, by being baptized, showed that they had become followers of Jesus. No less than 3,000 men and women joined the disciples that very day and they spent time with the apostles, learning from them and joining in their prayers and meals.

233

A Lame Man is Healed

Acts 3

Each day in Jerusalem more and more people believed, through the teaching of the apostles, that Jesus was the Son of God. They met together regularly in the Temple and in one another's homes.

Peter and John were on their way into the Temple one afternoon when they were stopped by a man at the entrance called the Beautiful Gate. He had never been able to walk and was sitting on the ground with his back against the wall, begging for money.

'Give me a coin, please, just a small coin,' he called out to the two apostles, looking at them hopefully.

'I have no silver or gold,' Peter explained, as the man's face fell. 'But listen,' Peter went on, 'I will give you what I have. In the name of Jesus of Nazareth, get up and walk!' He then held out his hand to the man, who took it, and with trembling legs he began to stand. Suddenly the man felt his feet and ankles becoming stronger until he could stand on his own. He stood still for a moment and then, shouting at the top of his voice, he began to walk and jump.

Peter and John were thrilled that God was able to use them to bring healing to the man and as they carried on into the Temple, the man ran alongside them, praising God as loudly as he could.

'Don't be surprised, friends,' Peter told people. 'This man has been healed by the power of the name of Jesus, the same Jesus who was crucified here in Jerusalem. God raised him from the dead and this man is proof of His living power.'

Peter and John Face the Council

Acts 4

Peter and John were still speaking when some Jewish leaders arrived on the scene. They were furious that the apostles were telling everyone that Jesus had risen to life again after his death. They called the Temple guards and had Peter and John arrested. In spite of this many of those who had heard what they had said believed their words. There were now about 5,000 people who had become followers of Jesus.

The two apostles were kept in prison overnight and in the morning they were escorted to a meeting of the Jewish Council together with the man whom they had healed. Most of the important leaders were there, including Caiaphas, the High Priest, who had arranged the death of Jesus.

Peter and John were made to stand in front of them all to answer their questions. They both knew that their lives were in danger, but God's Holy Spirit gave them a feeling of calmness as they faced the cleverest men in Jerusalem. 'We have heard that you healed this man in the Temple yesterday,' Caiaphas said. 'How did you do it?'

Peter looked at him and answered without fear.

'Sirs, you should all realize that the man is standing in this room through the power of Jesus of Nazareth—the one you crucified and whom God raised from the dead. He alone can give hope to the world; only he can save us.'

The Council members were amazed at the confidence of Peter and John and at the way such uneducated men spoke. There was little they could do because the man really had been healed and most people in the city knew about it. Caiaphas then turned to Peter and John. 'We order you never to speak or teach about Jesus again,' he said.

'We cannot do as you ask,' they both replied. 'Is it right to obey God or not? How can we stop speaking about things which we have seen with our own eyes?'

The Council decided to release them and straight away the two apostles went back to their friends, who had been waiting and praying anxiously for them. When they heard what had happened, they all gave thanks to God and went out into the city to speak about Jesus with the same boldness.

Peter's Vision

Acts 10

For a while Peter was not troubled at all by the Jewish leaders and he began to travel from Jerusalem to many other towns and villages. Wherever he went, he spoke to people about Jesus. All the new followers of Jesus were Jews. The apostles, who were Jews themselves, had thought that God wanted them to tell their message only to the Jews; in any case they were not supposed to mix with Gentiles, the name given to people who were not Jews.

Peter often used to visit a seaside town called Joppa, where several followers of Jesus lived. He was once staying at a house belonging to a leather-maker called Simon and, as was his custom, he went up on to the flat roof to pray. While he was up there he began to feel hungry and had a strange vision. It seemed as if a large sheet was being lowered towards him out of the sky. In it were all kinds of animals, including birds and reptiles. He then heard a voice.

'Get up, Peter! Kill them and eat them!'

'No, Lord,' Peter answered. Jews had strict rules about what they were allowed to eat and it seemed as if God was asking him to break them.

'If I allow it, then it is right,' the voice told him, and Peter was shown the animals twice more before the vision faded from view.

Peter was puzzling about what it all meant when Simon called up to tell him that three men had arrived to see him. As he walked down the outside staircase to meet them, he had the feeling that God wanted him to go somewhere with them. 'We've come from Caesarea, sir,' they explained, referring to a town north of Joppa. 'A centurion called Cornelius is stationed with the Roman garrison there and he had a dream about you. He is a good man who worships God, and he was told to send three men to invite you to travel to Caesarea to stay at his house. That is why we are here.'

Peter wanted to hear more from them, so Simon

invited them to stay in the house for the night. As they talked, Peter began to understand his own vision. Cornelius was not a Jew and for this reason Jewish people would not have approved of Peter's visiting him. But Peter remembered God's words, 'If I allow it, then it is right', and he made up his mind to set off with the men and a few friends the next morning.

It took a day's travel to reach Caesarea. Cornelius was expecting him and he had invited a number of friends and relatives to come to meet Peter. When the centurion greeted Peter at the door of the house, he knelt down and bowed to him. 'Please stand up,' Peter said. 'I'm just an ordinary person like you.'

The two men talked together before they went into the main room. Peter told him how he had only just learned that God's love was for the whole world and not only for the Jews. 'That,' Peter continued, 'was why I wanted to come.' Then Cornelius explained about his dream and thanked him for coming. 'We have all gathered here to learn from you about God.'

The main room was full of people eager to listen to Peter, so he stood and spoke to them about Jesus of Nazareth. 'I now realize,' he explained, 'that God treats all people in the same way. He loves and accepts anyone who worships Him and lives a life which pleases Him. It doesn't matter what national-ity or race that person is.'

Peter then went on to tell them all about the things Jesus had done and taught; he described how he had died and been raised to life by God. As he was speaking, God's Holy Spirit seemed to touch everyone in the room and the Romans began to praise God and speak in new languages as the dis-ciples had done in Jerusalem.

Peter and the friends who had gone with him from Joppa were amazed and in no doubt that their mes-sage about Jesus had to be taken throughout the world. They decided there and then to baptize Cor-nelius and all the others who wanted to become followers of Jesus. Peter stayed on for a few more days and then he travelled to Jerusalem to tell the apostles the news that God wanted them to tell every-one, whether they were Jews or not, about Jesus.

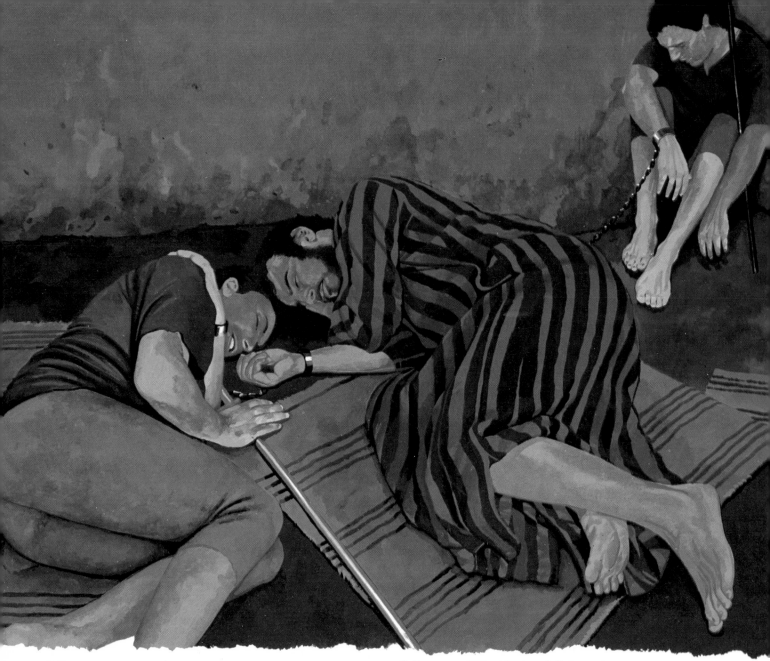

Peter in Prison

Acts 12

While the apostles were beginning to travel about more and more, opposition to them became fierce in places. Another King Herod, the nephew of the one who killed John the Baptist, was ruling at the time. He discovered that he could become popular with some of the Jewish leaders by attacking the followers of Jesus. He had one of the first disciples, James, executed by the sword and then he did his best to get rid of Peter.

Herod ordered Peter to be arrested in Jerusalem and kept in prison with soldiers guarding him. While Peter was there, his friends prayed constantly for him, asking God to be with him. On the night before his trial, Peter was sleeping, chained between two guards. Suddenly the cell was filled with light and an angel stood by him shaking his shoulder. 'Get up quickly!' he was told. 'Put on your belt and your sandals; then throw your cloak around you and

follow me.' The chains fell from Peter's wrists and he did as the angels had said. Then he followed him past several other guards and out into the city street. Peter thought he was dreaming, as he could no longer see the angel, but there was no doubt about it: there he was standing in a Jerusalem street in the middle of the night.

He went at once to a house where he knew that his friends were praying for him. He stood at the gate and knocked loudly. A servant girl called Rhoda came to see who it was and she was so excited to hear Peter's voice that she ran back to tell the others without letting him in! They didn't believe her at first, but they went to see for themselves and were overjoyed to find that it was indeed Peter. He quickly told them what had happened and then left them to hide somewhere else for safety.

The next morning Herod was enraged at Peter's escape and, when he could not be found anywhere, he ordered the guards to be killed. Soon afterwards Herod moved from Jerusalem to Caesarea, where he died. Peter himself continued travelling from place to place, tirelessly teaching all who would listen to him.

Philip and the Ethiopian

Acts 8

One day one of the apostles named Philip felt certain that God was telling him to travel into the desert along the road which goes from Jerusalem south to Gaza. Not knowing what he would find, he prepared for the journey and set off. When he had walked some way, he saw a strange sight. A splendid horse-drawn chariot was being driven slowly along the road and seated in the back was a well-dressed Ethiopian, reading from a scroll. It was so unusual to see anyone doing such a thing that Philip ran across to get nearer. To his surprise the man was reading aloud from the writings of the prophet Isaiah. Philip knew that this was why God had wanted him to come this way.

When the Ethiopian spotted Philip, he asked his driver to stop the chariot. 'Excuse me, sir,' Philip inquired. 'Do you understand those words?'

'I don't,' he answered. 'I need someone to explain them.' Philip said that he could help, so the Ethiopian invited him into the chariot. It turned out that he was an important official who served the Queen of Ethiopia and he was returning from worshipping God at Jerusalem. The chariot moved off, and as the two sat side by side, they read Isaiah's words:

'He suffered, but he said nothing:
He was taken like a lamb to be killed.'

Philip explained that the words described Jesus, who had been crucified, and he went on to tell the Ethiopian everything he could about him. When he had finished speaking, the Ethiopian was so sure that Jesus was the Son of God, that he made up his mind to follow him. They drove past some water, so the official asked to be baptized straight away. He stopped the chariot and then Philip baptized him.

After the baptism the Ethiopian continued his journey praising God, while Philip travelled to Caesarea, stopping to speak to people at every town on the way there.

Stephen

Acts 7

A follower of Jesus named Stephen became one of the leaders of the disciples who lived in Jerusalem. Strengthened by God, he did many wonderful things and became very well known in the city. A number of Jews were angry that he was attracting a great deal of attention and speaking so much to people about Jesus. They tried to argue with him in public, but Stephen's wisdom was a match for them all.

In their desperation to get rid of him, they bribed some men to say that he had said things which offended God. When the members of the Jewish Council heard these reports, they arrested Stephen, and made him appear before them.

He stood in front of the Council waiting to hear what accusations they would make. Then some more men who had been bribed, were brought in. They told several lies about him. They claimed that he had criticized the teachings of Moses and the activities of the Temple, and said that Jesus of Nazareth would do away with both.

The Council members looked at Stephen to see how he would reply. They were surprised at the calmness and happiness that seemed to radiate from him as, strengthened by God, he began to speak. He spent some time talking about how their ancestors had often turned away from God since the time of Abraham.

'You are no better,' he told them bluntly. 'You too

are deaf to hear what God is trying to say to you. You know God's law, but you do not obey it. Just as your ancestors killed God's messengers and prophets, you killed the Messiah when he came.'

This enraged the Council and an uproar of protests filled the room. Stephen was unmoved by their angry threats and as he stood there he felt as if God were very close to him. 'I can see heaven itself!' he said aloud. 'The Son of Man is standing with God Himself.'

The Council knew that Stephen was saying that he had had a vision of God and that Jesus was the Son of God. The words offended them so deeply that they put their hands over their ears and shouted with even greater rage. They then seized him and dragged him from the city to a rocky area nearby.

Stephen was thrown to the bottom of a slope and then the men hurled large stones and pushed boulders down on to him. He knelt for as long as he could as the rocks crashed into him. 'Lord Jesus!' he called out. 'Forgive them all. Into your hands I give my spirit!' With these prayers on his lips Stephen died.

Watching everything was a young man whose name was Paul. The men who actually carried out the stoning left their cloaks with him while they were doing it. He was against anyone who followed Jesus and was glad to see Stephen killed. He made up his mind to do all he could to stamp out all the talk about Jesus being the Son of God. With others he even went from house to house in many towns searching for followers of Jesus. When he found any, he had them arrested and put in prison. It became such a dangerous time for them all that most of them left Jerusalem and scattered to different areas for safety.

Paul at Damascus

Acts 9

To the north-east of Jerusalem is a town called Damascus. Paul heard that a number of Jews who lived there had become followers of Jesus, or 'Christians' as they were now called, so he asked the Jewish leaders for permission to travel there to arrest any he could find.

It was a long journey, so he and his companions were relieved when at last the city of Damascus came in sight. Suddenly, as they made their way along the road, the sky around Paul seemed lit up by a dazzling light. It was so brilliant that Paul fell to the ground, covering his eyes with his arm. None of them knew what was happening. Then they all clearly heard a voice. 'Paul, Paul!' it said. 'Why are you persecuting me?'

'Who are you, Lord?' Paul asked nervously.

'I am Jesus,' came the reply. 'I am the one you are persecuting and trying to destroy. Get up and go into Damascus. When you arrive you will discover what to do.'

As Paul got up, he opened his eyes, but saw nothing but total blackness. Then, to his horror, he realized that he could not see. His puzzled companions had to take him by the arm and lead him into the city. He was blind for three days and refused to eat or drink anything. During that time he thought a great deal about the things he had come to do. He had always hated anyone who said that Jesus was the Son of God; but after his vision he was beginning to think that perhaps they were right and he was wrong. He began to pray and as he did, he felt certain that someone would come to him to give him back his sight.

The Christians at Damascus had heard that Paul was in the city and they knew why he had come. News had reached them from other places about the cruel things he had done to the followers of Jesus, and they realized that their lives were in danger. On the third day after Paul's arrival a Christian called

Ananias had a dream in which God spoke to him very clearly. 'Go to Straight Street and find a house belonging to someone named Judas. Knock on the door and ask to see a man from Tarsus called Paul. He will be expecting you.'

Ananias couldn't believe his ears, 'Lord,' he said, 'I know about this man and about the way he has terrorized the Christians in Jerusalem.'

'Go to him, Ananias,' God answered. 'I have chosen him to serve me and the day will come when he will suffer for me.'

Wondering how it would all turn out, Ananias walked to Straight Street and he found the right house without any difficulty. He was intoduced to Paul and immediately explained his visit. 'The same person who spoke to you three days ago has told me to come here.' Ananias placed his hands gently on Paul's head. 'I have been sent so that you might be able to see again and be filled with the Holy Spirit.' At once light streamed into Paul's eyes and he began to see again. He was in no doubt that he wanted to become a Christian, so, as soon as he could see properly, he asked Ananias to baptize him. This was how one of the bitterest enemies of Jesus became one of his most outstanding followers.

Paul stayed on in Damascus and spent his time mixing with other Christians and teaching in the Jewish synagogues that Jesus was the Son of God. Everyone was amazed to see so great a change come over him. The Jewish leaders in Damascus became angry that he was now persuading people to follow Jesus and they were worried that he was being so successful. They met to arrange his death, but although the plan was supposed to have been a secret, news reached Paul. The Christians learned that the city gates were being carefully watched in order to capture and kill him, so one night they took him to an opening in the city wall and lowered him to the ground outside in a large basket.

After his escape Paul went straight to Jerusalem, where he lived with other Christians.

He carried on telling people about Jesus until his life was in danger again and he had to leave quickly for a safer place.

Paul at Philippi

Acts 16 & 19

Soon the Christians at Jerusalem and in Antioch realized how good Paul was at teaching other people about Jesus. God told them to send him with a man named Barnabas to the island of Cyprus and on to many other places. Paul and Barnabas had a very successful journey, encouraging new groups of Christians and helping many other people to become followers of Jesus.

Later Paul set off on a second journey with a friend called Silas. They visited the town of Philippi where they first talked to a number of Jews about Jesus. Among those who became Christians was a woman called Lydia who sold the expensive red cloth worn by wealthy people in those days. She invited Paul and Silas to stay at her house.

For several days as the two men were walking in the town they met a girl who made a great deal of money by telling fortunes. She kept pestering them both and Paul knew that the things she was doing were wrong. He ordered her in the name of Jesus to stop, and from that moment she was no longer able to see into the future. This meant that she couldn't earn any more money and so the men she usually gave it to were furious. They seized Paul and Silas and dragged them to the authorities. They were accused of causing a disturbance in the city and were ordered to be beaten and thrown into prison. This was done and, with their backs cut and hurting from the whipping, the jailer put them in the innermost cell and fastened their legs in wooden stocks. Paul and Silas amazed the other prisoners, for instead of being unhappy, they spent the night singing praises to God.

Suddenly the whole place shook with a fierce earthquake which flung open the cell doors and unfastened their stocks. The jailer, who had been asleep, woke with a start and was horrified to see the cell doors open. He thought that the prisoners had all escaped, and, knowing he would be punished for this, he drew his sword to kill himself. 'Stop!' shouted Paul. 'It's all right. We're all here!'

The jailer snatched one of the fire torches from its wall bracket and rushed towards the cells. He fell trembling in front of Paul and Silas. He had been impressed by the way they had behaved and, knowing that they were Christians, he asked how he too could become a follower of Jesus. They told him that

all he had to do was to believe in Jesus Christ. The jailer took them to his own rooms in the prison, where he bathed the wounds on their backs, and then asked them to talk to his whole family about Jesus. They were glad to do this and that same night all the jailer's family were baptized.

In the morning the authorities said that they could both be released. Paul sent a message back that as he and Silas were Roman citizens, they should be given an apology for the way they had been treated. The authorities knew that they could be in trouble for doing such things to Roman citizens, so they quickly apologized and let them go.

Paul continued travelling to different places bordering on the Mediterranean Sea. Sometimes he went alone and sometimes with companions like Barnabas and Silas. He was nearly killed at the splendid city of Ephesus, when he told the citizens that they must stop worshipping the goddess Artemis, in whose honour a magnificent temple and statue had been built there.

The people were angry at this and especially because many of them had become rich by selling silver models of the statue and the temple to the thousands of visitors who came to Ephesus each year. Two of Paul's friends, named Gaius and Aristachus, were attacked by a large crowd and dragged to the great amphitheatre. Paul wanted to go to help them, but, for his own safety, he was stopped from doing anything by some other Christians. The screaming mob looked as if it might only be satisfied with the two men's death, but then one of the city officials managed to calm everyone down and eventually they decided that there was no point in harming any of the Christians, so they let Gaius and Aristarchus go.

After this, Paul met all the Christians from the city and encouraged them to serve Jesus Christ without fear.

He told them all to trust God to give them strength and boldness in all the difficulties they might face. As he did wherever he went, he promised to write later to encourage them and to advise them as much as he could if they had any problems. He then left them and made his way through the magnificent buildings of the bustling city to the harbour, where he boarded a boat, which took him on the first stage of his journey back to Jerusalem.

Paul's Shipwreck

Acts 27

In Jerusalem several people stirred up trouble for Paul, so that a large number of Jews turned against him. One day he was in the Temple when a crowd began to shout at him. They were angry because he kept telling everyone that Jesus was the Son of God. When Claudius Lysias, the Roman commander, heard about the disturbance, he sent his soldiers to arrest Paul at once. Claudius questioned Paul, but he was puzzled by him because he didn't seem to have broken any laws. Paul then frightened him by saying that he was a Roman citizen and should not have been arrested.

One night Paul's nephew heard about a plot to kill Paul, so he went at once to Claudius with the news. As soon as the commander was told, he ordered 200 spearmen and 70 horsemen to get ready to escort Paul to the coastal town of Caesarea. They were to take Paul into custody for his own protection.

Paul was held in prison for over two years, and during this time several Roman governors and officials tried to decide what to do with him. When a governor called Festus was thinking of handing him back to the Jews in Jerusalem to be put on trial, Paul asked to be sent to Rome to let the Emperor himself decide about his case. This was arranged and an officer called Julius was given the job of escorting Paul and some other prisoners to Rome.

Their sea voyage went well until they were transferred on to a grain ship and were forced by strong winds to sail close to the island of Crete. For some days they had to anchor at a place called Safe Shelter, because the wind and the sea were still very rough. Paul suggested that they should spend the winter in the harbour, but no one else wanted to. They all wanted to sail along the coast to a better port called Phoenix. One day the wind settled a little, so the captain weighed anchor and they began to make their way along the coast to Phoenix.

They had only sailed a short distance when the wind changed and, to their horror, the ship was blown off course and right out to sea. It was imposs-

ible to head into the wind, so that captain let the wind drive them forward. With the gale howling around them, the ship was one moment lifted to the tops of the mountainous waves and then with a sudden lurch was hurled down into the deep troughs between them. It was impossible to plot the course they were taking, because the sun, moon and stars had been hidden behind the heavy clouds for many days.

Nearly everyone felt sure that the ship would be destroyed and that they would drown. The pounding waters began to weaken the wooden hull, so they had to pass long ropes right around it to hold it together. Paul knew that, as well as having no hope, the crew, the soldiers and the prisoners were all weak from having had no food for days. But Paul did not feel disheartened, so the captain gathered everyone together to listen to Paul. 'Don't lose heart,' he shouted about the roar of the wind. 'God has told me clearly that we will all reach Rome safely! I trust God: His words will come true.'

The ship stayed afloat for two weeks in the storms. Then one night the sailors heard the sound of waves crashing on to rocks. They were nearing land. Some of the crew tried to take the small ship's boat to reach safety on their own, but on Paul's advice, the soldiers cut it loose, so that everybody stayed on the ship. Just before dawn Paul persuaded all the 276 people on board to build up their strength by eating some bread, then, to make the ship ride higher in the water, they threw the cargo overboard: every sack of grain went into the sea.

As dawn broke they saw a beach ahead of them and they hoisted the sail, hoping that the wind would carry them ashore. For a while they surged forward, but then the bows stuck fast in a sandbank and the vessel began to break up. Some of the soldiers wanted to kill the prisoners to stop them escaping, but Julius ordered them not to harm anyone. Then, one by one, they all jumped overboard into the sea. Those who could not swim, clutched pieces of wood to stay afloat. No one drowned and 276 people waded ashore, glad to be alive and thanking God that He had saved their lives. They soon discovered that they were on the island of Malta. They stayed there for the whole of the winter and then travelled safely on to Rome.

Paul and Onesimus

The Book of Philemon

When Paul reached Rome, he was not put in prison, but was placed under guard in an ordinary house. His friends could visit him and he was allowed to send as many letters as he liked. He was able to teach and encourage the many Christian groups he knew by writing to them. Very often a secretary helped him by writing down Paul's words for him.

One day he began this letter to the Christians at Philippi: 'I thank my God for you whenever I think of you. I want you to know that coming to Rome has helped more people to hear about Jesus Christ. All the officials know what I believe, and the Christians here have become fearless in telling others what they know. I do not fear death: if my blood has to be shed, I shall not be sad and you must not be sad either. I have been willing to lose everything, because I have gained so much from serving Jesus Christ. I have learned to be happy, whatever happens to me, for I can do anything through Christ who gives me the strength.'

One of Paul's last letters was sent to Philemon, a Christian friend of his who lived at a place called Colossae. It was about a young man who had once worked as a slave for Philemon. The slave's name was Onesimus and a few months earlier, to Paul's surprise, he came to see him. Paul had probably met him before at Philemon's house. We don't know exactly what they said to each other, but judging from Paul's letter to Philemon their conversation possibly went something like this.

'Is your master here in Rome?' Paul asked.

'No, sir,' Onesimus replied. 'I'm on my own.'

'Has he sent you to me with a message then?'

'No, nothing like that,' the slave went on. 'You see, I ran away, sir.'

'You did what?' Paul exclaimed.

'I know it's wrong and Philemon could have me punished, but I stole some money from him. Then I came to Rome, hoping no one would find me among so many people. The trouble is, I ran out of money and didn't know what to do until I heard about you, sir.'

'About me? How?' Paul inquired.

'Some Christians, sir,' Onesimus explained. 'They told me that you were in Rome and I remembered the times you came to my master's house at Colossae, so I thought I'd take a chance and come here. I thought perhaps you could help me.'

Paul realized that runaway slaves had to be returned to their owners, but he knew that Onesimus

would be punished if he returned. For a while Onesimus came to talk to Paul regularly, and, one day, to Paul's delight he said that he wanted to follow Jesus and become a Christian. As a result of this Paul became like a father to Onesimus and he advised him to go back to Philemon and to apologize to him. In order to make his return easier, Paul decided to give Onesimus a letter to take to Philemon. We can still read this letter today.

'My friend Philemon,' he wrote. 'I want to ask a favour from you for Onesimus. He has become a Christian through me and I would dearly like him to stay here with me as my assistant. I cannot make you do this, but I would like you to welcome him back as warmly as you would welcome me.

'I am willing to pay back however much he took from you. Remember, by the way, how much you owe to me! I ask you to do this for the sake of our Lord Jesus. Onesimus is not just a slave; he is now a Christian friend. If you take him back, you will then have gained not only your slave again, but also another follower of Jesus for your household. I am sure that you will do what I ask and even more. May the grace of the Lord Jesus Christ be with you always.'

Onesimus took the letter and, wondering what would happen to him, he said goodbye to Paul and set off on the long journey to Colossae. No one knows how Philemon reacted when he returned, but he probably welcomed Onesimus as Paul had asked, for Christians became known for one thing above all else—their love and care for each other, even if they were very different sorts of people. Paul once wrote to some Christians in Galatia: 'There is no difference between Jews and non-Jews, between slaves and free-men, between men and women; you are all united through Jesus Christ.'

Paul the Letter Writer

I Corinthians 12 & 13; Galatians 5; II Timothy 2; Philippians 2; Ephesians 6

Paul wrote letters to other Christians long before he was arrested. Sometimes he sent them to one person, like his letter to Philemon, but usually they were meant for groups of Christians. Often they were passed from person to person and many copies were made, so that large numbers of Christians could read them. These growing Christian groups came to be known as 'churches'. At first they had no special buildings for worship, as most of the 'churches' were small enough to meet in ordinary houses.

In a letter to the Christian church at Corinth Paul insisted that they needed the love of God more than anything else:

'Even though I speak with the power of God, unless I have love, my words are as empty as a clashing cymbal. I may have great wisdom, but if I have no love, I am nothing. I can sacrifice my possessions and even my life, but unless I do it for the love of God, it is all pointless.

'Love is patient and kind, not jealous or boastful; love is not irritable or resentful; it puts up with everything and lives in hope. Love never ends and can never be destroyed.

'We can't understand everything now: it's like looking at a puzzling reflection in a dull mirror. One day God will help us to see clearly, so that all our questions and doubts will be answered. Until then, we have three things: faith, hope and love. The greatest of these is love.'

In his letter to the Christians at Galatia, Paul said that they were each like a plant, which would grow good or bad fruit. He told them that a person who is filled and controlled by God's Holy Spirit would produce the 'fruit of the Spirit'. 'The fruit of the Spirit is love, joy, peace, patience, kindness, goodness, faithfulness, humility and self-control.'

Paul did not want Christians to let God down by the way they lived. He believed that they should lead the best possible lives for God. A young Christian called Timothy once received this advice in a letter from Paul: 'In a large house there are dishes made of wood, clay, silver and gold: only the best are used on special occasions. Serving God is a special honour. Christians should remember that only the best is good enough for God.'

Paul once reminded the Christians at Philippi that in everything they did they should follow the example of Jesus Christ. 'Be like Jesus,' he wrote. 'Although he had the nature of God, he humbled himself like a servant and came to the world as a human being. He accepted God's plan for his life and obeyed Him even when it meant dying on a cross. Because of the way he lived, God honoured him and

has made him greater than any other person, so that at his name every knee should bow.'

The Christians at Corinth had begun to disagree among themselves, so Paul told them to remember that every single Christian needs his fellow Christians as much as one part of a body needs another. 'A body isn't made up of just one part,' he said. 'Each body has many parts. The eye can't say to the hand, "I don't need you", and the head can't say to the feet, "I don't want you". Every part is needed. The whole body should work together happily. If one limb suffers, then the whole body will feel the pain. Christians are like the different parts of a body: you all have different gifts and a different part to play, but you need one another.'

From the hardship he had faced in his life, Paul realized how difficult it could be to live as a Christian. He pictured it as a battle, which always has to be fought against wrong in each Christian's life and in the world. When he wrote to the church at Ephesus, where he and his friends had nearly been killed, he could perhaps see his Roman guard standing nearby. 'Put on every piece of God's armour. Then you will be able to fight off any evil attack and stand firm. Fasten the belt of truth around your waist and cover your chest with the breastplate of goodness. On your feet you must have travelling boots to take you everywhere with the good news about Jesus. Make sure that at all times you have the shield of faith with you, for by trusting God you will be safe against the burning arrows of evil. Put on your head the helmet of God's salvation and grip in your hand the sword of God's word. As you wear this armour make sure above all that you pray and then God will give you His help and His strength.'

Christian Letters

James 2 & 3; Hebrews 12

Paul was not the only Christian who wrote important letters to the churches growing during his lifetime. A man called James wrote to Christians everywhere with some very blunt advice. 'Treat everyone as equals because of your faith in Jesus Christ,' he said. 'For example, imagine that two men come into a meeting of Christians, one wearing gold rings and expensive clothes and the other shabbily dressed. If you pay more attention to the richer of the two, by offering him a special seat while ignoring the second man, then you have become like judges whose minds are full of evil thoughts. A poor person who loves God is rich in God's eyes. By treating the poor man in the way you did, you have insulted him. You will serve God well if you carry out His command to love your neighbour as much as you love yourself.'

James had seen so much trouble caused by people saying harsh or unkind things that he asked Christians to guard their tongues. 'We need to put bits into horses' mouths to control their movements; in the same way, if we can control our tongues, we will be able to control everything else we do. Think of a ship: a small rudder can guide a great vessel through stormy winds. That's just like our tongues: they may be tiny, but they can bring about great disasters or great successes. Putting it another way, a tongue can start things which no one can stop, just as a small fire can grow into a forest blaze.'

One great Christian letter-writer, whose name we don't know, looked back at the many great people like Abraham and Moses who had trusted God through past centuries and he asked his readers to do the same: to put everything into following Jesus Christ, as an athlete puts everything into a race. 'Let us strip away everything which might hold us up, especially the wrongs which drag us back, and let us run the race ahead without flinching. Let us keep our eyes fixed on Jesus, trusting no one else. Nothing could make Jesus give up—not even a cross! Since then God has given him honour and glory. Think of what he went through and don't ever give up.'

Everything is New!

I Corinthians 15; Revelation 21

Jesus Christ taught his disciples that everyone who followed him would find their lives changed by God. They would find a new hope, a new strength and a new purpose in all that they did. 'If anyone puts his trust in Jesus he is a new creation,' Paul wrote. 'The old life has passed away and everything is new!'

Because Christians believe that God raised Jesus from the dead, they also believe that their lives will not end when they die. God will raise them to new life. They look forward to enjoying forever a new life with God, when there will be no more pain or wrong. Paul once told the Christians at Corinth about this.

'I would like to remind you, my friends of the good news, which I taught to you. Everything we believe is based on this: Jesus Christ died for our wrongs; three days after his burial, he rose to life again. He then appeared to close friends and to over 500 of his followers. I also saw him alive.

'The truth is this: as surely as Jesus Christ rose from the dead, so we can be certain that we too will live on after we die. Who says that death destroys? Death has no power to harm us. God had destroyed death. We thank God who will make us victorious over death through our Lord Jesus Christ!'

So Christians have hope for the future, and many believe that one day Jesus himself will return to the world to make it a new and better place.

Once on the island of Patmos a Christian called John was praying in the cave where he lived. Suddenly he had a dream in which the risen Jesus seemed to speak to him. 'Don't be afraid,' he said. 'I am the one who is alive! I was dead, but now I am alive for ever!'

Among the many things which John saw in his dream was a wonderful picture of the new world which God would one day give to all who serve Him.

'I saw a new heaven and a new earth; the first heaven and the first earth had passed away.
And I saw the Holy City, new Jerusalem, coming down from heaven:
It was as beautiful as a bride ready to meet her husband.
Then I heard a great voice speaking from the throne:
"From now on, God will live closely with all mankind.
They will serve Him as His people and He will be their God.
He will wipe all tears from their eyes.
There will be no more death or sorrow or pain.
Everything old has disappeared—
Now I make all things new!"'

251

The Story Behind the Bible

The Message of the Bible

The Bible is really not one book only: it is made up of 66 books, which were written by many different people who lived at many different times. It is like a library where you can find stories, poems, prayers, laws, history, diaries and letters.

Although all the books are about God, they teach about Him in different ways. Through the history of the People of Israel for instance, we can learn how God cares for everyone who follows Him. Sometimes, people have not understood all the great stories of the Bible. For example, the story of the Creation of the World is not trying to tell us exactly how life came about; chiefly it is telling us that the world has been made by God and that He wanted it to be a good place in which to live; the story of the Garden of Eden is not mainly about a serpent and two special trees: it is saying that the sadness and suffering in the world have come about mainly because people have ignored God and His laws.

The New Testament is all about Jesus Christ and also about the men and women who became his first followers. Throughout the centuries, Christians have believed that, most of all, God showed his love for the world through the things Jesus did and said. That is why they have read the stories about his life more than any other part of the Bible. These stories are in the first four books of the New Testament and are called the Gospels, which means 'the Good News'.

The Writing of the Bible

At first the words of the Old Testament were not written down. They were passed on from one person to another as stories or songs.

When they came to be written down this was

on rolls of parchment made from the skins of animals. They were written during a period of about 1,000 years in Hebrew, the ancient language of the People of Israel.

The New Testament also began as spoken stories which people told. They began to be written down during the lifetime of some of Jesus' friends. Although some of the stories may have been passed on in Aramaic, which was the language Jesus himself spoke, Greek was the language in which the New Testament was written down.

The parchments, which were made from a plant called the papyrus, were often stored in sealed jars to protect them.

After many years, leading Christians considered the writings and decided which were the most important ones to keep. These then became known as the 'New Testament'.

The Bible Moves On

Although Greek was the language used in the eastern part of the Roman Empire, in the western part, Latin was the main language. The whole Bible was therefore translated from Hebrew and Greek into Latin. In the fourth century AD, Jerome produced his famous Latin translation which was called the 'Vulgate'. The Bibles which the first Christian missionaries brought to Britain were in Latin. They were carefully copied by monks who decorated the manuscripts.

By the 8th century AD, parts of the Bible had begun to be translated into the Anglo-Saxon language, which was spoken by the people of Britain, but it was not until 1380 that the whole Bible was put into English by a clergyman called John Wycliffe, who was helped by several friends. At this time all the copies were still being hand-written. In the middle of the 15th century printing was invented, so that copies of books could be made more quickly.

The Bible was one of the first books to be printed in large numbers. The first complete Bible to be printed in a modern language was a German one in 1466. Although some people were against ordinary men and women reading the Bible for themselves, soon printed copies were to be found all over Europe in the languages of the different countries. Then, as Christians began to explore other parts of the world such as Asia and Africa, they began to translate the Bible into many languages.

Life in Biblical Times

The Home

Many ordinary homes in Jesus' day were like this. The family could reach the flat roof by going up the outside staircase. The roof was a useful place to dry crops such as corn or grapes. In warm weather people ate and slept there too. The inside of the house usually consisted of only one or two rooms. There was often a raised area which could be used for cooking, and, in colder weather, for eating and sleeping. The lower area was where the animals could be kept at night.

In the day time if the owner of the house was, say, a carpenter or a potter, he would probably work in the lower part, unless it was warm enough for him to work outside. Notice the jars of oil, which was used for cooking, lighting and for bathing wounds. The oil lamps would be in alcoves or on lamp stands.

On the side of the door is a little container called a 'mezuzah'. It contained some writing which said 'The Lord alone is our God. You shall love and trust your God with all your heart, with all your soul and with all your mind.' It was placed on the door post to remind the family to think of God as they went in and out and lived their daily lives. Jewish families still use them.

Farming

Farmers who grew corn would usually plough the soil with oxen. The seed was scattered by hand from a basket or bag. When they worked, the men generally tucked up their long robes to help them to move more easily. They kept their heads covered because of the heat.

At harvest time, the corn was cut with sickles. The grain was separated from the ears of corn by two sorts of threshing: sometimes it was beaten with flails or whips; sometimes donkeys pulled metal-bottomed sledges over and over the corn until the husks broke and the grain came out. Then, on a windy day it was winnowed: as the separated grain and husks were thrown into the air, the wind blew the husks away and the grain fell straight back to the ground again.

Olive-growing has always been important in the Middle East. Ripe olives are picked and then crushed in special presses to obtain the oil which they contain. The vineyards, where grapes were grown, were often protected by guards posted in watchtowers.

Sheep farmers had to take great care lest either wolves or thieves managed to take any of their flock. Shepherds guarded them with a strong stick or staff and at night they would protect them by leading them into a walled sheepfold. Instead of closing it with a door, the shepherd might lie across the entrance all night, so that no animal or person could go in or out without his knowledge.

ITALY

• Rome

SICILY

Extent of the Roman Empire

CRETE

MEDITERRANEAN SEA

Extent of the Roman Empire

THE BIBLE LANDS AT THE TIME OF CHRIST

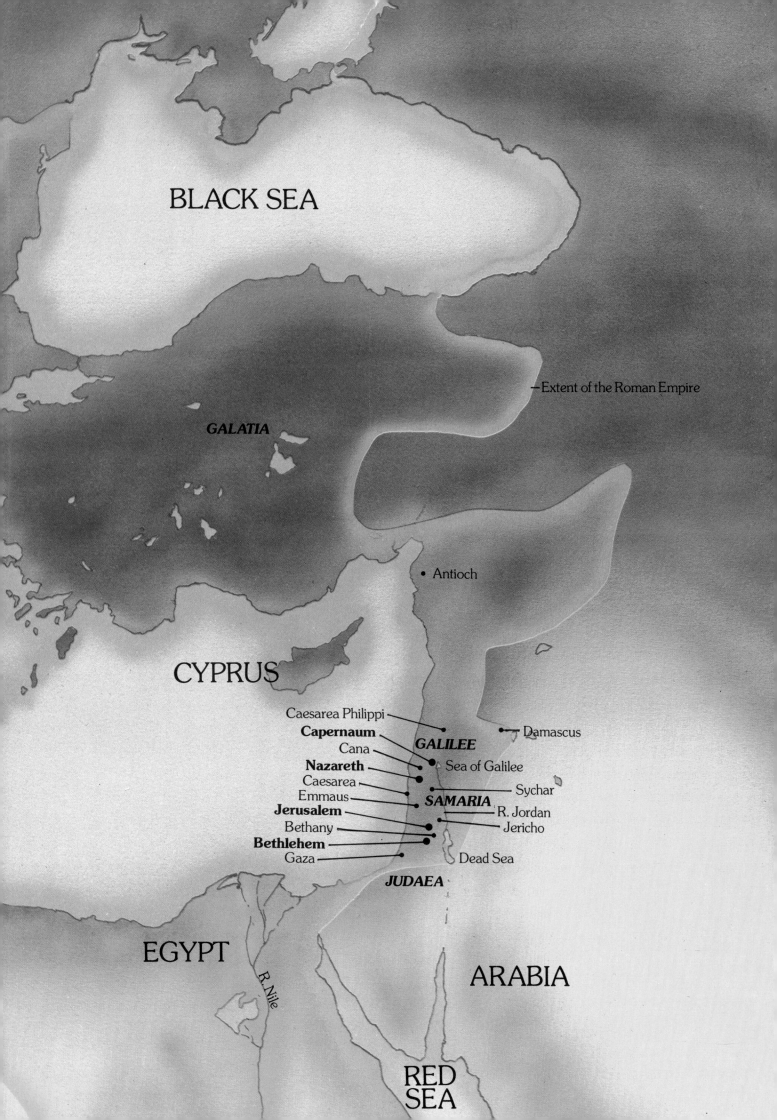

BLACK SEA

GALATIA

—Extent of the Roman Empire

CYPRUS

Antioch

Caesarea Philippi

Capernaum

Cana

GALILEE

Damascus

Nazareth

Sea of Galilee

Caesarea

Emmaus

Sychar

SAMARIA

Jerusalem

R. Jordan

Bethany

Jericho

Bethlehem

Gaza

Dead Sea

JUDAEA

EGYPT

R. Nile

ARABIA

RED
SEA

First published 1980 by
Octopus Books Limited
59 Grosvenor Street
London W1

ISBN 0 7064 0861 6

Produced by Mandarin Publishers Limited
22a Westlands Road, Quarry Bay, Hong Kong
Printed in Hong Kong

Acknowledgments

The author wishes to express his thanks to the following
people for their help on this book:
Dr Douglas de Lacey, lecturer at the London Bible College, for
acting as historical consultant.
Sister Martina, O.P., headmistress of St Catherine of Siena
School, Watford, for her help as Roman Catholic adviser.
Rev. Geoffrey Curtis, Communications Adviser, Diocese of
Guildford, for his help as Anglican adviser.

Artists

Andrew Aloof: pages 10–13, 38–57, 94–117
Jon Davis: pages 58–71, 86–7, 120–1
Dick Eastland: pages 250–3
Colin Shearing: pages 14–37, 72–85, 88–93, 118–19, 122–48
Barrie Thorpe: pages 150–249

PDO 81-127